CRE**A**TIVE
HOMEOWNER®

BEGINNERS' GUIDE TO

gardening

CREATIVE HOMEOWNER®, Upper Saddle River, New Jersey

THE BEGINNER'S GUIDE TO GARDENING

WRITERS	Roger Holmes, Eleanore Lewis
SUPERVISING EDITOR	Timothy O. Bakke
INTERIOR DESIGN CONCEPT	Glee Barre
COVER DESIGN CONCEPT	Kathy Wityk
LAYOUT	David Geer
PRODUCTION	Scott Kraft
INDEX	Ellen Davenport
ILLUSTRATORS	Vincent Alessi (*site plan, petal color wheels, bird feeders, spading fork, stirrup hoe, colinear hoe, hand cultivator, hand weeder*)
	Michelle Ferrar (*plant habits, parts of tree to bare roots, containerized roots*)
	Todd Ferris (*all other tools*)
	Mavis Torke (*pruning illustrations, rose anatomy, foolproof fence design*)
FRONT COVER PHOTOGRAPHY	Dreamstime: T
	Neil Soderstrom: BL BC BR
BACK COVER PHOTOGRAPHY	Grant Heilman (Larry Lefever: T BL, Jane Grushow: BC); Michael Thompson BR

Manufactured in the United States of America

Current Printing (last digit)
10 9 8 7 6 5 4 3 2 1

The Beginner's Guide to Gardening
Originally published as *Creating Good Gardens*
Library of Congress Control Number: 2012931478
ISBN-10: 1-58011-563-2
ISBN-13: 978-1-58011-563-6

CREATIVE HOMEOWNER®
A Division of Federal Marketing Corp.
24 Park Way
Upper Saddle River, NJ 07458
www.creativehomeowner.com

Photo Credits

Health and Safety Considerations

All projects and procedures in this book have been reviewed for safety; still it is not possible to overstate the importance of working carefully. What follows are reminders for plant care and project safety. Always use common sense.

▌ Always consider nontoxic and least toxic methods of ad-dressing unwanted plants, plant pests, and plant diseases before resorting to toxic methods. Follow package application and safety instructions carefully.

▌ Always substitute rock phosphate and gypsum for bonemeal when amending soil. Authorities suggest that there's a hazard in using bovine-based products such as bonemeal, blood meal, and cow manure because they could harbor the virus that causes Mad Cow disease in cattle and humans.

▌ Always read labels on chemicals, solvents, and other products; provide ventilation; heed warnings.

▌ Always wear eye protection when using chemicals, sawing wood, pruning trees and shrubs, using power tools, and striking metal onto metal or concrete.

▌ Always wear a hard hat when working in situations with potential for injury from falling tree limbs.

▌ Always wear appropriate gloves in situations in which your hands could be injured by rough surfaces, sharp edges, thorns, or poisonous plants.

▌ Always wear a disposable face mask or a special filtering respirator when creating sawdust or working with gardening dusts and powders.

▌ Always protect yourself against ticks, which can carry Lyme disease. Wear light-colored, long-sleeved shirts and pants. Inspect yourself for ticks after every session in the garden.

▌ Always determine locations of underground utility lines before you dig, and then avoid them by a safe distance. Buried lines may be for gas, electricity, communications, or water. Contact local utility companies which will help you map their lines.

▌ Always read and heed tool manufacturer instructions.

▌ Always ensure that the electrical setup is safe; be sure that no circuit is overloaded and that all power tools and electrical outlets are properly grounded and protected by a ground-fault circuit interrupter (GCFI). Do not use power tools in wet locations.

▌ Always keep your hands and other body parts away from the business end of blades, cutters, and bits.

▌ Never employ herbicides, pesticides, or toxic chemicals unless you have determined with certainty that they were developed for the specific problem you hope to remedy.

▌ Never allow bystanders to approach work areas where they might by injured by workers or work site hazards.

▌ Never work with power tools when you are tired or under the influence of alcohol or drugs.

▌ Never carry sharp or pointed tools, such as knives or saws, in your pocket.

Contents

Introduction

Few pastimes are as rewarding as gardening. With a little bit of ground and a few seeds or plants, anyone can be a gardener, and almost any collection of plants can be a garden. To the child who planted it, a tiny patch of marigolds, zinnias, and beans, started from seeds planted in milk cartons, is as rewarding as an extensive perennial border is to her grandmother, for whom the garden has been a 40-year labor of love.

Gardening can be a refreshingly simple activity in an increasingly complex world. But you'll have greater success and more fun if you start with an understanding of basic gardening practices. The techniques in this book are easy to follow and suitable for all gardeners—from beginners to advanced. Ecologically friendly methods are included so that you can create a garden that eventually helps to sustain itself.

Chapter 1 presents the principles of garden design and gives tips to help you plan almost any type of garden. In Chapter 2, you'll learn how to get started with plants and how to install garden beds. Chapter 3 explains how to care for your garden through the seasons and control weeds, pests, and diseases. Subsequent chapters introduce the plants in your garden—annuals, perennials, bulbs, herbs, shrubs, and trees—and take a closer look at the roles they each play. You'll learn the basics of growing and caring for each type of plant and find descriptions of proven performers in each category. The book's final chapters tell how to attract birds and butterflies to your garden, how to make and care for a water garden with a small pond and water plants, and how to grow and maintain a vegetable garden.

The tools and materials you'll need are included with each step-by-step project, and each is rated for difficulty; *easy*, even for beginners; *moderate*, somewhat difficult but able to be done by beginners who have patience and willingness to learn; *challenging*, requires a serious investment in time and tools—consider consulting a professional.

A well-designed garden can transform problem spots such as this cul-de-sac, above, into secluded niches for privacy and relaxation.

Good gardens are easy to create on any part of your property. As shown opposite, a garden can transform a potential eyesore, such as a garden shed, into a bright cheerful spot.

CHAPTER 1

Design Basics

Garden design is simply figuring out what plants go where, for what purpose, and to what effect. This aspect of gardening is a pleasure for some gardeners and challenging for others. But no matter what your approach, design becomes much easier once you learn a few basics.

Good plans are crucial. Poorly conceived plantings often perform poorly, are unattractive, or get in the way of other activities on your property. But well-designed gardens are a joy. A good design makes the garden both beautiful and easy to maintain. Take the time in the beginning to draw and redraw your plans until your design meets all your family's needs.

Getting Started

Few people would begin building a house without some sort of blueprint or plan. Having a plan is no less sensible when making a garden. Fortunately, gardens are less complex than houses. Simple gardens require only simple plans. Some are simple enough to exist solely in your head. For example, a seasonal planting of daffodils and crocuses by the front door—followed by petunias with a skirt of candytuft—hardly needs to be sketched on paper. But larger areas involving many plants benefit from more thought and, often, a plan on paper. Coordinating colors, textures, and seasons of bloom to provide eye-catching displays for months at a time demands even more effort, not to mention experience and knowledge.

DESIGN PLANS

The most challenging design task is planning an entire property. This plan should address your family's full range of outdoor activities. Consider entertainment for adults and children, access to entrances and storage areas, privacy from neighbors and passersby, and so on. Whole-landscape planning may involve positioning outdoor structures such

Make a Site Plan

A site plan allows you to leave space for all the areas you may want to develop. Draw in children's play areas and adult lounging and recreational spaces. Avoid future problems by drawing in the mature size of plants, and leave room for specialty areas such as a berry patch or water garden.

Vegetable Garden

Swing Set

Dining Area

Space for Berries

Kitchen Herb Garden

Flower Beds

Flower Beds

as arbors, fences, and paths; grading the entire lot; and some-times locating, or siting, a new house, garage, and driveway. It's far easier to plan just the individual beds and other plant-ings that are the main focus of this book. For a sample site plan, drawn to approximate reality, see opposite.

Starting Small. The best way to succeed at design is to start small. The experience and knowledge you acquire with each project will help in the next. The danger of this ap-proach is ending up with a landscape of unrelated elements, rather like acquiring a set of dishes by purchasing a different pattern every year. So at each stage, take the time to think about the bigger picture. Before you start out, consider your family's favorite outdoor activities and where these might take place. Then pick a spot for your first garden bed that takes these areas into account. For instance, if you already have a patio, your first project might be a bed of colorful, fragrant annuals and perennials near that area. If you don't have a patio but plan to build one, locate your first garden bed outside the potential patio area so that you don't have to tear out the bed later.

A harmonious color scheme, repetition of form and color, and wise use of structural focal points, above left, are the design elements that make this garden lovely.

Start small gardens when you are beginning to develop your land-scape, above right. As they become established, you can expand on them or add new plantings in different parts of the yard.

Plan for Tomorrow. Over time, beginning gardeners be-come experienced gardeners, and their landscapes evolve. This developmental process is one of the great pleasures of gardening. Many garden plants adjust easily to change. If you want them somewhere else, you can dig them up and move them. However, trees and large shrubs are less ac-commodating. If you want to transform a significant part of your home landscape with woody plants, consider engag-ing an experienced gardener or hiring a landscape designer to help you establish a long-range plan. Such a plan can al-low you to experiment and grow as a gardener, while saving you the trouble and anguish of needing to transplant a tree or uproot a flower bed a few years farther along.

Fundamentals of Garden Design

The qualities people enjoy in individual plants and plant combinations are easy to identify. *Color, texture, form,* and, sometimes, *fragrance* of flowers and foliage are high on the list. People also respond to seed heads and seed pods; fruits and berries; and shapes and colors of leaves, stems, branches, and bark, as well as the overall shapes of plants. Plant forms are also called *growth habits.*

When you design a garden bed, try to select and arrange plants so that these qualities produce a pleasing effect. This is easier said than done. Professional landscape designers have two important advantages—familiarity with the qualities of plants and a storehouse of design examples to draw on for ideas and inspiration. Yet you have an advantage over a professional designer who works for numerous clients because you have only yourself to please. You can also take advantage of tricks professional designers use. Two—repeating specific design elements and creating focal points—are discussed later in this chapter.

Every accomplished garden designer was once a beginner. If you start small, mistakes are usually easy to correct. You'll be surprised at how quickly you can become acquainted with a useful range of plants. For inspiring examples, consider the photographs in this book and others. Also study attractive garden designs in your travels. Visit public gardens, and private ones if you can arrange an invitation. Keep a file of photos of plant combinations you like.

As you plan your first garden and begin to note other plantings, try to identify and understand the qualities that you like or dislike. The following will get you started.

COLOR, CONTRAST, AND HARMONY

For many people, color is the defining characteristic of a garden, from early spring, when tiny crocuses sprinkle the still-dormant countryside with color, into fall, when the entire landscape seems to explode with fiery foliage. Flowers, of course, are a prized source of color. But don't forget foliage. Most of the time the dominant colors in a garden—if not the most eye-catching—are those of the leaves.

It's possible to use color boldly without being haphazard about color combinations. Explore combinations of contrasting colors, such as yellow daylilies with blue salvia. Also try harmonizing colors, such as purple coneflowers with pink garden phlox. White flowers, such as Shasta daisies, or plants with gray or silver foliage, such as artemisias and lamb's ears, can soften the impact of clashing colors within a group or smooth the transition between groups of plants that don't quite harmonize. Consider the color wheels on these pages when selecting your combinations.

Try to make full use of foliage colors in a planting, too. Some help tie a planting together, while others can be featured performers. The dense greens of evergreen shrubs, such as yews, arborvitae, and rhododendrons, make a superb backdrop for colorful flowers. The varied greens, blues, and golds of hosta leaves and the russets and golds of ornamental grasses in autumn are eye-catching in their own right. And don't forget about other colorful plant parts. For example, hollies, crabapples, and sedums produce attractive berries, fruit, and seed heads, while red-twig dogwood has distinctive red stems.

A variety of textures and forms makes this garden a visual feast.

Harmonious colors, close to each other on the color wheel, create never-fail combinations in the garden. Here, the pink of 'Bejeweled' daylilies magnifies the impact of colorful 'Cerise Queen' yarrow.

A variety of greens, set off by the whites on leaves and flowers, is a restful sight for weary eyes.

COLOR THROUGH THE YEAR

Once you've got the feel for color combinations, consider ways in which you can achieve a succession of colorful displays through the seasons. With some thought and planning, gardeners who live in areas with cold winters can have bloom from spring until frost and then enjoy colorful foliage, bark, and berries through the winter. Warm-winter gardeners can have color from flowers and foliage year-round.

The Range of Plants. It is possible to provide three- or four-season color using just annuals and perennials, but you'll increase your choices and produce more interesting results if you include shrubs and trees in your plans.

Annuals flower prolifically—many bloom from the time you plant them until frost kills them in the fall. Grown in beds or placed in pots, annuals can provide a quick color fix for a drab spot. Most perennials flower for weeks rather than months, but their year-to-year longevity makes them indispensable design elements on which to build. And their limited bloom times allow you to plan for a succession of color schemes that can travel through a perennial border as plants come into and out of bloom. For example, perennial blue-and-white columbine might bloom at the front of the border in late spring, giving way in the summer to clumps of golden yarrow at each end, followed in fall by a tall stand of deep-purple asters at the back. Using season and sequence, you can transform the color scheme of your garden from soft pastels in spring to vibrant shades in summer to rich earth tones in fall, without fear of clashing colors.

Foliage. Plants in every season can present a palette of colorful leaves in myriad greens, as well as a wide range of yellows, reds, oranges, golds, purples, and more. Annuals, perennials (including ornamental grasses), shrubs, and trees all offer numerous plants with excellent foliage potential for your garden. And in snow-covered winter landscapes, evergreen trees and shrubs and the fountain-shaped clumps of dried ornamental grasses become colorful accents.

Plants with Multiseason Interest. With so many attractive flower and foliage plants to choose from, strive to get the most out of your garden space by growing plants that have interest in at least two seasons. For example, many shrub roses bloom from late spring to frost. Dogwoods offer pretty pink or white flowers in spring and then cranberry red leaves in fall. Perennials such as hostas, astilbes, and lady's mantle contribute a few weeks of bloom but months of handsome foliage color.

Multiseason interest is guaranteed with dogwood trees. Their graceful spring blooms are followed by brightly colored autumn leaves. The textured bark is lovely all through the year but becomes most noticeable in winter.

White flowers and gray or silver foliage can soften the impact of contrasting or clashing colors while unifying a garden, above.

A succession of blooms keeps this garden lovely from spring to fall, below. Spring bulbs and early summer irises and peonies preceeded this midseason view. In the fall, 'Autumn Joy' sedum will take center stage.

SEASONAL COLOR

Flowering shrubs and trees, planted in mixed beds as featured individuals or massed in the landscape, greatly increase the potential for continuous displays of color.

- There are scores of spring-blooming trees and shrubs, including rhododendron, forsythia, lilac, dogwood, crabapple, and cherry.
- For summer bloom, try crape myrtle, southern magnolia, hydrangea, and butterfly bush.
- Flowering in fall are chaste tree and autumn cherry. Glossy abelia also continues blooming into fall.
- A number of trees and shrubs grown in warm climates, such as acacia, camellia, and Carolina jasmine, bloom in winter. And in northern climes, witch hazel provides flowers in winter.

FORM AND TEXTURE

The tall spikes in this garden contrast nicely with the shorter, more mounded forms.

While color may be the first feature to catch the eye, gardens need other, often more subtle, design elements to sustain and deepen interest. Long after the initial impact of the color scheme, other qualities hold your attention. These include the shapes of individual flowers and leaves, the forms of plants or groups of plants, and the surface textures.

Like color, the forms and textures of plants can be combined to heighten contrasts or create harmonies. Low velvety mounds of lamb's ears contrast with the smooth plump leaves of 'Autumn Joy' sedum. The delicate horizontal limbs of Japanese maple trace a spidery pattern on a dense backdrop of conifer foliage, and spikes of larkspur punctuate mats of ajuga.

It takes time to develop an appreciation for the subtleties of form and texture, and a bit longer to learn how to combine plants to exploit these characteristics.

Both appreciation and skill increase with your gardening experience, so don't get bogged down in subtleties. Instead, consider height and spread. Pay attention to the overall shapes and forms, or growth habits, of plants. As you plan, try to create combinations of plants as interesting for their shapes and textures as for their colors.

PLANT GROWTH HABITS

A plant's form and texture are as important as color, size, or bloom time. As you design, imagine how the shapes of various trees, shrubs, and herbaceous plants will fit into your landscape.

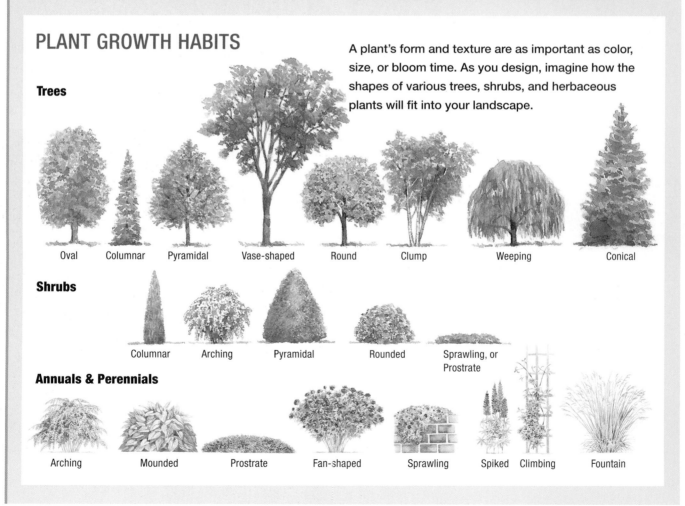

Trees

Oval   Columnar   Pyramidal   Vase-shaped   Round   Clump   Weeping   Conical

Shrubs

Columnar   Arching   Pyramidal   Rounded   Sprawling, or Prostrate

Annuals & Perennials

Arching   Mounded   Prostrate   Fan-shaped   Sprawling   Spiked   Climbing   Fountain

REPETITION

Beginners sometimes want to grow as many different plants as possible. Too often, this results in a bed containing one of each of dozens of plants. The gardener gains valuable experience with a lot of plants. But the bed looks helter-skelter. Too many different plants in one bed can make you dizzy. The remedy is repetition, one of the most useful tools in the design repertoire.

Repeating the same plant or color several places in the same bed helps tie a planting together by giving the other plants context and introducing order into the composition. Repetition can be especially useful in large beds, where the repeated elements divide the planting into smaller, easier-to-grasp units while lending continuity to the entire composition.

Repetition alone won't reduce the dizzying effect of too much variety in too small a space. It works best when you also simplify your planting scheme.

First, reduce the number of different plants. If you must grow two dozen kinds of them, make more beds. Then increase the numbers of each of the plants that remain. Instead of planting one lady's mantle and one bleeding heart, for example, plant groupings of three, five, or seven of each. (Odd-numbered groupings seem to please the eye more than those that are even-numbered.) Larger groupings of fewer plants are easier to notice and easier to work into coherent schemes of color or form. Of course, some plants are so large that a single specimen commands attention. Others are best deployed in masses. For example, a ground cover weaving through a planting provides a cohesive background, visually tying the garden together.

FOCAL POINTS

Whether it's a small flower bed or an entire landscape, any composition, or design scheme, can benefit from having one or more focal points. These are elements that quickly catch the eye, providing a starting point for the viewer's exploration.

A focal point need not be large, but it does need to attract attention. A reflecting ball set on a low pedestal in a planting of towering ornamental grasses is effective, as is a single clump of grass towering over a planting of perennials. In a landscape, a specimen tree, such as a weeping cherry or a cutleaf Japanese maple, is often a striking focal point. Structures such as gazebos, arbors, or wooden benches can also be focal points.

Repetition of color and form in this garden create a sense of unity and cohesion.

Focal points, such as this birdbath, attract attention and provide interest through the seasons. Place the focal point where you want to draw the viewer's eye.

CHAPTER 2

Getting Started

A well-designed garden, started with healthy plants and fertile, well-prepared soil, is on its way to being successful. You'll find that all aspects of getting started, from browsing in nurseries to digging and amending your garden beds, are truly enjoyable.

Buying Healthy Plants

While many annuals and some perennials are easy to start from seed, the majority of the plants most gardeners want are only sold as plants.

Look for a nursery or garden center that supplies quality plants and sound advice about selecting and growing them. At a good local supplier, you can inspect the plants before purchase and learn from knowledgeable staff how specific plants perform in your area.

Seek recommendations about suppliers from veteran gardeners in your area. When you're deciding where to shop, look for suppliers that offer plants and gardening supplies year-round, or at least for the entire growing season, rather than those that sell plants only seasonally. Also, inquire about the store's policy on replacements. Some suppliers provide a replacement or give a credit if a plant dies within the first year, depending on the plants and the circumstances. If you're buying large, expensive plants such as shrubs and trees, a performance guarantee is prudent as well as reassuring.

Selecting Size. Many plants are sold in containers ranging from an inch to a foot or more across or, as discussed in Chapters 5 and 9, bare-root or balled and burlapped. In general, large plants are older and more expensive than the same types of plants at a smaller size. However, a perennial purchased in a quart pot and the same kind of perennial in a gallon pot will often be the same size after each has been in the ground for a year. The size gap usually closes more slowly for shrubs and trees. When buying annuals, beginners are often tempted to pick the biggest plants or those already in flower. Resist the urge. Younger plants without blooms are more likely to perform better.

Choose plants carefully. Smaller plants that have not yet bloomed usually outperform those in flower, especially those with small rootballs, left. Larger rootballs can offset the stress that early blooms create.

Getting started on creating a garden like this, opposite, involves tasks as diverse as choosing plants appropriate to the site, laying out and designing garden beds, and improving the soil by adjusting the pH and adding organic matter and nutrients.

PLANT-BUYING KNOW-HOW

Whether you're buying annuals, perennials, or a tree, examine each plant carefully according to the following criteria:

- Foliage should have consistent color. Avoid plants with discolored or missing leaves and those with limp or wilted foliage.
- The plant's overall shape should be well-branched and bushy, uniform and symmetrical. Avoid plants with a few long, sprawling shoots or shoots that appear stunted; also avoid plants with broken or bent shoots, stems, or branches.
- The size of the container should be in proportion to the plant. Big plants in small pots are likely to be pot-bound, as shown below to the left.
- A few small roots protruding from the drainage holes in the bottom of the container are acceptable. Avoid plants with long, thick, protruding roots. Also avoid plants with roots coiling on or near the soil surface.
- Soil should fill the pot to within 1 inch of the rim. Avoid plants in dry soil that has pulled away from the sides of the container.
- Avoid plants showing symptoms of insect or disease damage, including misshapen flowers and contorted stems or branches.
- Look for an identification tag securely attached to the plant or inserted into the pot. Plants are sometimes mislabeled, but those with no label at all are too risky.

Pot-bound plants often have a mass of roots protruding from the drainage holes at the bottom.

Tease circling roots apart with your fingers before you transplant to keep them from strangling the plant.

Match the Plant to the Site. Lastly, as you select plants, remember to match their preferences for growing conditions to the places where you'll plant them. The grower's label or tag sometimes tells how much sun and what type of soil and moisture the plant needs. If you're not sure what conditions a plant requires, ask for advice at the nursery or garden center. Many gardeners like to try growing new plants, and some enjoy the challenge of growing plants in adverse conditions. If you decide to place a plant in a potentially unfriendly situation, be sure your yen for gambling suits your wallet. It's disappointing to spend several years tending an expensive shrub or tree only to have it die because it wasn't hardy enough or received too little sun.

smart tip

WATER-WISE GARDENING

Communities throughout North America have become increasingly conscious of the need to conserve water. From the arid Southwest to lush New England, no region has been spared water shortages during the last 20 years, and droughts have become more commonplace. Prodded by regulation, the increasing cost of water, or environmental concern, gardeners have become more sensitive to water use in their yards and gardens. The suggestions on page 19 can help reduce the amount of water your landscape requires. For more extensive and detailed information, contact your Cooperative Extension Service or your city, county, or state water board.

WHAT'S IN A NAME? COMMON VS. BOTANICAL

Botanical names often come as a surprise when you are beginning to garden. Many people are put off when they learn that the black-eyed Susan they admired in grandmother's garden is more properly called *Rudbeckia fulgida* 'Goldsturm'. This discovery can make the pleasant flower bed they were planning seem more like a botany field trip.

Don't let plant names flummox you. First, be assured that common names like black-eyed Susan are perfectly acceptable means of identifying and discussing plants. As long as you and the person with whom you're talking are using the same names for the same plants, common names serve just as well as botanical ones. But distinctly different plants can share a common name, and one plant can be known by several different common names. For example, at least three familiar plants share the name black-eyed Susan: one is a vine, one is a short-lived perennial often grown as an annual, and one is a hardy perennial. If you want to be certain when discussing and ordering plants, it's a good idea to use the botanical name.

Fortunately, gardeners need not master the intricacies of botanical nomenclature. For the black-eyed Susan mentioned earlier, *Rudbeckia* is the plant's ge-

nus; *fulgida* is its species; and 'Goldsturm' is the name of the particular cultivar. The genus and species are classifications scientists have devised to distinguish and group plants with similar botanically significant features. Cultivars (short for cultivated varieties) are names plant breeders have given to unique versions of a plant that were created by breeders, researchers, or even gardeners. Many garden plants are not cultivars and so are identified just by their genus and species name, as for the flowering dogwood, *Cornus florida*. Some plants may be identified by a genus and cultivar name only, as in *Sedum* 'Autumn Joy'. You'll encounter other variations in botanical nomenclature. Remember that you needn't know what the botanical names mean in order to use them when identifying or ordering plants, just as you needn't know what people's names "mean" when using them.

In this book, you'll find common names used in general discussion. In profiles of specific plants, you'll also see the botanical names so you can be certain when you go shopping for them. Many gardeners find that they use common names at some times and botanical names at other times, depending on which is most helpful in the particular situation.

***Rudbeckia fulgida* 'Goldsturm'** is the botanical name for these black-eyed Susans.

'Autumn Joy' sedum is one of the plants more widely known by its cultivar name than by its botanical name.

Plant Hardiness

When choosing plants, select those that will be able to withstand the rigors of your climate. The most common measure of this ability is the minimum temperature a plant can survive. The U.S. Department of Agriculture has divided North America into 13 "hardiness zones" based on average minimum winter temperatures. Horticulturists and expert gardeners have rated many plants according to the zone in which they will dependably survive the coldest temperature. The hardiness zone rating is frequently given on plant labels, in catalogs, and in books. Annuals aren't rated, unless they are actually perennials grown as annuals in the north and are hardy only in warm zones.

More than a decade ago, more attention began to be paid to the effects of heat on plants. The American Horticultural Society (AHS) developed a heat zone map, and increasingly, plant labels indicate ratings for heat zones. You'll find maps showing the North American cold-hardiness zones and the United States heat zones on pages 20–21. If you're uncertain at which zones your area is rated, ask at a local nursery or at the Cooperative Extension Service.

COOPERATIVE EXTENSION

The Cooperative Extension Service is one of the best sources of information about all aspects of gardening in your area. Drawing on the resources of state-funded universities, extension service offices in more than 3,500 cities and counties include or have access to horticulturists, entomologists, and soil scientists. Extension agents are excellent sources of local information—which plants perform best, which pests are most problematic, and which controls are most effective.

For information on the Cooperative Extension Service in your area, search the Internet, look in the phone book under County Government, or contact the nearest land-grant university.

If plants at local nurseries and garden centers aren't labelled for cold hardiness or are rated for a different zone than yours, check with staff to determine what conditions they might require.

smart tip

BE WATER WISE

- Seek out plants native to your region. These plants thrive on the moisture nature usually provides.
- With non-native plants, look for those that are well-adapted to your region's conditions. However, even drought-tolerant plants require regular moisture during their first year or two in the garden.
- Group plants with similar water needs in the same bed.
- Plant perennials and woody plants in fall in warm-winter regions and in early spring in cold-winter regions to take advantage of natural rainfall.
- Mulch garden beds to conserve moisture.
- Monitor soil moisture so you can water when necessary, not according to a schedule.
- Water with soaker hoses or install a drip irrigation system to minimize waste and evaporation loss.
- In container plantings, use plastic instead of porous clay pots, which dry out faster, or conserve moisture by putting a plastic pot inside a clay one or a clay pot inside another clay pot. Fill the space between the pots with peat moss, and water this stuffing to help keep roots cool and moist.

Moderate to heavy water needs link the gloriously diverse plants in this garden bed.

Hardiness Zone Map

Average Annual Extreme Minimum Temperature 1976–2005		
Temp (F)	Zone	Temp (C)
-60 to -55	1a	-51.1 to -48.3
-55 to -50	1b	-48.3 to -45.6
-50 to -45	2a	-45.6 to -42.8
-45 to -40	2b	-42.8 to -40
-40 to -35	3a	-40 to -37.2
-35 to -30	3b	-37.2 to -34.4
-30 to -25	4a	-34.4 to -31.7
-25 to -20	4b	-31.7 to -28.9
-20 to -15	5a	-28.9 to -26.1
-15 to -10	5b	-26.1 to -23.3
-10 to -5	6a	-23.3 to -20.6
-5 to 0	6b	-20.6 to -17.8
0 to 5	7a	-17.8 to -15
5 to 10	7b	-15 to -12.2
10 to 15	8a	-12.2 to -9.4
15 to 20	8b	-9.4 to -6.7
20 to 25	9a	-6.7 to -3.9
25 to 30	9b	-3.9 to -1.1
30 to 35	10a	-1.1 to 1.7
35 to 40	10b	1.7 to 4.4
40 to 45	11a	4.4 to 7.2
45 to 50	11b	7.2 to 10
50 to 55	12a	10 to 12.8
55 to 60	12b	12.8 to 15.6
60 to 65	13a	15.6 to 18.3
65 to 70	13b	18.3 to 21.1

Puerto Rico

0 10 20   40 Miles
0 15 30   60 Kilometers

Alaska

0   75   150   300 Miles
0   100   200   400 Kilometers

Hawaii

0 25 50   100 Miles
0 45 90   180 Kilometers

0   40   80   160 Miles
0 50 100   200 Kilometers

The Hardiness-Zone Map developed by the Agricultural Research Service of the USDA divides the country into 13 zones according to average minimum winter temperatures. Hardiness zones are used to identify regions to which plants are suited based on their cold tolerance, which is what "hardiness" means. Many factors, such as elevation and moisture level, come into play when determining whether a plant is suitable for your region. Local climates may vary from what is shown on this map. Contact your local Cooperative Extension Service for recommendations for your area. Or go to www.planthardiness.ars.usda.gov to find your hardiness zone based on your zip code. Mapping by the PRISM Climate Group, Oregon State University.

AHS Heat-Zone Map

Zone	Average Number of Days per Year Above 86°F (30°C)
1	< 1
2	1 to 7
3	> 7 to 14
4	> 14 to 30
5	> 30 to 45
6	> 45 to 60
7	> 60 to 90
8	> 90 to 120
9	> 120 to 150
10	> 150 to 180
11	> 180 to 210
	> 210

The American Horticultural Society Heat-Zone Map divides the United States into 12 zones based on the average annual number of days a region's temperatures climb above 86°F (30°C), the temperature at which the cellular proteins of plants begin to experience injury. Introduced in 1998, the AHS Heat-Zone Map holds significance, especially for gardeners in southern and transitional zones. Nurseries, growers, and other plant sources will gradually begin listing both cold hardiness and heat tolerance zones for plants, including grass plants. Using the USDA Plant Hardiness map, which can help determine a plant's cold tolerance, and the AHS Heat-Zone Map, gardeners will be able to safely choose plants that tolerate their region's lowest and highest temperatures.

AMERICAN HORTICULTURAL SOCIETY
7931 East Boulevard Drive
Alexandria, VA 22308 U.S.A.
(703) 768-5700 Fax (703) 768-8700

Coordinated by:
Dr. H. Marc Cathey, President Emeritus

Compiled by:
Meteorological Evaluation Services Co., Inc.

Underwriting by:
American Horticultural Society
Goldsmith Seed Company
Horticultural Research Institute of the
American Nursery and Landscape Association
Monrovia
Time Life Inc.

Copyright © 1997 by the American Horticultural Society

Scale for Alaska
Scale for Hawaii

Canada's Plant Hardiness Zone Map

Canada's Plant Hardiness Zone Map outlines the different zones in Canada where various types of trees, shrubs, and flowers will most likely survive. It is based on the average climatic conditions of each area. The hardiness map is divided into nine major zones: the harshest is 0 and the mildest is 8. Relatively few plants are suited to zone 0. Subzones (e.g., 4a or 4b, 5a or 5b) are also noted in the map legend. These subzones are most familiar to Canadian gardeners. Some significant local factors, such as micro-topography, amount of shelter, and subtle local variations in snow cover, are too small to be captured on the map. Year-to-year variations in weather and gardening techniques can also have a significant impact on plant survival in any particular location.

Plant Hardiness Zones

0a	0b	1a	1b	2a	2b	3a	3b	4a	4b	5a	5b	6a	6b	7a	7b	8a

Building Good Gardens

Successful gardening doesn't start with picking the loveliest or even the most robust plants. Instead, it starts with narrowing your plant choices to those that are right for each of your sites. As mentioned earlier, the quality of the soil, as well as exposure to wind, sun, or shade, may vary from place to place on your property. Sun-loving plants such as yarrow will hardly grow or flower in a shady spot. And a dry, sunny site can cause shade-lovers such as impatiens to wither and die. Other conditions, such as winter cold and summer heat, affect whole regions. Before you start digging a garden bed, learn about all the possible bed sites on your property and the kinds of plants that will grow well in each of them.

SOIL PREPARATION

Few gardening tasks are as beneficial to plants as good soil preparation. Healthy soil creates healthy plants. It is firm enough to anchor roots but loose enough to allow them to spread; retains enough water to supply plant needs but not so much that roots rot or are starved of oxygen; supplies adequate plant nutrients without requiring large doses of supplemental fertilizer; and supports a large and diverse population of earthworms, soil fungi, insects, and micro-organisms that, working together, help keep it healthy.

In general, soils with a high clay content drain slowly but are nutrient-rich. Sandy soils drain rapidly and are often nutrient-poor. Loam—consisting of balanced amounts of clay, silt, and sand liberally mixed with organic matter—is the ideal garden soil. It drains neither too quickly nor too slowly, has plenty of air spaces for oxygen and root penetration, and retains sufficient nutrients to support healthy growth.

Approaches to Preparation. All new garden beds benefit from some form of soil preparation. If your native, unimproved soil is largely loam, you can do as little as remove the existing vegetation and loosen the underlying soil. But most soils require additional work to improve their structure, fertility, and drainage. Fortunately, these qualities can all be improved simply by adding organic matter and minerals in sufficient quantities. Many gardeners produce good soil by working grass clippings, rotted manure, or compost into the top few inches of garden beds. In vegetable gardens, yearly additions of organic matter can transform poor soil in a few seasons. Soil in beds of perennial plants can't be extensively reworked each year, but supplements of mulch, compost, and necessary fertilizer can maintain and even improve soil quality.

TESTING THE SOIL

Gardeners can test their soil and amend it according to the test results. Although easy-to-use kits are available at garden centers, their results will usually be less extensive and less accurate than those from a professional laboratory. Soil tests are offered through some Cooperative Extension Services, as well as through university and private laboratories. Cooperative extension tests usually fall within the price range of simple home test kits. Private labs usually do more extensive testing and charge more for it. A few home test kits are quite elaborate and approach or exceed the costs of having a test performed by a commercial lab.

Soil tests vary in the factors they evaluate. Those conducted by labs and some of the more extensive home tests measure nutrients, and some labs recommend amendments or fertilizers to rectify deficiencies for the plants you're growing. All soil tests measure the soil's pH, or its degree of acidity or alkalinity as expressed on a scale of 1 to 14. Of all the tests provided by home test kits, the most useful and accurate are those for pH. Generally speaking, the soil's pH affects the ease with which plants can use nutrients in the soil. A pH of 7 is neutral, neither acid nor alkaline. Numbers lower than 7.0 indicate increasingly acidic soil, while those above 7.0 indicate soils that are increasingly alkaline.

Testing the soil with a home kit is fast and easy. Using the same type of kit every year gives you a good indication of changes in your soil.

Soil texture is determined by the percentage of sand, silt, and clay. It's difficult to change the texture, but you can improve soil structure with compost and organic mulches.

COLLECTING SOIL SAMPLES

To collect a soil sample for testing, brush any debris off the soil surface, and use a clean trowel (plastic if possible) to dig a hole 4 to 6 inches deep. Then take a ½-inch slice of soil from the side of the hole, and put that soil into a clean plastic container. (Because the samples are so small, a metal container or trowel can affect the results of the test.) Take a number of samples like this from different spots around the planting area. Thoroughly mix the samples in the container, and send at least a cup of this mixture to the lab. To compare soil from different parts of your property, prepare separate samples for separate tests. Label samples with the intended use (vegetables, perennials, etc.).

Dealing with pH

Garden plants will tolerate soil with a pH between 4.5 or 5 and 8.0, though most perform best at 6.0 to 6.5. Because most garden plants tolerate a fairly wide range of soil pH, some gardeners never need to adjust the pH. Occasionally, gardeners need to balance naturally acidic or alkaline soil, increase acidity for plants such as rhododendrons and camillias, or increase alkalinity for those that prefer a pH closer to neutral.

To adjust soil pH, follow the recommendations of the soil-testing lab or consult with your Cooperative Extension Service. The materials generally used to adjust soil pH—lime to decrease acidity and sulfur, peat moss or woody organic amendments to increase acidity—are inexpensive and widely available. But the types, quantities, and frequency of application will vary according to your soil and circumstances.

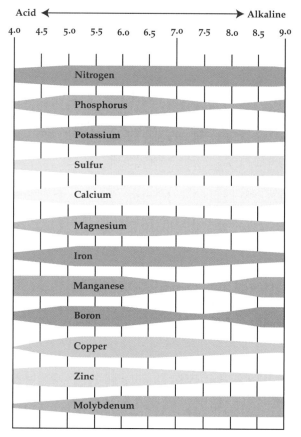

Nutrient availability as a result of soil pH is indicated by the width of the various bars on this chart. The wider the bar, the more nutrient that is available. It's easy to see why most plants grow best at a soil pH of 6.0–6.5.

DRAINAGE

Soil drainage is as important to plants as soil fertility. Roots rot and are deprived of needed oxygen in soggy soil and wither if it's too dry.

When you're planning a bed, test the site's drainage. Dig one or more holes 1 to 2 feet deep, fill them with water, let them drain, and fill them a second time.

- If the water is gone after 24 hours, the drainage should be adequate for most plants.
- If a few inches of water remain, plants described as preferring "very well-drained soil" may find this soil too wet. In this case, you can improve drainage by double-digging and adding large amounts of organic matter. (See "Dig a Garden Bed," page 31.) Both soil type and conditions influence the quantities and ma-

terials you should add, so your best bet is to consult with a knowledgeable person at your nursery or garden center.

- If more than a few inches of water remains in the test hole after 24 hours, relocate the bed. If you have no alternative site, construct a raised bed, as discussed on page 29.

Note: When you test for drainage, you may discover a hard, impervious layer of soil at the bottom of your hole. Called *hardpan,* this layer is often created by heavy equipment that has compacted the soil or by tillers used repeatedly when the soil was too wet. In the Southwest, hardpan occurs naturally and is called *caliche*. If you discover hardpan, consult with a landscape contractor.

Many woodland species thrive in soils that are exceptionally wet in spring and fall.

Drainage is easy to check with test holes. If water remains in the hole a day after the second filling, correct the drainage before planting.

AMENDMENTS VS. FERTILIZERS

The terms *amendment* and *fertilizer* are often used interchangeably. But there are differences. For the purposes of this book, amendments are materials that improve soil structure, drainage, and nutrient-holding capacity. Some add nutrients. All fertilizers supply nutrients. Peat moss is strictly an amendment, and a bag of 5-5-5 granular fertilizer is strictly a fertilizer. Some materials, such as compost, act as both a fertilizer and an amendment.

Organic Soil Amendments. Soil amendments include both organic and inorganic materials. Organic amendments are the decomposing remains of once-living organisms. Finding organic amendments can be aseasy as collecting grass clippings and leaves from your own yard or buying compost in bags. Some useful amendments, such

as oyster and crab shells, or buckwheat and rice hulls, are available on a regional basis. Many of these materials are excellent additions to your soil, but some, such as cotton gin waste or leather meal, can contain potentially harmful residues of pesticides or heavy metals.

Organic materials improve aeration and drainage in both clay and sandy soils and increase nutrient retention in sandy soils. As they decompose, organic materials also provide plant nutrients. You can add organic amendments liberally to any soil with beneficial results. For example, if you're digging 12 inches deep, you can add up to 6 inches of organic amendments. Use only well-decomposed materials, such as compost that is dark and crumbly, or peat moss, which is partially decomposed sphagnum peat. Materials with high concentrations of chemical salts, such as raw manure, or those with high concentrations of carbon, such as fresh sawdust, can damage or stunt the growth of plants. Mulching an existing bed with a few inches of dried grass clippings or chopped-up leaves, on the other hand, is a good way to incorporate these organic materials.

You can make your own compost, as described on page 37. If you need large quantities, buy it from a nursery. An increasing number of towns and cities compost organic waste. Leaf and yard waste composts are generally safe. But be cautious about municipal waste composts; avoid those of mixed municipal wastes unless they don't contain plastic and have been tested and shown to be free of harmful levels of heavy metals.

Inorganic Soil Amendments. Inorganic materials include greensand, which supplies potassium, and rock phosphate, which supplies phosphorus, in addition to lime, sulfur, and gypsum. Greensand and rock phosphate are becoming more widely available at nurseries, and almost all outlets sell lime, sulfur and gypsum.

Using Inorganic Materials. While it's almost impossible to add too much decomposed organic material to soil, be careful to add only the correct amounts of inorganic amendments. To adjust pH, apply lime, sulfur, or gypsum in the precise quantities recommended by a soil lab or extension service.

Many fertilizers are made of inorganic materials that provide the mineral nutrients required by plants. A new bed amended with a lot of well-rotted organic compost should grow healthy plants without additional fertilizers. However, if you're uncertain about the fertility of the soil, you can add a balanced fertilizer blend made of rock powders and organic materials, or up to 2 pounds per 100 square feet of a 5-5-5 synthetic granular fertilizer without fear of overdoing it. But remember that too much fertilizer can damage plants. Applying fertilizers according to a soil test is the best course of action.

Fertilizers containing organic materials are more widely available than ever. Before buying, check to see if they are approved for organic growers.

FIGURING OUT FERTILIZERS

The wide range of fertilizers can be baffling. They're usually distinguished from each other by the nutrients they provide, the materials that make them up, and the form in which they come. There are fertilizers for specific plants and situations as well as general-purpose fertilizers. Some are made from organic materials, others from inorganic; some come from "natural" sources (plants, rocks, and animals), others are synthesized in chemical factories. Many are granular, but liquids and powders are also common. Additionally, certain fertilizers, usually made from minimally-treated natural products, are approved for use by organic gardeners, while others (usually synthetic) are not.

All fertilizers provide nutrients in the form of inorganic ions. Organic fertilizers tend to take effect more slowly than synthetic ones but can improve the soil structure and contribute to the long-term health of the soil.

Plants require nitrogen (N), phosphate (P), and potassium (K) in larger amounts than other nutrients (called micronutrients), so fertilizers are labeled according to the relative concentrations of these *macronutrients,* or *primary* nutrients. The ratio of N to P to K (always in that order) is usually displayed prominently on the label: 10-10-10, for example. A 10-10-10 fertilizer will have twice as much of each of the three primary elements as a 5-5-5. When preparing a planting bed and for ordinary care, a fertilizer with roughly the same amounts of these three elements usually fills the bill. Such fertilizers are sometimes called *balanced.* If a soil test shows a nutrient deficiency, ask the staff at the nursery which fertilizers will meet the recommendations of the test and how much to apply. If you want to avoid synthetics, ask for an organically acceptable fertilizer.

Garden Tools

Gardening can be a low-tech activity. You can garden for years with just the tools shown here. Better tools may cost more initially but are less expensive in the long run since they don't break and need replacement. Look for garden spades and forks with blades, tines, and ferrules (the part that houses the handle) forged from a single piece of thick steel.

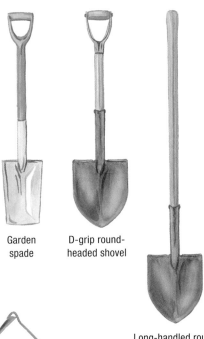

Garden spade

D-grip round-headed shovel

Long-handled round-headed shovel

Garden Spade and Shovels. The most important digging tool for many gardeners is the versatile flat-bottomed garden spade. It is used for initial bed preparation, transplanting, and maintaining bed edges. The blade of a round-headed shovel has a greater curve across its width than the garden spade, making it more useful for very sandy soils and for scooping and moving piles of gravel or rock. Tools with short D-grip handles are convenient and provide more than enough leverage, but taller people may find a long-handled tool easier on the back.

Garden (Spading) Fork. This tool loosens compacted earth that a spade won't budge and is ideal for mixing amendments into the soil or reworking the loose soil of a vegetable garden in the spring or fall. Thick square-section tines resist bending better than flat tines, though a thick-tined tool is heavier.

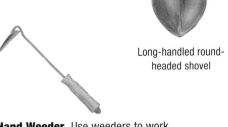

Hand Weeder. Use weeders to work wherever plants are close together.

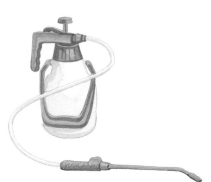

Hand Sprayer. Buy two sprayers, one for liquid fertilizers and the other for pesticides. Wash them well after every use to keep the nozzles clear.

Tiller. A small tiller is ideal for working fertilizers into the soil and making a smooth seedbed.

Garden rake

Lawn rake

Garden and Lawn Rakes. Garden rakes can smooth the soil surface in preparation for setting out plants or sowing seeds. They are also invaluable for spreading surface amendments. For removing leaves, twigs, and general tidying up, use a lawn rake with a wide fan of long tines.

Garden Cart. A sturdy cart is the best choice for hauling heavy loads. Some have removable front panels for easy dumping.

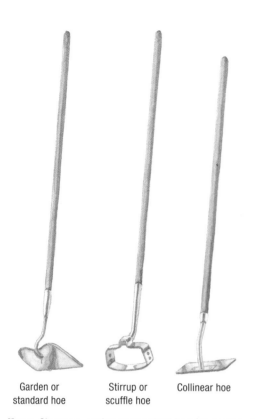

Garden or standard hoe

Stirrup or scuffle hoe

Collinear hoe

Hoes. Choose a garden or standard hoe for routine work, a stirrup hoe for small weeds and a collinear hoe for very fine, tight work. Sharp blades make work more efficient; sharpen your hoes before every use.

Wheelbarrow. Use wheelbarrows for hills and easy maneuvering. Buy the strongest available model for durability.

Bypass

Anvil

Pruning Shears. A pair of bypass pruning shears will handle almost all the pruning chores you'll encounter. Bypass shears (above, left) have two curved blades that cut like scissors; a good pair will cut through living stems and branches up to about ½ inch thick. Anvil-pattern shears (above, right), in which one straight blade cuts against the soft metal surface of the other blade, tend to crush stems and leave wounds that aren't as clean.

Hand Cultivator. The strong tines on this tool loosen and aerate soil and are invaluable for removing weed roots and rhizomes.

Trowel. You can dig small planting holes using a sturdy trowel with a fairly narrow blade. Trowels are also handy for removing tenacious tap-rooted weeds.

how to

Clear a Site Using a Spade

DIFFICULTY LEVEL: EASY

Tools and Materials: spade, tarp (optional)

1 **Remove the sod** by cutting blocks about the same size as your spade. Push the spade under the sod layer and lift.

2 **Pile sod pieces,** grass sides together, in a compost pile or place them face down at the bottom of the bed.

LAYING OUT AND CLEARING THE SITE

The first steps in starting a new garden bed are laying it out and clearing it of vegetation. Begin by outlining its perimeter. For beds with straight sides, you can tie string to stakes. For beds with curved or undulating outlines,   use a garden hose or powdered horticultural lime.

Remove whatever vegetation is currently growing inside the bed's perimeter (usually lawn grasses and weeds). Don't be tempted to dig or till the sod or weeds into the bed because many grasses and weeds spread by creeping roots that can sprout new plants. Instead, cut plants as close to the ground as possible and skim off the sod with a spade. Bury the pieces of sod upside down at the bottom of the new bed or in a compost pile. If you're removing pernicious weeds such as quack grass or Bermudagrass, it's safest to get rid of them in the trash.

If the bed is large or especially weedy, you may want to kill the vegetation first. You can smother plant roots by spreading sheets of black plastic over the site for five to six weeks in the heat of the summer.

Using Herbicides. If your site is infested with intractable weeds such as poison ivy, digging or smothering may be too difficult or ineffective. Another option is a nonspecific herbicide. Products based on the chemical glyphosate can kill persistent weeds that are difficult to remove by other means. These herbicides kill by moving through the entire plant from leaves to roots. **Caution:** *Use herbicides exactly as the label specifies, including wearing protective clothing.*

It may take a week or more for herbicide-sprayed plants to die, and it may take several applications to kill all the vegetation. Once all vegetation is dead, you can till the remains into the soil. While the manufacturer's tests show that glyphosate quickly breaks down into nontoxic substances, others cite research disputing this claim. Organic gardeners often avoid glyphosate because of damage it may do to soil organisms.

Leaves of nearby plants must be protected from herbicide oversprays. If possible, apply the herbicide on a windless day. You can use a large sheet of cardboard to shield nearby plants. If you're applying it to weeds in an existing bed, apply the herbicide with a sponge or brush.

how to

Till to Clear a Site and Plant a Garden Bed DIFFICULTY LEVEL: MODERATE

Tools and Materials: tiller, trowel, plants, fertilizer, water, mulch

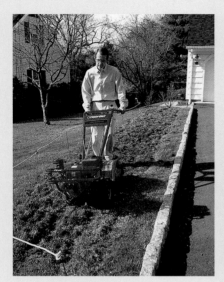

1 Till the sod only if you are certain that it contains no grasses, such as quack grass or Bermudagrass, that spread by rhizomes. When you till these grasses, you increase their populations and your weed problems.

2 Wait a week or so before transplanting. During this time, root fragments and weed seeds will sprout. Disturb the soil as little as possible when you remove these weeds; place transplants according to your plan.

3 Mulch to eliminate weed problems through the season; fertilize and water as needed; and stand back to watch the show. Before long, your new garden bed will be brimming with attractive flowers and foliage.

MAKING A RAISED BED

If your soil is less than ideal, you can still make a garden with raised beds. Consider this solution if your soil isshot through with heavy clay, exceedingly sandy, poorly drained and boggy, underlain by tough hardpan, laced with greedy tree roots, or packed with rocks.

By building up good garden soil on top of the problem soil, you can avoid the problems these conditions create. Raised beds are also an effective way to meet the special soil conditions required by acid-loving plants without trying to amend large areas of native soil.

To create a raised bed, use soil from your property, or buy topsoil. Regardless of its source, test and amend the soil to make it suitable for the plants you want to grow. You can build raised beds simply by mounding soil up to 8 inches above the surrounding area and firming the edges with the back of a rake. If

Raised beds are popular for vegetable gardens because plants in these beds tend to be healthy and yield well.

the plants you want to grow require deeper soil or if you'd like a tidier look, enclose the bed with stones, bricks, or landscape timbers.

HAND-TESTING SOIL BEFORE DIGGING

With the site cleared, you're ready to dig—but only if the soil is also ready. You can destroy a soil's structure by working it when it is too wet or too dry. Test the soil by squeezing a handful. If it crumbles into powder when you open your hand, it's too dry. Water the area

thoroughly and try the squeeze test again in a day or so. If the soil forms a tight wet ball, it's too wet to dig and you'll have to wait a day or more to let the soil dry. If the soil forms a ball that breaks apart easily when you tap it gently with your fingers, it's ready to dig and amend.

For most soils, *single digging* to a depth of 8 to 10 inches (the length of the spade) is sufficient. This kind of digging aerates the soil, gives you a chance to remove rocks and roots, and lets you add several inches of organic amendments. *Double digging* refers to the process of aerating the soil at the trench bottom as shown opposite. It is the best method for improving poorer soils and those with inadequate drainage.

The best tools for digging a new bed are a garden spade and fork. In compacted soil, using a gas-powered tiller can be more work than digging by hand. Because single and double digging involve many of the same steps, they can be described together, as shown opposite.

Begin by taking a handful of soil and squeezing it.

A

Soil that won't hold together is too dry to work.

B

Soil that holds together when squeezed . . .

. . . but compresses when tapped, is too wet to work.

C

Soil that holds together when squeezed . . .

. . . but crumbles apart when tapped, is just right to work.

OUTSMARTING THE WEEDS

A newly dug garden bed is a satisfying sight. Unfortunately, the digging and raking that produced that lovely manicured surface also dredged up millions of weed seeds. All it takes is a little warmth and moisture to make them germinate. If you can bear to postpone planting, you can get rid of this unwanted crop by using a farmer's technique called a *stale seedbed*. Since you won't spend so much time weeding later in the season, this method is well worth the wait. Let the soil sit undisturbed for a week or two, until the little weed seedlings are about an inch high. Then dislodge them with a rake or hoe, and rake them off the surface of the bed. Take care not to stir the soil any more than you have to, or you'll bring more weed seeds close to the surface. Unless your soil is unusually weed-free, you'll need to repeat this process a few times to eradicate a significant portion of the annual weeds. This weed-control method works best in spring and summer. In fall, seeds don't germinate, even though they may be present.

how to

Dig a Garden Bed

DIFFICULTY LEVEL: EASY

Tools and Materials: spade or shovel, tarp, fertilizer, soil amendments

1 **Remove the sod** by cutting through the roots in blocks that are about the same size as your spade. Push the spade under the sod layer and lift.

2 **Single- and double-digging** start by digging a 2-foot-wide trench, one spade deep, across one end of the bed. Move soil from this first trench to the other end of the bed.

3 **Spread a layer of amendments** on the trench bottom. If double-digging, use a spading fork to loosen the soil at the trench bottom to another spade's depth.

4 **Dig a second trench,** filling the first with soil from the second. Repeat this, using the soil from the first trench to fill the last one.

CHAPTER 3

Garden Care

After giving your garden a good start, you'll want to ensure that the plants stay healthy and attractive as the garden matures. Keeping plants well watered, well fed, and well groomed is, or can be, part of the fun of gardening. Tending your plants gives you a good excuse for being outdoors, and observing plants at close range deepens your appreciation and understanding of them.

Observation, in fact, is one of the most important aspects of plant care. Problems seen early are much easier to remedy than those that have progressed far enough to be visible across the lawn. Try to take a slow stroll around your plantings every day or so—morning and evening if possible. As you grow more familiar with your plants, you'll be able to anticipate things that need doing and spot problems in the making.

Routine Care

Gardens require routine maintenance, as described on pages 34 through 38, to stay healthy, beautiful, and productive. As a garden becomes established, you'll find that it requires less and less care, but only if you've done a thorough job in the beginning.

Organic mulches, such as the straw used in this garden below, add beauty, increase soil health, and cut your work time.

Garden care becomes less time consuming and more enjoyable as the season and the years progress, opposite.

WATERING

Although mulch helps hold existing water in the soil, it doesn't add moisture. Most gardeners have to supplement natural rainfall to keep plants healthy. In some regions, irrigation is a regular requirement; in others an infrequent one. In any region, young plants in new beds need regular watering to get established. (See "Water-wise Gardening," Chapter 2, page 17.)

Frequent Inspection. Check on water needs daily. Wilted leaves often indicate water stress, and dull or curling leaves are pre-wilting symptoms. But the condition of leaves can be misleading, even for experienced gardeners. Symptoms common to water stress may be due to disease or insect damage instead. The best way to determine when to water is to check the soil. If the soil beneath the mulch feels dry to the touch, dig down and see if it is moist 2 or 3 inches below the surface. If you don't want to disturb roots, shove a thin stick of light-colored, unfinished wood 2 or 3 inches into the soil. (The wooden stirrers given out by paint stores make fine moisture-testing sticks). Pull up the stick after an hour. If the bottom few inches is not discolored by moisture, you need to water.

Water Thoroughly. When you water, water deeply. Garden plant roots can grow from 1 foot to more than 5 feet deep. Wetting just the top few inches of soil encourages shallow root growth, making it necessary to water more frequently. You can water small plants or widely separated plants adequately with a hand-held hose. But hand-watering an entire bed for even as long as an hour can provide less water than ½ inch of rainfall. Providing enough water to soak down a foot or more into the soil requires a sprinkler or irrigation system.

Sprinklers as Watering Tools. Sprinklers are inefficient tools because water is blown away by wind, runs off sloped or paved areas, or falls too far away from individual plants to be of use to them. The water soaks leaves as well as the soil, and damp foliage can be a breeding ground for disease. But sprinklers are inexpensive and easy to use, so many people find them convenient when they are just getting started.

smart tip

HOW MUCH WATER DO YOU NEED?

You can determine your soil's absorption rate by watering an area and digging to determine penetration, but this is messy and imprecise. As a general rule of thumb, 1 inch of slow, steady rainfall soaks about 4 to 5 inches deep in clay soil, 7 inches deep in loam, and 12 inches in sandy soil. So if you want to water 12 inches deep in loam, you'll need to provide a little less than 2 inches of water.

To make best use of your sprinkler, determine the rate at which it delivers water and the rate at which your soil absorbs water. To determine the sprinkler's delivery rate, set a number of empty cans (empty tuna cans work well) in a line from the sprinkler to its farthest reach. Note how long it takes to deposit an inch of water in any one of the cans. You'll see that water accumulates in the cans at different rates; few sprinklers deliver water evenly.

Efficient Watering Systems. Soaker hoses and drip irrigation systems both apply water directly to the roots. Very little water is lost, and the risk of water-borne foliage problems is reduced. Drip irrigation systems are the more expensive and involved option, but most people can install a simple system. For an overview of drip systems, see page 35.

Soaker hoses are inexpensive, easy to install, and easy to use. Made of perforated plastic or water-permeable material, soaker hoses seep or drip water along their length. They deliver water much more slowly than sprinklers, so you'll have to check the manufacturer's information for delivery rates. Soaker hoses are well suited for watering plants grown in rows, as in vegetable or cutting gardens. In ornamental plantings, you can encircle large shrubs or trees and snake the hose beside smaller plants. Because water doesn't spread very far sideways as it soaks into soil, plants that are not next to the hose will not get watered.

Watering needs are easy to determine by using an unfinished wooden stick as a gauge of soil moisture, left.

Soaker hoses allow water to seep out into the soil, while sprinklers, right, spray droplets into the air and onto the leaves.

Drip Irrigation Systems

Drip irrigation systems deliver water at low pressure to plants through a network of plastic pipes, hoses, tubing, and a variety of emitters. In addition to ground-level emitters that drip water in controlled amounts, systems can include porous soaker tubing and sprayers or sprinklers positioned at ground level or up to several feet above the soil surface. Simple drip systems can be attached to regular garden hoses and controlled manually from an outdoor faucet, just like a sprinkler. The most sophisticated systems include their own attachment to your main water supply, a system of valves that allows you to divide your property into zones, and an electronic control system that can automatically water each zone at preset times for preset durations.

A person with modest mechanical skills and basic tools can plan and install a simple drip irrigation system. Unless you're mechanically inclined, leave complex systems to professional installers. You can buy kits or individual system components from garden centers, nurseries, or specialty suppliers. The main components are outlined below. Good criteria for choosing among different suppliers are their knowledge of system design and installation and their willingness to help you with both. They may charge for this service, but good advice is worth the money.

- A drip system connected to a domestic water supply needs a backflow prevention device (also called an antisiphon device) at the point of connection to the water supply to protect drinking water from contamination. Backflow devices are often specified in city building codes, so check with local health or government officials to determine whether a specific type of backflow prevention device is required.

- Install a filter to prevent minerals and flakes from coming off metal water pipes and clogging the emitters. You'll need to clean the filter regularly. Between the filter and emitters, all hoses and tubing should be plastic because metal an flake off and clog the system.

- To reduce the water pressure supplied by the household pipes to the low pressure required by the emitters, every drip system needs a pressure regulator.

- Install a timer or electronic controller for convenience. Unlike you, it won't forget and leave the water on too long. It irrigates during the day or while you're away. However, without resetting, it may also water in a rainstorm.

- To automate your gardening further, consider installing fertilizer injectors to deliver nutrients to your plants along with timed watering.

- Water is delivered from the pipes to the emitters by flexible plastic tubing, sold specifically for drip systems. Systems installed just under the soil surface often have an air/vacuum relief valve placed at the high point in the line (as shown below).

- A range of emitters and mini-prinklers is available for different kinds of plants and garden situations. Consult with your supplier about which best meet the needs of various gardens.

Typical drip system shown installed on a 4-in. subgrade. It can also be installed on the surface or under mulch.

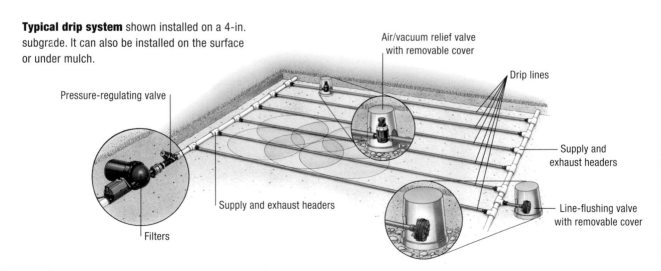

Pressure-regulating valve

Air/vacuum relief valve with removable cover

Drip lines

Supply and exhaust headers

Supply and exhaust headers

Filters

Line-flushing valve with removable cover

MAINTENANCE FERTILIZING

Most ornamental plants get a good start if their beds are prepared and amended as discussed in Chapter 2 (beginning on page 28). In subsequent years, you can maintain healthy soils and provide nutrients by spreading a couple of inches of well-rotted compost on the surface of the soil. The decomposition of regularly renewed organic mulch also builds and maintains soils.

Many gardeners augment these good soil-husbandry practices during the season by fertilizing their entire gardens or only a few selected plants such as bulbs, annuals, roses, and rhododendrons. Applied at the right time and in the correct amounts, additional fertilizer can help to establish sturdy stems and foliage, boost bloom, and build up reserves for dormancy and reemergence in the spring. *Balanced,* or complete, fertilizers generally suit these purposes. (See Chapter 2, pages 24–25, for an overview of fertilizers.) Sub-par performance is sometimes remedied by additional nutrients, though it is often difficult to pin a problem on a single cause, and fertilizing a plant that doesn't need it can do more harm than good. Excess nitrogen, for example, can promote foliage growth at the expense of flowers and fruit. Whether you're seeking to boost healthy plants or rejuvenate ailing ones, it's best to seek advice at a good local nursery or from your Cooperative Extension Service on what type of fertilizer, if any, is most appropriate for your plants. Follow package instructions precisely for application and dosage.

Fertilizing Vegetable Gardens. Many gardeners rework the soil in their vegetable gardens every spring. During this process, nutrients can be augmented and adjusted, either with specific nutrient sources or by the addition of liberal amounts of well-rotted manure or compost. Gardeners seeking to boost yields often apply supplementary fertilizers to all or some of the plants. The principles are the same as those described for ornamentals, as is the caution to avoid overfertilization.

Granular fertilizers, whether organically derived or synthetic, are easy to measure out and apply to ornamental and vegetable garden beds. Sprinkle granules around the base of the plants, taking care to keep them away from stems and off leaves. Work the granules into the soil with your fingers or a *hand cultivator,* and apply water to begin dissolving them. *Slow-release* fertilizers can be spread as little as once a year, in the spring. They're especially valuable for plants that become increasingly difficult to get to or to work around as the season progresses. In general, slow-release fertilizers are more expensive to use than ordinary formulations. Most organically derived fertilizers release their nutrients slowly, although their labels don't usually advertise them as slow-release fertilizers. While these fertilizers may also cost more, many contribute to the long-term health of the soil and supply important trace elements missing from synthetic fertilizers.

Fertilizing Other Plants. Potted plants need regular doses of fertilizer. The nutrients in potting soil are quickly taken up by the plant or leached out by watering. *Liquid fertilizers* are easy to apply to container plants. Although these fertilizers are expensive, potted plants require relatively small amounts. Slow-release granules are also handy and can reduce the number of applications considerably.

Young trees and shrubs can benefit from fertilization until they're near full size. But many do well with no fertilizer at all. Trees and shrubs grown in garden beds or in the lawn will benefit from fertilizer you apply to annuals and perennials in the beds or to the turf around the trees. To boost bloom in flowering shrubs, apply additional balanced fertilizer or spread 1 inch of compost every spring.

Fertilize plants according to their needs, left. Here, a gardener is applying wood ash, which supplies potassium, to asparagus beds in early spring.

Add fertilizers carefully. Learn plants' nutrient requirements before fertilizing with materials other than compost, right.

COMPOST FOR MAINTENANCE FERTILIZING

Well-rotted organic matter, or compost, is an excellent soil amendment and mulch. It's easy to compost plant waste collected from your yard, garden, and kitchen. The simplest method is to pile plant wastes together in a homemade wire bin. Make one from sturdy wire mesh; chicken wire is too flimsy to stand on its own. A piece 4 feet wide by 14 feet long will make a bin 4 feet in diameter, the smallest volume that works well. A grid up to 1½ inches by 3 inches or so will hold material inside. The smaller the grid, the tidier the composting area will be.

Toss in grass clippings, plant material from the garden, and plant wastes from the kitchen. If you add fallen leaves, first shred them by running over the pile a few times with a lawn mower. Farm-animal manure and straw are excellent compost materials, if you can get them. Don't add animal bones or flesh from the kitchen, because they attract carniverous rodents and other unwanted animals. Dog and cat waste may contain parasites or disease organisms that can affect humans; don't add them to your compost piles. Don't compost diseased plant parts or weeds with seeds either. Some disease organisms survive the composting process, so burn them or toss them in the trash.

Within six months to a year, depending on the ingredients and your climate, much of the material in the bin will have decayed into a crumbly, rich brown substance. To harvest the compost, just remove the wire bin and set it up nearby. Transfer the uncomposted material on top of the pile into the bin to start the next batch, and dig out the composted material from the center of the old pile. You can increase the speed of composting by turning the pile regularly with a garden fork. If the art of composting intrigues you, ask your Cooperative Extension Service for information on more-sophisticated methods.

Compost bins made from wire or plastic mesh (as shown here) are easy to set up. They prevent compost ingredients from blowing around, keep animals out, and allow moisture and air movement.

Composting transforms ordinary kitchen and yard waste into a valuable soil amendment and fertilizer. Pile a 6-in. layer of dry material on the bottom of the bin. Add 4 in. of fresh materials, as shown in the top photo, add a sprinkling of garden soil, and repeat the layers. In a month or so, materials will have started composting, as shown in the second photo from the top. The third photo shows fully finished compost, which takes 6 months to a year to develop in ordinary conditions.

MULCHING

Mulch is the garden's miracle material. Organic mulches a few inches deep help soil retain moisture, keep plant roots from getting too cool or too hot, hold weeds in check, provide nutrients as they decompose, and contribute organic matter to feed soil organisms and improve soil structure. As a bonus, mulches give the garden a neat, tidy appearance.

Many loose organic materials can be used as mulch—chopped leaves, straw, grass clippings, newspaper, shredded or chipped wood or bark, and seed or nut hulls and shells. You can collect leaves and grass clippings from your own property and buy other mulching materials in bags or bulk from a nursery or garden center. Shredded wood (and bark) is an ideal mulch because it's unobtrusive, easy to spread, heavy enough to stay put when the wind blows, and non-compacting (unlike grass clippings). Shredded wood also decomposes relatively slowly and needs renewing only every year or so.

Gravel is effective at keeping plant roots cool and helping to retain soil moisture, but it doesn't supply organic matter or appreciable nutrients. Water-permeable landscape fabrics are useful for mulching shrub borders and other low-maintenance landscape plantings, but they're difficult to cut through and impractical in plantings where you're occasionally adding or moving plants around. Plastic sheeting isn't a good mulch material for ordinary gardens for numerous reasons. It doesn't allow water to penetrate, can overheat plant roots, and is difficult to work with and remove. It also deteriorates after a few seasons into shreds that blow around.

Beds started with young plants, rather than by direct seeding, should be mulched at the time of planting. Layer the mulch no more than 3 inches deep, and leave a few inches around the stem of each plant mulch-free. You can mulch direct-seeded plants once the seedlings have been thinned and are at least a few inches tall. Depending on climate and materials, organic mulches may last for several years or mere months. Hot, humid conditions tend to speed decomposition, and fresh, moist materials such as grass clippings decompose more quickly than dry ones.

Pull mulches back a few inches from plant stems, left, to avoid rotting problems.

Good mulches, above, include such materials as newspapers, straw, cardboard, compost, autumn leaves, and shredded wood.

Garden Hygiene

In addition to watering, fertilizing, and mulching, there are a variety of garden maintenance tasks that need to be done from time to time during the course of the year.

SEASONAL CARE

Spring and fall are busy gardening times, particularly in cold winter climates. In fall, you prepare plants for winter. Cut old leaves and stems of most deciduous perennials back to the ground, and remove the debris from the garden. To protect roses from the cold and drying winds of winter, mulch the plants loosely or set up protective covers and barriers around them.

In spring, you clear away winter's detritus and prepare the plantings for a new growing season. Remove or pull back protective coverings from emerging plants, renew mulches, and give the beds a general tidying up. Inspect the shrubs and perennials whose stems and foliage have overwintered, and prune out dead, diseased, or weak stems and foliage.

If you live in a warm-winter climate, you'll perform many of the same seasonal tasks, but you'll have to work around plants that grow year-round.

During seasons of active growth, some plants need to be cut back to control their size or promote bushy growth. Removing spent flowers, called "deadheading," encourages reblooming in annuals and a number of perennials. The plant descriptions in the following chapters will note if these practices are recommended.

Good garden hygiene discourages pests and diseases that live in debris both during the season and over the winter months.

WEED PATROL

No matter how carefully you prepare the bed and mulch the soil, your garden will still harbor at least a few weeds. Keep an eagle eye out for weeds on your regular inspection tours. Weeds are far easier to control if you pull them when they're just a few inches high and their roots haven't spread far and wide.

Detected early enough, most weeds can be easily hand pulled. Tap-rooted weeds, such as dandelions, may require assistance from a garden knife or trowel. Try to get the entire root, or you'll be pulling the same weed in a few days. Weeds that spread by their roots, such as bindweed, can grow quickly, so you may need to remove them from an area using a scuffle hoe. Then smother the soil with mulch. Even well-mulched weeds may resprout from root fragments. Check the area frequently, and keep pulling new plants out. Eventually you'll get rid of them.

Some weeds, such as Bermudagrass, are so tenacious that chemical controls (discussed in Chapter 2, page 28) are just about the only line of defense.

Pest and Disease Control

Pest and disease control starts with prevention. Select plants that are adapted to the conditions of your region, and whenever possible, resistant to pests and diseases common in your area. Prepare the soil well, keep plants well watered and fed, and keep the garden tidy. Healthy plants have greater recuperative powers, and well-tended gardens provide fewer areas for insects to breed and congregate. Be vigilant. During your daily garden strolls, be on the lookout for insect damage. Similar to weed control, it's easiest to correct insect problems at the beginning. When you see a little damage, don't mount a war. Monitor the problem. The forces of nature may resolve it for you or keep the damage to an acceptable level. If the problem gets worse, identify the culprit before taking action. A chewed leaf, for example, may be obvious, but unless you actually catch the culprit in the act, it can be difficult to determine which insect is to blame. If you're uncertain, catch the insect you feel is causing the damage and take it to a nursery or the Cooperative Extension Service for identification and help in determining the extent of the problem and the best treatments.

INSECT PESTS

Increased concern about the effects of toxic chemicals has shifted the emphasis on garden pests from eradication to control. Today, we're encouraged to view the garden as a natural system, where a balance of good, bad, and benign insects is maintained by natural processes with assistance from the gardener.

Gardens abound in insect life. Some insects, such as aphids, grubs, grasshoppers, and spider mites, can damage and sometimes kill plants. Others, such as lady beetles and certain wasps, are beneficial; they destroy or disable plant-damaging insects. Still others, such as caterpillars and the butterflies they become, cause some damage as well as provide beauty and enjoyment.

Controlling insect pests involves determining which pests are unacceptably harmful to the plants (most plants being able to withstand some damage) and which methods of control are least harmful to the benign, beneficial, or beautiful insects and other creatures in the garden. Common pests are shown on pages 44–47.

Control Methods. When you've determined that something needs to be done about an insect pest, consider the least-toxic methods of control first. Some insects are easy to pick off plants with your fingers. Squash them or drop them in a jar of soapy water. Other insects, such as aphids, can sometimes be kept under control by knocking them off leaves with a blast of water from the garden hose. You can protect plants in vegetable or cutting gardens by using barriers such as floating row covers, which are made of a thin fabric permeable to light, rain, and air but not to bugs.

Least-toxic materials include diatomaceous earth, household detergents or specially formulated insecticidal soaps, and horticultural oils. Biological controls, including certain insects and insect diseases that destroy garden pests, can be purchased and releasedin the garden. (See the box at right for common biological controls.)

If these methods prove impractical or ineffective, you can turn to a wide range of insecticides. Some, such as sabadilla, ryania, neem, and pyrethrin, are made from substances produced by plants. Organic gardeners prefer these pesticides because of their plant origins and because they break down quickly into nontoxic materials. Other pesticides are synthetic. Many of the newer synthetic pesticides are safer for the environment than older synthetic products. To use an insecticide, identify the pest you're after. Pesticides are formulated and registered for use only on specific plants. It is illegal and inappropriate to use them on plants other than those listed on the label. Whether organic or synthesized, ***all insecticides are toxic and should be handled and applied exactly as described on the product label, including wearing protective clothing and a mask.*** (See "Taking Cover," page 43.)

Encourage beneficial insects by growing plants with small flowers, such as this bee balm, or mint, yarrow, or salvia.

Prevent insect damage with row covers. Drape the material over hoops, as shown here, or simply lay it over plant rows. Use soil, rocks, or ground staples to hold it in place.

BIOLOGICAL PEST CONTROLS

Lace wing: Both larvae and adults feed on aphids, mites, and other small, soft-bodied pests. Adults require nectar and pollen in order to reproduce.

Lady beetle (ladybug): Both larvae and adults eat a wide range of soft-bodied insects. Provide a pesticide-free environment to grow your own because purchased beetles tend to fly away when released.

Trichogramma wasps: Larvae feed inside caterpillars before emerging and pupating on them, as shown here.

Parasitic nematodes: These microscopic worm-like creatures eat grubs, webworms, and hundreds more soil-dwelling pests.

Predatory mites: These tiny arachnids feed on other mites and thrips that wreak havoc with some plants.

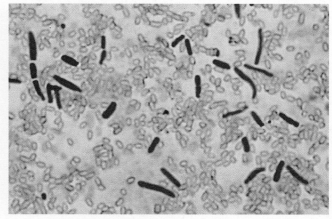

BT (*Bacillus thuringiensis*): This bacterium kills caterpillars and is harmless to humans (can be used on all food crops).

ANIMAL PESTS

Some gardeners make a special effort to attract animals to their plantings. Others work equally hard trying to keep them out. Whether welcomed or repulsed, deer, woodchucks, rabbits, squirrels, chipmunks, voles, ,moles, and other animals can do considerable damage to garden plants, both above- and below-ground. Few of the products that claim to repel these animals are effective, and then usually only if the animals aren't really hungry. The most effective controls are fences and traps. Electric fences up to 18 inches high, with strands placed at 4- to 6-inch intervals, can discourage small aboveground animals. Deer can jump tall fences but are held at bay by wide ones. One excellent design consists of poles set at about a 30- to 40-degree angle and strung with electric wires at 1-foot intervals, with the top wire being about 5 feet off the ground.

To stop burrowing animals, dig a 1-foot-deep (2-foot-deep for gophers), ½ foot-wide trench, and erect a chicken-wire fence that extends from the bottom of the trench to 2 to 3 feet above the ground. Fill in the trench with soil. At the top of the fence, leave an additional foot of fencing material unattached to the posts so that it will flop out and discourage small climbing animals. Traps are available that kill animals or capture them for release somewhere else. In some areas, local animal-control authorities may provide such traps. In other areas, it's illegal to trap and relocate wildlife.

Foolproof Animal Fencing

Fences that extend belowground will keep digging animals out of a garden and loose fencing on top discourages climbers. Use chicken wire on the underground portion and for about 2 feet above the soil surface. For deer, add a second, electric, fence 5 feet outward from the first. Attach aluminum foil covered with peanut butter to the electric fence; deer get a jolt they don't soon forget.

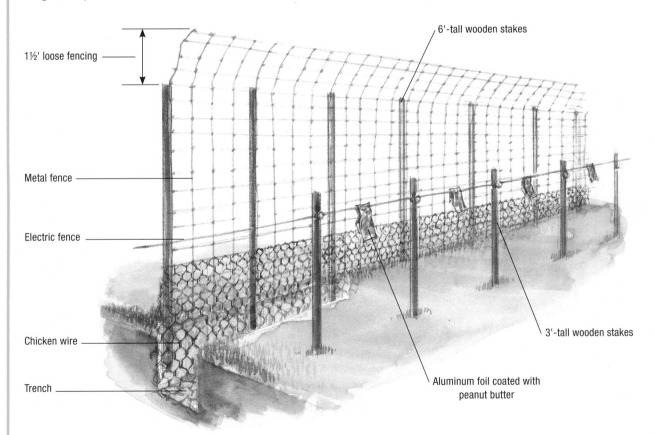

1½' loose fencing

6'-tall wooden stakes

Metal fence

Electric fence

3'-tall wooden stakes

Chicken wire

Aluminum foil coated with peanut butter

Trench

PLANT DISEASES

Bacteria, fungi, and viruses disfigure or discolor leaves or flowers, produce powdery or moldy films or spots, and rot stems and roots. Knowing whether a disease is fungal, viral, or bacterial helps you treat it. But a variety of problems besides diseases can cause symptoms of ill health—including insect pests, water stress, air pollution, nutrient problems, and too much or too little sunlight. Additionally, while diseases such as powdery mildew have characteristic signs or symptoms, many others cause similar-looking damage, making them difficult to identify. (See pages 45–47 for photos of some of the most common plant diseases.) In cases when you can't be certain of the identity of a disease, take samples of the diseased tissue to a nursery or your local county Cooperative Extension Service.

Plant diseases can be difficult to treat, so it's best to do everything you can to avoid them in the first place. Rotate annual plants so that their diseases don't have a chance to build up in the soil. Seek out resistant cultivars. Take good care of your plants; well-watered, well-fed plants grown in good soil are less susceptible to and better able to tolerate many diseases. Poor air circulation breeds fungal diseases; plant at recommended spacings and thin out dense growth. Monitor plants regularly for disease. When you spot a disease, cut away the affected plant parts, or remove entire plants. Remove and discard the diseased material, but put it in the trash; don't compost it. After cutting diseased tissue, disinfect pruning shears with alcohol to avoid spreading the infection.

TAKING COVER

Using insecticides and herbicides derived from botanical, biological, mineral, or synthetic materials requires basic precautions. Read product labels thoroughly, and apply these products with great care. If your clothing becomes wet with pesticides, remove it immediately and shower before changing into uncontaminated clothes. Following is a list of basic protective clothing and gear that you may need.

- Long-sleeved shirt, pants, and socks made of tightly woven material (all cotton). Do not leave skin exposed!
- Waterproof, unlined gloves
- Waterproof footwear
- Hat, scarf, or hood to completely cover scalp and to overhang face
- Goggles
- Disposable dust mask designed for pesticide dusts
- Tight-fitting respirator when using liquid sprays. Respirators contain activated-charcoal cartridges that filter pesticide vapors from the air. Make sure it's approved by the National Institute of Occupational Safety and Health (NIOSH).

Note: Be sure to rinse off your waterproof gear and pesticide applicator with plenty of clean water before removing your protective apparel. Avoid handling the outside of the contaminated clothing—use gloves if necessary—and if it will not be laundered immediately, place the clothing in a sealable plastic bag. Wash these garments separately from your regular laundry. Pre-soak them in a pre-soaking product; then wash them on the highest temperature setting for a full cycle with detergent. If the clothing has any residual pesticide odor after the rinse cycle, repeat the washing procedure until the odor is gone. Air-dry the wet clothes on a line. Clean the washing machine by running it through the wash cycle with detergent but without clothes. Or simply throw the clothes away.

Protect hands from accidental chemical or toxic splashes or sprays. Heavy-duty rubber latex gloves, not just household gloves, allow needed flexibility while giving good protection. Gloves that extend to the forearm and fit snugly around the wrist provide the best protection.

COMMON PESTS AND DISEASES

Japanese beetles are an eastern and midwestern pest. Beginning in midsummer, adults quickly skeletonize leaves of many ornamental plants and vegetables. Control by handpicking the adults into a can of soapy water. Japanese beetle pheromone traps may or may not be effective.

Japanese beetle larvae eat many types of roots but prefer those of lawn grasses. After a year or sometimes two, they pupate. Adults emerge in midsummer. Control larvae by treating the lawn with beneficial nematodes or, south of Zone 5, milky spore disease (both available from garden centers).

Caterpillars, the larvae of moths and butterflies, feed on many plants, from cabbages to roses. Because they grow into butterflies and moths, you may not want to kill them. For pest species such as gypsy moth larvae, use BT (*Bacillus thuringiensis*) while the caterpillars are small.

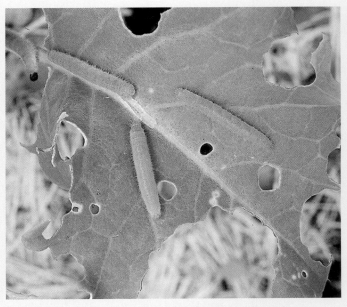

Leafhoppers spread diseases as they suck cell sap. Affected plants are often distorted. Avoid problems with floating row covers or, in small areas, aluminum foil mulches. Dust foliage with diatomaceous earth (available from garden centers or feed stores). Renew the dust after every rain.

Imported cabbage moth larvae eat cabbage crops from Canada to Florida. Protect plants with floating row covers. Handpick the caterpillers into a jar of soapy water. If the infestation is severe, spray plants with BT when the cabbage worms are small.

Mexican bean beetles and their larvae skeletonize the leaves of bean plants in most regions of North America. Adults lay clusters of yellow eggs on the undersides of bean leaves. Soft-bodied larvae and adults eat from leaf undersides too, but populations build so quickly and damage is so severe that you will see them. Use floating row covers, but monitor them daily. If the bugs appear, handpick adults, and squash larvae and eggs, wearing gloves if you're squeamish. Dust leaves with diatomaceous earth. In serious infestations, spray with neem or ryania.

Thrips are too small to see with the naked eye, but you can sometimes see their small dark droppings. They suck cell sap from leaves, fruit, and flowers, making the affected leaves look silvery or bleached and wilted and the fruit look scabby or russeted. Some species spread spotted wilt virus. Spray dormant oil on fruit trees in late winter. Dust plants with diatomaceous earth when you first see damage. Predatory mites control them and are worth the trouble on fruit trees. Spray insecticidal soap or, as a last resort, neem or pyrethrins.

Crown gall bacteria live in all regions of the continent and attack many different plants. Roots or stems near the soil line develop abnormal growths, usually covered by roughened tissue. Remove whole plants, including the roots, and throw in the trash. Inspect all planting stock carefully.

Slugs and snails live in moist regions and under organic matter. They eat ragged holes in plant leaves and flowers and leave slimy trails. Set boards in the garden, and capture resting pests each morning. They won't cross copper. You can trap them in shallow pans of beer set flush with the soil surface.

COMMON PESTS AND DISEASES (Continued)

Bacterial leaf spot diseases attack plants all over North America and are difficult to diagnose because so many diseases cause spotted leaves. Prevent outbreaks with good cultural practices. Excess nitrogen levels make plants susceptible. Pick off affected leaves at the first sign of attack, and discard them. Use copper spray on fruit trees when buds open and until temperatures reach 85°F. Rake up and destroy dropped leaves.

Spider mites are pests all across North America. Although they are difficult to see, their webs are quite visible. Other pest mites do not make webs, but all species suck cell sap, giving plants a papery appearance. If you suspect mites, use a hand lens to inspect leaf undersides and new growth. If the mites are present, mist plants with water every morning. Release predatory mites. Use insecticidal soap spray or ryania as a last resort.

Powdery mildew produces white patches on leaf surfaces. It requires less moisture than most fungi to germinate and grow. It thrives in all parts of North America and tends to attack older leaves or stressed plants after midseason. It rarely kills plants but weakens them and looks unattractive. Good soil nutrition helps to prevent attack as does proper spacing. Use baking powder spray from midseason on or horticultural oil spray when infection first strikes. Repeat sprays every 7 to 10 days until fall.

Mosaic viruses are common in all regions and attack everything from vegetables to roses. Leaves develop light green, yellow, or white areas, giving them a mottled "mosaic" look. Plants are often stunted. Tomato fruit may have yellow patches or may ripen unevenly. Different types of viruses cross easily, and some crosses produce thin, *shoestring* leaves or leaf curling. There is no control. Prevent viruses by controlling insects (aphids and leafhoppers) that spread them. Choose resistant cultivars when possible. Remove diseased plants from the garden.

Fusarium wilt fungus is most common in Zone 6 and southward. Symptoms include general wilting, yellowing, and eventual death. Choose resistant cultivars. Remove plant tissue from the garden in fall. Rotate crops, and plant only in well-drained soil.

Corn earworms (tomato fruitworms) live in every region. Choose corn cultivars with tight husks to prevent earworms from entering them. Apply 10 drops of mineral oil on ear tips when silks begin to dry. Dig out larvae at husk tips when they are small.

Botrytis blight attacks plants in humid conditions in every region. Prevent it with good spacing and high air circulation. Plant only in well-drained soils, and water carefully. Prune off infected plant tissue at the first sign of attack, and put in the trash.

Cedar-apple rust lives in the east but at least one rust disease lives in every region. Many rusts have two alternate plant hosts. Rusts can form galls on plants or show as rust-colored spots on leaves or fruit. Separate hosts by at least 4 miles. Choose resistant cultivars. Remove and burn galls; rake up and destroy all infected leaves.

Aphids live in all parts of North America. They suck cell sap, spread diseases, and often distort plant growth. Many beneficial insects prey on them, including ladybugs, lacewings, and beneficial wasps. Plant small flowers for the beneficials. Squash; for severe infestations, spray with insecticidal soap. Use pyrethrins as a last resort.

Blackspot fungi attack only roses, primarily in moist regions in eastern North America. Pick off affected leaves, and put them in the trash. At the end of the season, rake up old mulch and leaves, spread compost, and remulch with new material. Baking soda often controls this fungus. Use sulfur sprays as a last resort. Select resistant roses.

Annuals and Perennials

When most people think of flower gardens, they think of annual and perennial plants. These two vast groups provide colorful flowers and handsome foliage in almost unlimited variety. Whether your gardening aspirations involve a simple window box or backyard acreage, basic understanding of annuals and perennials is vital.

What Are Annuals and Perennials?

Technically speaking, an annual is a plant that lives for only a single growing season, during which time it flowers, sets seed, and dies. Perennials are plants that don't die after setting seed; they keep growing year after year unless killed by drought, temperatures beyond their tolerance, or other adversity. Some perennials stay green all year, especially where winters are mild. Others go dormant; that is, their tops turn brown or die down to the ground, but the roots live on and send up new shoots the next year.

The distinction between annuals and perennials isn't clear-cut, because many plants that are used as annuals are actually perennials in frost-free environments. These plants, called tender perennials, are often grouped with annuals or bedding plants. Gardeners in warm-winter climates can grow them outdoors year-round, while gardeners in cold-winter climates can keep them from year to year by bringing them indoors for the winter.

A few garden plants are biennials, meaning that they form leaves but no flowers or seeds the first season. The following year, they make flowers and seeds before dying. Fox-

Annual flowers at the front of this bed, above, bloom for the season, providing color no matter which of the perennials is in flower.

Annuals and perennials combine to make a season-long display in this lovely garden, opposite.

gloves and many hollyhocks are common garden biennials.

Annuals produce an abundance of flowers, typically for long periods during the growing season. Perennials also produce beautiful flowers but often for a shorter season, giving them time to store energy to fuel their yearly rejuvenation.

Annuals give quick results in the garden, but you need to start from scratch again the next year. Although some perennials produce flowers in their first growing season, many take two or three years to become established and bloom well. After that, they commonly live for years. A good way to start a garden is by growing annuals interspersed among a few perennials, adding more perennials as your garden and gardening interests grow.

Choosing Plants

Annuals and perennials are most often prized for their flowers. But despite this, the prevailing colors in a garden are the various greens, grays, and other hues of the foliage. For perennials that flower only a short time, foliage is a crucial consideration when you're deciding which plants deserve precious garden space. Select foliage as a backdrop for flowers or as a focal point on its own.

In addition to a plant's appearance, consider its growing requirements. Plants adapted to your climate usually thrive with only routine care. Cold hardiness isn't a factor when selecting annuals, although some perform better during the fall and winter in warm-winter areas. However, cold hardiness is of considerable importance for peren-nials. They

Choose plants with lovely foliage to set off your flowers.

must be able to survive the lowest temperatures common in your region. (See the USDA Cold Hardiness Zone Map, Chapter 2, page 20.) Knowledgeable staff at a nursery or garden center can offer valuable help in identifying plants well adapted to your region.

Creating a Cutting Garden

Part of the fun of growing flowers is cutting them for indoor display. You can, of course, mix flowers for cutting into any garden bed. But if you don't want to ravage your outdoor displays, plant a cutting garden.

A cutting garden doesn't need to be "designed." Lay out your rows for convenience, with taller plants placed to the north so that they don't shade the shorter ones. If you have space, plant at least one rose bush—hybrid tea, floribunda, or shrub type. Most of the annuals and perennials grown for cutting thrive on being picked—the more flowers you cut, the more they produce. In fact some, like cosmos, will stop flowering if blooms aren't removed. The accompanying box, "Plants for a Cutting Garden," lists a selection of easy-to-grow annuals and perennials that produce excellent cut flowers.

Cutting gardens are generally laid out in straight rows to make routine care and harvesting fast and efficient.

PLANTS FOR A CUTTING GARDEN

ANNUALS

Ageratum (tall cultivars)	Pansy
Calendula (pot marigold)	Shirley poppy
Celosia	Snapdragon
China aster	Statice
China pinks	Stock
Cosmos	Sweet pea
Gloriosa daisy	Sweet William
Larkspur	Zinnia

PERENNIALS

Artemisia	Cottage pinks
Baby's breath	Feverfew
Balloonflower	Globe thistle
Bellflower, peach-leaved	Japanese anemone
Black-eyed Susan	Obedient plant
Butterfly weed	Purple coneflower
Coral bells	Yarrow

SPRING- AND SUMMER-FLOWERING BULBS

Calla lily	Grape hyacinth
Camassia	Lily
Crocosmia	Lily-of-the-valley
Daffodil	Ranunculus
Dahlia	Tuberose
Gladiolus	Tulip

PRETTY PLANT COMBINATIONS

Mixing plants in a garden takes imagination, skill, and a bit of daring. Look at other people's gardens to find combinations you like—and those you don't. Select plants with varied heights, shapes, textures and colors, and plan for harmonious or complementary color schemes. Note time of bloom so that you will know how the garden will look through the season. Remember that foliage with interesting texture or color can carry a garden through times when no perennials are in bloom. Well-chosen annuals will give color through the season, too. Group at least three of the same plants together. Groupings or specimen plants can be repeated in large areas. Gardens evolve over time. No matter how much you like your initial plan, you're sure to change it and add to it over the years.

Variation in color and form gives interest to this Southeastern garden.

Groupings of ajuga and rhododendrons light up a shady corner.

Cottage gardens are noted for the diversity of plants they contain.

Harmonious colors make this garden feel calm and restful.

Container Gardening

Many annuals and tender perennials make excellent plants for container gardens. Grown in pots, window boxes, or even a pair of old boots, container plants can transform any area of your home or yard. Though hardy perennials, shrubs, and even trees may be grown in containers, keeping them healthy for many years requires special care. Seek advice at a local nursery if you're interested in this type of container gardening.

Nurseries and garden centers carry a good selection of annuals and tender perennials that grow well in containers. Choose from pansies, petunias, snapdragons, cockscombs, lobelias, geraniums, daisies, spike plant, and dusty miller. Finding interesting containers is part of the fun. Buy containers, or use a favorite pot or un-usual found object. Make sure the container has drainage holes; if not, drill ½-inch holes in the bottom.

Potting soil should have a crumbly texture and retain moisture without becoming soggy. While it's possible to make your own, many gardeners get best results by purchasing bagged potting soils. Most types work well for annuals and tender perennials.

You can display one plant or many in a single pot. Don't be afraid to crowd a pot. Dense displays look better than sparse ones, and commonly used container plants perform well when crowded if well-watered and fertilized. Good container combinations mix colors, textures, and heights just as in gardens, but on a smaller scale.

Planting Containers. Begin by moistening the soil mix until it is damp. Add some slow-release fertilizer if you wish, in recommended quantities. Place screening or old nylon stocking material over the drainage holes, and fill your pot to within 2 to 3 inches of the rim. Insert the plants into the soil, working from the center out. Keep individual root balls as intact as possible, but disentangle roots that have wound around themselves. The tops of the root balls should be about ½ to 1 inch below the rim of the pot. As you add plants, fill

Grouping container plants, above, can provide needed variety.

Container gardens require variety as much as any others, left. Choose plants that complement each other's form, texture, and color.

in around them with potting soil. Then water the pot deeply.

Caring for Container Gardens. Caring for container plants requires more vigilance than work. Plants in well-fertilized potting soil usually perform well if you keep them watered. Check moisture levels daily. In hot, breezy summer weather, the small amount of soil in a pot, particularly one made from porous terra-cotta, can dry out quickly. You may need to water several times a day. Flexible-tube drip-irrigation systems designed for containers can save you time and plants, particularly if you're away for a few days in hot weather.

Commercial potting mixes ordinarily contain few, if any, nutrients, so you'll have to fertilize from the beginning. What kind of fertilizer, how much to use, and how often to use it depend on the plant, the container, and the conditions on your site. In general, you're safe following dosages recommended on fertilizer packages. If you're uncertain, ask at your nursery.

Starting Plants

You can start annuals and perennials from seeds or purchase plants from a nursery or garden center. Starting from seeds is less expensive than buying plants but takes more time and effort. Many hybridized perennials must be purchased as plants, because seed-grown plants may not produce the desired characteristics. Such plants are usually produced commercially by root division or stem cuttings. Division is an easy process and is discussed later in this chapter.

Annuals and a few perennials are sometimes sown directly where they are to grow; in fact, some plants do best when direct-sown. Seed packets are dependable sources of basic information on planting—when and how deep to plant, and how long until germination.

how to

Direct Seed

Tools and Materials: rake, water sprinkler, seeds, sand, row cover material (or burlap or straw), scissors

1 **Prepare the soil** as described in Chapter 2 (pages 28–31). Rake it smooth, and sow the seeds evenly on the surface if you're carpeting an area with plants. If you wish to grow a single plant, sow three to five seeds in a spot, and thin to the strongest seedling after the first true leaves have expanded. When planting a group, sow two to three seeds for every desired plant and thin as necessary.

2 **If you're carpeting an area** with small seeds, such as those of sweet alyssum or poppies, mix the seeds with a few teaspoons of dry sand. The extra bulk will help you scatter the seeds more evenly. Some seeds require light to germinate and should be left uncovered (the packet will specify). Just press them firmly into the soil. Cover larger seeds with a fine layer of soil, if recommended, and then water thoroughly.

3 **The key to success** is keeping seeds moist until they germinate. You may need to check the site several times a day and water as necessary. Apply water as a gentle sprinkle so that you don't dislodge the seeds. To conserve moisture, cover the seeded area with a thin layer of straw, row cover, or burlap, and water through the material. Remove burlap or row cover material after the seedlings have germinated.

4 **When the plants** are several inches tall, thin them to the recommended spacing. To thin, carefully snip off unwanted plants; pulling or digging risks disturbing the roots of those left in place. Continue to water regularly, even if the plants are drought-tolerant, until growth is well established. For perennials, supplemental water may be needed throughout the first season.

FLOWERS FOR DIRECT SEEDING

Bachelor's button	Lupine, annual	Nasturtium	Sunflower
Blanketflower	Marigold	Shirley poppy	Sweet alyssum
Cosmos	Mexican sunflower	Stocks	Sweet pea
Larkspur	Morning glory	Strawflower	Zinnia

STARTING SUMMER-BLOOMING BULBS AND TUBERS

The bulbs and tubers of lilies, dahlias, gladiolus, cannas, and similar plants can be planted directly into the garden or started indoors in pots for later transplanting. (See Chapter 6, page 81 for spring-blooming bulbs.) In cold-weather climates, tender summer-blooming bulbs such as gladiolus and dahlias are planted in spring each year. Lilies are planted in spring or fall.

Plant bulbs or tubers in the garden after danger of frost has passed. Be sure to plant them at the depth recommended by the supplier, and don't let the soil dry out while they are sprouting underground. Plant as many bulbs or tubers as you want plants.

To get a head start on bloom time, plant bulbs or tubers indoors a few weeks before the last frost. Plant in 4-inch pots, using one bulb or tuber to a pot. Keep the potting soil moist at all times. When shoots or leaves appear, put the pots in a warm bright window or under lights as described below in "Start Seeds in Containers." Water and fertilize regularly as the plants grow, and carefully transplant the started plants into garden beds or display containers after all danger of frost has passed.

---

how to | Start Seeds in Containers

DIFFICULTY LEVEL: MODERATE

Direct seeding can be risky. A sudden cold spell, a torrential rain, or hot drying winds can reduce germination or wipe out little plants. Avoid these problems by starting seeds inside. Check the seed packets to determine timing.

1 Sow seeds in containers filled with moist soil mix. Shake the seeds onto a piece of paper and use the tip of a pencil to space them correctly. Depending on the size of the seeds, you can sow from 4 to 12 seeds in each 4-inch pot. In flats, allow up to an inch between seeds. Cover the seeds with soil—unless the packet says they need light to germinate. Wet the sown seeds gently by misting with water from a household spray bottle, and set the pots out of direct sunlight in a warm part of the house. Commercially-available soil heating mats can keep the soil mix warm.

2 Keep the soil moist by misting and covering with a plastic dome or by enclosing the containers in plastic bags. Use sticks to keep the bag from sagging onto the soil. When the seeds germinate, remove the plastic and gradually expose the containers to bright light. If possible, place them beneath a fluorescent fixture with ordinary tubes, suspended a few inches above the seedlings. Keep it lit for 12–16 hours a day. Setting seedlings on a sunny windowsill provides light but also heat. Make sure the seedlings don't dry out or roast.

3 Bottom water the containers by using a propagation unit with a wicking mat or by setting containers in a shallow, water-filled tray until the top surface of the soil mix glistens. Bottom watering minimizes fungal diseases and encourages deep rooting. Feed the seedlings once or twice a week with a water-soluble fertilizer, diluted to one-half the ordinary rate. If your plants are under fluorescent lights, keep the tubes raised about 2 inches above the top leaves. If the seedlings are in a window, turn the containers frequently to keep stems growing straight.

Gardeners in cold-winter areas will need to dig up tender corms and tubers in the fall and store them indoors. (See Plant Gallery entries, pages 58–65.) When you place these plants in a garden bed in the spring, be sure they're accessible and positioned so that the fall digging won't disturb neighboring plants. Because of this disruption, some gardeners prefer to grow tender bulbs in separate beds or cutting gardens or replace them annually.

Summer-blooming dahlias in pink and red set off the purple petunias and white and purple salvias in this planting.

Tools and Materials: seed containers, soil mix, water mister, soil heating mat (optional), small sticks, plastic bags, fluorescent light fixtures (optional), water soluble fertilizer, plant pots, pencil

4 After the plants have developed their second set of leaves, transplant them into individual containers. You can transplant small plants into four- or six-cell plastic packs; use 4-inch pots for plants that grow large quickly. Fill the cells or pots with fresh, moistened potting soil. Holding a seedling gently by a seed leaf, prick its roots out of its pot with a sharpened pencil—taking care not to disturb the roots and attached soil—or gently remove all the plants and carefully tease apart roots of plants growing close together.

5 Use a pencil to poke a hole in the soil of the new cell or container. Holding the seedling by the root ball or leaves, place it in the pot, and fill around it to bury the roots. Suspend larger seedlings in an empty cell while you add moistened potting soil around their roots. Gently firm but do not pack the soil mix; seedling roots need oxygen as much as they need water. Place the cell packs or individual containers under lights or on the windowsill again. Water and feed as before. Turn plants in a window a quarter turn each day to keep the stems straight.

6 When the seedlings are large enough to put in the garden, they need to be "hardened off," or acclimated to conditions outdoors. Begin by setting the plants outside for a few hours every day, in a spot protected from direct sunlight and wind. Over the period of a week or so, gradually increase the time and exposure to sunlight and wind. Leave them out all night if there is no frost danger. Transplant tender plants after all danger of frost has passed. Cold-hardy seedlings often tolerate light frosts but can be stunted by them.

Transplanting Outdoors

Transplanting to the garden is a simple procedure, as long as you follow a few guidelines. Always space the plants according to their mature size, following recommendations. You can fill the spaces between slow-growing perennials with annuals for the first one or two seasons. Make sure the annuals are shorter than the perennials so that they don't retard the perennials' growth. Water is crucial for new plants. If nature doesn't oblige, provide an inch per week throughout the growing season—even for drought-tolerant plants—until they are established. Mulch around the plants to retain water, keeping the mulch back from the stem to avoid disease problems.

Transplanting outdoors during the summer can be hard on seedlings. Cover them with shade cloth, or erect a temporary lath house for filtered light.

how to

Transplant
DIFFICULTY LEVEL: EASY

Tools and Materials: trowel or shovel, water

1 If you're transplanting into a new bed, prepare the soil as described in Chapter 2, on pages 28–31. If you're transplanting into an old bed, amend the soil with compost where the new plant will go. Water the container, and let it drain. Before you remove the plant from its pot, use a trowel or shovel to dig a hole in the bed a few inches wider than the plant's root ball and not quite as deep.

2 Gently slide the plant from the container, keeping the root ball as intact as possible. Don't pull on the stem. Instead, slip your fingers on either side of it, and turn the container upside down. Tap on the container with the other hand or a trowel to loosen the root ball. If your plants are in packs, squeeze the bottom of each cell, and push from the bottom to slide the root ball out of the pack.

3 Gently loosen congested roots on the bottom and lower sides of the root ball; unwrap any that encircle the ball. Place the plant into the hole, firm the soil around it, and water thoroughly. For large plants, set the plant in the hole, and fill the hole about halfway with soil. Then soak the root ball with water, and let it drain. Add the remaining soil, firming it gently around the stem. Water thoroughly.

Propagating Perennials

There are various ways, aside from starting seeds, to increase your perennials. The easiest method is division.

Many perennial plants form a dense concentration of stems, called a crown, at their base. As the number of stems increases each year, the plant increases in diameter. You can produce two or more new plants from a single plant by dividing the crown and its attached root and top growth. Some plants, such as daylilies, hostas, and irises, have thick stems and roots that are easy to imagine as separate plants when you look at the root ball. Other plants, such as yarrows, asters, and Shasta daisies, have finer roots and stems that appear as a more-or-less undifferentiated mass. Never-

theless, they will form new plants when divided. Although small plants can be divided, you'll get a better show more quickly if you divide mature plants into several good-size clumps.

Divide perennials in the early spring or early fall. In cold-winter climates, spring division offers new plants a full growing season to become established. In mild-winter climates, fall division provides months of mild weather for establishment and avoids subjecting divisions to hot, dry summer weather. Before you divide plants, prepare the areas where the divisions are to be transplanted.

Division isn't always done to increase your plants. Some perennials become unhealthy when they grow too large. Division rejuvenates these plants.

how to

Divide Perennials

DIFFICULTY LEVEL: MODERATE

Tools and Materials: scissors, garden fork or spade, knife, trowel, mulch

1 The day before you intend to divide the plant, water it well to make the soil easier to dig. If necessary cut back the foliage to 6 to 10 inches to make the plant more manageable.

2 Using a garden fork or spade, dig up the whole plant with as many of its roots intact as possible. This is easier if you work in a circle around the plant.

3 Pull the roots apart by hand, cut them with a knife, or pry them apart with two garden forks. Divide them so that each piece has a stem or growing point and a supply of roots.

4 As quickly as possible, plant the new divisions. Position the crowns at the depth they were previously growing. Water and mulch well, and fertilize if necessary.

Gallery of Annuals and Perennials

Following is a select list of popular, easy-to-grow annuals and perennials.

Calendula

ANNUALS

CALENDULA (*Calendula officinalis*)

Calendula cultivars offer single or double daisy-like flowers in creamy white, yellow, or orange. They grow 1 to 2 feet tall. Good cut flowers, they can be grown in flower beds, cutting gardens, or large containers. They need **full sun.** They are hardy annuals, so they won't be killed by a mild frost. Calendulas will bloom all winter in mild climates. In early spring, sow seeds outdoors (or indoors in pots) and transplant into the garden.

CANNA (*Canna* hybrids)

These tropical plants bear large, striking, deep red, pink, bronze, or yellow flowers on sturdy stalks with large, equally striking (and sometimes colorful) leaves. Plants range in height from 2 to 6 feet tall; clumps are attractive additions to perennial borders, or they can stand on their own. Dwarf plants 2 to 3 feet tall make fine centerpieces for large container plantings. Plant in **full or partial sun** in well-drained but moist soil. Grow as a perennial in Zone 8 and warmer climates; divide rhizomes when clumps become crowded. In colder climates (Zones 3–7), grow cannas as annuals, planting the rhizomes in spring when the soil has warmed (or start them indoors in pots). Dig rhizomes after the first hard frost in fall; dry them and store over winter in a box of barely damp peat moss.

Canna

Coleus   Cosmos

COLEUS (*Solenostemon scutellarioides,* formerly *Coleus* x *hybridus*)

Prized for their colorful, variegated foliage, coleus have serrated, ruffled leaves in combinations of red, rose, pink, bronze, yellow, cream, lime, or green. Plants for **shady spots,** they grow from 10 to 18 inches high with an equal spread. They're particularly effective in mixed container plantings with other shade-lovers and as edging for a flower bed. They do bloom, but the unimpressive flower stalks are best cut off so thatthey don't spoil the neat look of the plants. Coleus are not drought-tolerant; they do best in well-drained soil kept evenly moist. Because overfeeding may result in less colorful variegation, apply compost (a slow-release nutrient source) once at the beginning of the season. If you grow coleus from seeds, don't cover them because they need light to germinate; it's much easier to buy started plants. Zone 10.

COSMOS (*Cosmos sulphureus, C. bipinnatus*)

Synonymous with country gardens, cosmos are upright, airy plants with simple but beautiful single or semidouble blooms. Cosmos range from foot-tall dwarf varieties to cultivars reaching 5 feet or more. The taller cultivars add a lacy effect to the rear of a border as they seem to float among the other flowers; shorter cultivars do well as edgers. They need **full sun.** Sow seeds outdoors in late spring or early summer. Cosmos self-sow readily and may pop up anywhere in the garden in late spring. Although they resent being transplanted, seedlings can be moved if you get all the roots and water the plants deeply after transplanting them. There is a perennial cosmos, *C. atrosanguineus,* known as chocolate cosmos because of its dark maroon, chocolate-smelling flowers; it grows to about 3 feet tall but is consistently hardy only to about Zone 7.

DAHLIA (*Dahlia* hybrids)

Dahlias are long-time favorite bedding plants and cut flowers. Hybridized for centuries, they come in a vast range of flower shapes and sizes in every color but blue. Plants range in height from about 1 foot to 6 feet. Smaller plants make colorful edgings for flower beds; in containers, they brighten a patio or deck. Tall plants show up well at the back of a flower bed; or give them a bed of their own. Dahlias bloom from midsummer to frost. They need **full sun** and well-drained, fertile soil. You can grow dahlias from seeds, and the shorter cultivars are often grown this way; seed-grown plants will bloom the first summer. Dahlias are also grown from tuberous roots. Plant them 4 inches deep and about 8 inches apart after danger of frost is past. Tall cultivars need support, so install a stake when you plant and use narrow strips of fabric to tie the plant to the stake as it grows. Pinch off the shoot tips of shorter cultivars to promote maximum flower production. Keep plants well watered; if it doesn't rain, give them about 1 inch a week. Where winter temperatures stay above 20°F (Zone 9), dahlias can overwinter outside. But even in warm-winter climates, most gardeners dig up the tubers after the foliage has been killed by hard frost. Cut off the stems a few inches aboveground before digging. Each clump will have several tubers attached to the stems. Leave the tubers attached, clean off the soil, and let the clumps dry for several days. Store tubers and stalks in a cool, dry place, covered with dry sand, sawdust, or peat moss. Several weeks before spring planting, cut tubers from the stems, making sure that each tuber has a growth bud or "eye" (visible just below the tuber's connection to the stem). Discard withered or stunted tubers, and plant the rest.

GAZANIA (*Gazania rigens*)

Yellow, orange, red, or multi-colored daisylike flowers appear on gazanias' bright green, silvery green, or gold-variegated foliage in even the hottest, driest gardens. Growing to 12 inches tall, they are useful as edging or fillers in a flower bed, as a ground cover in warm climates, or as a bright accent in containers. They need **full sun.**

Sow seeds utdoors or indoors in pots. Plants are commonly available in garden centers. A tender perennial hardy to Zone 9, gazanias are grown as annuals elsewhere.

GERANIUM (*Pelargonium* x *hortorum*)

One of the most useful annuals for the garden and containers, geraniums are easy to grow. Large clusters of long-lasting single, semidouble, or double flowers rise on stiff stalks above large round leaves. Flowers range from orange and red to pale pink and white—just about every color except blue and true yellow. Compact cultivars grow up to 16 inches tall. They prefer **full or partial sun** and an enriched, well-drained soil. Buy plants, or start them from seeds indoors about 12 weeks before the average last spring frost. Set seedlings in the garden when soil and weather have warmed up. Remove spent blooms to encourage reblooming, and pinch back the stem tips of the larger cultivars to keep them from getting straggly. Bring a few plants indoors before the first frost to have blooms over winter, or take stem cuttings from the plants and root them indoors for planting the following spring. Geraniums are tender perennials, hardy to Zone 9.

Geranium

Cactus dahlia

PomPom dahlia

Gazania

Gladiolus

Impatiens

Marigold

GLADIOLUS (*Gladiolus* hybrids)

Prized by flower arrangers for their spectacular flower spikes, gladiolus are often grown in cutting gardens. If you can resist harvesting them for indoor display, they can lend drama to flower beds and borders with their sword-shaped foliage and showy flowers in a wide range of colors. Plants can reach 5 feet tall and flowers may be up to 7 inches across. Smaller species and varieties are less widely available but may be better suited to beds and borders. They need **full sun.** Plant in spring after the soil has warmed; set corms 6 to 8 inches deep and 1 to 2 feet apart. You can plant closer together if you're not growing plants for cutting. Install stakes for tall cultivars at planting time, and tie the growing stalk with narrow strips of fabric. Newer cultivars may not need staking. If you're growing for cutting, plant new corms every week or two for a month so that you'll have flowers for a longer season. Cut flower spikes for display when the first buds start to open. (Spikes bloom from the bottom up.) Remove cut-flower plants after they bloom, and dig garden plants at season's end. If you plan to keep the corms, the foliage must be allowed to stay in place until it naturally yellows. Discard the withered old corm, and set new corms aside to dry before storing them in a cool, dry place for planting the following spring. Although the plants are perennial in Zone 8, gardeners in warm-winter climates almost always dig corms and store them over winter.

Petunia

IMPATIENS (*Impatiens walleriana*)

A favorite for shade gardens, impatiens make a fine annual ground cover, bed edging, or container plant. Mounds of foliage 12 to 18 inches tall are covered with delicate-looking flowers from late spring until the first fall frost. Cultivars offer single or double flowers in many shades of pink, purple, red, orange, and white, as well as bicolors. They need **partial shade.** Buy plants, or start them indoors from seed ten weeks before the last frost. Impatiens are tender perennials, sensitive to frost; plant after danger of frost is past. New Guinea impatiens (cultivars of *I. hawkeri*) are taller than common impatiens and need some sun to produce their variegated leaves and bright flowers. Zone 10.

MARIGOLD (*Tagetes erecta, T. patula*)

These popular annuals have long provided children with their first flower-gardening experience. The rich green, pungently scented foliage and compact, brightly colored flowers enliven flower beds, containers, and even vegetable gardens. African marigolds (*T. erecta*) form large clumps up to 3 feet tall and bear double flowers up to 5 inches across. French marigolds (*T. patula*) are shorter, to 18 inches, and bear smaller single or double flowers. They need **full sun.** Sow seeds outdoors after all danger of frost has passed, or sow indoors six weeks before the last frost. Thin or transplant at a 10- to 12-inch spacing. Remove spent flowers to encourage reblooming.

PETUNIA (*Petunia* x *hybrida*)

Long-time garden favorites, petunias are staples in flower beds, containers, and hanging baskets. Plants bloom from late spring to fall and come in a wide range of colors. Flowers range from 2 to 5 inches across and can be single, double, or highly ruffled. Some cultivars are fragrant. The sticky leaves are borne on stems that are compact in some cultivars; others are sprawling, making them ideal for hanging baskets. They prefer **full sun.** Buy plants or start seeds indoors 10 to 12 weeks before the last frost. Remove spent flowers to encourage reblooming. Pinch off the tips of stems to control sprawl or make bushier plants. Petunias are tender perennials but are almost always grown as annuals. Zone 9.

SNAPDRAGON (*Antirrhinum majus*)

Spikes of delightful hooded flowers in pastels and bright shades of pink, red, maroon, yellow, orange, or white appear in early summer and continue until frost if deadheaded. A range of sizes, from 6 inches to 4 feet tall, gives snapdragons a place almost anywhere in the garden as well as in containers. Cut partly opened spikes for indoor bouquets. Plants need   Buy plants, or grow from seeds started eight to ten weeks before the last frost. Stake taller cultivars. Deadhead to encourage reblooming. In mild-winter climates, plant in fall for bloom in winter or early spring. Protected snapdragons sometimes survive cold winters. Zone 8.

TUBEROUS BEGONIA (*Begonia* hybrids)

Prized for their remarkable flowers, which can reach 8 to 10 inches across, tuberous begonias brighten lightly shaded spots. Flowers include ruffled, frilled, single, double, variegated, edged, and bicolors in every shade but blue. Plants grow upright or trailing and are most commonly grown in hanging baskets, window boxes, and other containers. They need **dappled shade.** Tuberous begonias thrive where summers are cool and moist and do poorly in hot, humid conditions. Plant tubers indoors two or three weeks before the last frost, or earlier if you want to grow the plants indoors longer. Transplant to containers or beds when the shoots are about 3 inches tall. Upright types need stakes to support the heavy flowers. Be careful about watering; keep the soil moist but not soggy. Too little or too much water may cause bud drop or stem rot, respectively. To keep the plants from year to year, unpot the tubers in fall, after the leaves have yellowed and dropped. Let them dry out; then store them indoors in a cool, dry spot through the winter. Zone 8.

WAX BEGONIA (*Begonia* hybrids)

These small plants form many-branched mounds of colorful foliage topped for months with bright flower clusters. Cultivars offer green or bronze leaves and pink, red, coral, or white single or double flowers. They are excellent candidates for flower beds and containers, both indoors and out. They thrive in **sun or partial shade.** Wax begonias are easy to grow from cuttings or seeds. Plants are commonly available at garden centers. Set plants outdoors in spring after all danger of frost has passed. Plant 8 to 10 inches apart. Zone 10.

ZINNIA (*Zinnia elegans*)

Zinnias are the perfect annual—easy-to-grow plants that provide cheerful flowers for months. Plant them in beds, containers, or a cutting garden. Long known as "cut and come again," the more zinnias are picked, the more flowers they produce. Flowers from 1 to 6 inches across come in every color but blue and are borne on plants ranging from under 1 foot to 3 feet tall. Larger types produce lovely cut flowers. They perform best in **full sun.** Start seeds indoors six weeks before the last frost, or sow in the garden when the soil has warmed up. Well-watered plants tolerate hot weather. Pinch the ends of stems to promote bushy growth.

Tuberous begonia

Wax begonia

Zinnia

Snapdragon

Zinnia

Astilbe

Columbine

Coral bells

PERENNIALS

ASTILBE (*Astilbe* x *arendsii*)

Among the best perennials for **shady or partly shady** sites, astilbes produce plumes of tiny white, pink, rose, red, or magenta flowers. The blooms turn brown in late summer. Some people cut them off; others like the looks of the dried flowers and leave them in place until spring cleanup. The glossy, much-divided leaves form bushy mounds up to 3 feet tall and wide and are attractive all season. Dwarf forms that grow smaller than a foot tall can edge beds or serve as ground covers. Astilbes can be started from seeds planted early indoors, but it is easier to buy 1-year-old plants. Grow astilbes in well-drained soil rich in organic matter, and ensure that the soil is always moist. Cut the foliage to the ground in early spring or after frost. Divide overgrown plants in very early spring. Zone 3.

COLUMBINE (*Aquilegia* species and cultivars)

Lovely spurred, single or double blooms hang above lacy foliage on this perennial. Several species and numerous cultivars offer a range of flower colors and plant sizes, from 6 inches to 3

Coreopsis

feet tall. Among the most common are a group of hybrid cultivars that includes the 'McKana Giants', tall plants bearing large flowers in a number of colors on sturdy stems. The Canada columbine (*A. canadensis*) has red-and-yellow flowers that attract hummingbirds. Columbines prefer **full sun or partial shade;** in hot climates, some shade is advisable. Grow from seeds or purchased plants. Columbines self-seed, and you'll find new plants scattered about in spring. Simply dig them up while they are still small, and move them where you want them. Zone 3 or 4.

CORAL BELLS (*Heuchera* x *brizoides*)

Delicate little bell-shaped flowers seem to float on thin stems above a mound of deep-green foliage. Coral bells grow 1 to 1½ feet tall with white, light pink, or red flowers. Because the foliage is attractive for months, coral bells are good for highly visible spots or massed as a ground cover. They prefer **partial shade but tolerate full sun** in areas with cool summers. Buy plants, set them in well-drained soil, and keep them well watered. Remove spent flowers to encourage reblooming. Divide coral bells every few years, replanting the divisions 1 to 2 inches deeper than they were growing before. *H. micrantha* 'Palace Purple' is one of several cultivars grown in shady gardens primarily for their attractive bronzy-purple leaves. Zone 4.

COREOPSIS (*Coreopsis grandiflora*, *C. verticillata*)

From late spring to September, these plants produce cheerful daisylike flowers by the hundreds, especially if you keep picking or shearing off the older flowers as they fade. Look for compact cultivars, such as *C. grandiflora* 'Early Sunrise' and *C. verticillata* 'Moonbeam' and 'Zagreb'; the last two form well-behaved mounds of fine foliage from 1 to 3 feet tall sprinkled with small yellow flowers. They prefer **full sun.** Plants can be started from seeds, but it's easier to buy them. Divide plants in early spring every couple of years. Zone 4.

Top: Lady fern
Middle: Hart's tongue fern
Bottom: Japanese painted fern

DAYLILY (*Hemerocallis* cultivars)

No garden should be without daylilies. Few perennials are as carefree, as long-lived, or as easy to mix with other plants in the garden. The trumpet-shaped flowers come in hundreds of colors and are borne on stalks ranging from under a foot to 5 feet or more. Lasting just a day, the flowers are always fresh, and a single plant can produce dozens of buds over a period of weeks. By choosing early-, mid-, and late-blooming cultivars, you can have daylilies in bloom from early summer into fall. (The remarkable cultivar 'Stella d'Oro' blooms almost continuously during that entire period.) Plants' narrow straplike foliage is an attractive addition to the garden in its own right. They prefer **full sun but will grow well in partial shade.** Buy plants, and set them 1½ to 2 feet apart. Many cultivars multiply quickly; divide them every couple of years, and fill your garden. In warm-winter areas, many daylilies are evergreen. Daylilies are rarely bothered by pests or diseases. Zone 3.

FERNS

Despite their delicate appearance, ferns are among the most durable and trouble-free plants you can grow in shade. Species range in size from about 1 foot to over 5 feet. Fronds can be delicately divided or coarse, narrow or broad. Colors encompass a wide range of greens; Japanese painted fern (*Athyrium nipponicum* 'Pictum') cancombine shades of green, silver, and maroon. Ferns require shade. Buy plants, and set them in moist soil that has been amended with extra organic matter. After they're established, ferns need no routine care and often spread to form colonies. Ask at a local nursery about the ferns that do best in your region. Zone 3.

HARDY GERANIUM (*Geranium* species and cultivars)

Perennial geraniums, also called cranesbills, are delightful, usually clump-forming plants that flower profusely in early summer and sometimes sporadically until fall. Low-growing types make excellent ground covers or edgings for beds. Taller plants make eye-catching specimens. The five-petaled flowers, up to 2 inches across, can be pale pink, red, magenta, or blue. ('Johnson's Blue' is one of the most popular cultivars.) They tolerate conditions from **full sun to partial shade,** though most are best when protected from hot afternoon sun. Buy plants. Divide every few years to rejuvenate. Zone 3 or 4.

HOSTA (*Hosta* species and cultivars)

Hostas are one of the best perennials for shady sites, where they are grown as specimen plants or ground covers. Long-lived and easy to grow, they are prized for their beautiful leaves, which come in a wide range of shapes, sizes, textures, and colors—green, blue-green, chartreuse, gray-blue, variegated white, cream, yellow, and gold. Plants form clumps up to an incredible 6 feet wide or as small as a foot. Stalks bearing white, lavender, or purple flowers rise above the foliage in mid- to late summer. The flowers of *H. plantaginea* cultivars are fragrant. Hostas prefer **partial sun to shade.** Buy plants, and set them in well-drained soil amended with a lot of organic matter. Keep the soil moist. Plants seldom need dividing. Hosta's biggest enemies are slugs and deer. Zone 4.

Daylily

Geranium

Hosta

Bearded iris

Siberian iris

Crested iris

Lily

IRIS (Bearded hybrids, *Iris sibirica, Iris cristata*) Irises, with their elegant flowers, are garden royalty. The flowers have 6 petals, 3 inner (called "standards") and 3 outer (called "falls"). Bearded irises are among the most popular types. Their flowers are borne on sturdy stalks and have upright standards and downward curving falls with distinctive fuzzy "beards." The many hybrid cultivars offer a wide palette of colors, and some are fragrant. Plants range in size from miniatures as small as 6 inches to plants with flowers on stalks 3 feet tall. They need **full sun or afternoon shade.** Plant in well-drained consistently moist soil amended with a lot of organic matter. The thick rhizomes should rest right at the surface of the soil, though the roots must be buried. Bearded irises will tolerate hot, dry summer weather. Remove the spent blooms for a neater appearance. Divide plants every few years in late summer. Zone 4.

Siberian irises (*Iris sibirica*) produce smaller, less ornate but no less beautiful flowers than their bearded kin. Following their early summer bloom, the large arching clumps of tall, slender leaves are a striking feature in the garden for the remainder of the growing season. Flowers may be dark purple, pale blue, white, or yellow; there are many cultivars. They prefer **full sun or partial shade.** Plant the rhizomes 1–2 inches deep, and divide clumps in early spring. Soil conditions and care are similar to those for bearded irises, but Siberian irises also tolerate wetter sites. Zone 4.

Crested irises (*Iris cristata*) are tiny plants, growing only 4 to 6 inches tall, that spread by slender rhizomes to form patches that look good in informal plantings or "natural" landscapes. Flowers may be blue or white and appear in late spring. Plant in **partial shade.** They prefer moist, well-drained soil but will tolerate dry spells and summer heat. The rhizome creeps along the surface of the ground; anchor the roots in soil when you plant, but don't cover the rhizome with soil. Zone 3 or 4.

LILY (*Lilium* species and hybrids)
Regal plants with dramatic flowers, lilies make striking accents in any planting. Slender leafy stalks bear large flowers in white, yellow, gold, orange, pink, red, or magenta. There are hundreds of wonderful cultivars. It's possible to have different lilies in bloom from May through August. Grow them with other perennials in beds and borders, or plant shorter or fragrant cultivars in pots on the deck or patio. You can buy species plants or choose from a number of hybrid groups, of which the Asiatic and Oriental are most common. Asiatic hybrids (Zone 4) have scentless flowers on 2- to 4-foot stalks and bloom in early summer. Oriental hybrids (Zone 5) have sweetly scented flowers on 3- to 5-foot stalks in late summer. Lilies need **full sun.** Plant bulbs about 6 inches deep in fertile, well-drained soil in late fall or early spring. When planting, insert stakes to support tall cultivars. Lily bulbs are sold in bags with a moisture-retentive material; they should be plump and moist when purchased. Don't let them dry out before planting. Lilies multiply slowly and can remain in the same place for years. Sprinkle a complete fertilizer on their soil each fall. Zone 4 or 5.

PEONY (*Paeonia lactiflora*)

Peonies are very long-lived, multistemmed plants with beautiful large, fragrant white, pink, or rosy flowers in late spring. After the blooms are gone, the dark green foliage, which grows 2 to 3 feet tall, is a handsome companion for other perennials. The foliage turns purple or gold before it dies down in fall. Peonies need **full sun.** Plant the thick rootstock no more than 1 inch deep in well-drained soil heavily amended with organic matter. New plants take two or three years before blooming. Most peonies need supports—wire hoops or multiple wooden stakes—to carry the weight of the heavy flowers, although single-flowered kinds stand up fairly well on their own. Select the site carefully. Peonies take a few years to reach their prime and are hard to transplant, but once established they continue for decades. Most peonies need winter chilling and do not grow well in areas where freezing temperatures are rare (Zone 8 or higher). Buy crowns, and propagate plants by division in very early spring. Zone 3.

SEDUM (*Sedum* species and cultivars)

The distinctive foliage and unusual flowers of these easy-to-grow plants look good in combination with a variety of other perennials as well as in massed plantings. The widely available cultivar 'Autumn Joy' forms neat mounds up to 3 feet tall and wide of succulent gray-green leaves. Tightly packed, flat-topped clusters of tiny flowers appear in late summer, changing color over many weeks from almost white through pink to rusty red. Other sedums, such as 'Vera Jameson' and 'Rosy Glow', with smaller leaves and flower heads, make smaller, looser mounds and are good ground covers and edging plants. They prefer **full sun.** Buy plants. Divide in early spring if they become crowded. You can leave the seed heads on the plants for winter interest. Zone 3.

SHASTA DAISY (*Leucanthemum* x *superbum*, formerly *Chrysanthemum superbum*)

These are versatile perennials because their pure white flowers, up to 4 inches across, look good in combination with flowers and foliage of almost any color in the garden or in arrangements. Erect stalks from 12 to 36 inches high, each bearing one flower, rise above a low mat of deep green foliage. They prefer **full sun.** Grow plants from seeds, or buy named cultivars as plants. Plant in well-amended, well-drained soil. Stake taller plants. Remove spent flowers, and cut flower stalks to the ground after the plant has finished blooming. Renew plants by dividing them every two years, in spring. Zone 4.

Shasta daisy

Peony

Sedum

CHAPTER 5

Roses

Roses may be the best known and most popular garden plants. Perhaps more than any other plant, roses entice us with their beautiful flowers—their color, form, and fragrance. But because roses have a reputation for being finicky and subject to pests and diseases, many gardeners hesitate to grow them. If you're one of those, take heart. People have grown roses since Roman times, proof that these are strong and adaptable plants. Whether you're drawn to old-fashioned species or the newest landscape and shrub types, you'll discover roses that will thrive in your area when given good soil, adequate water, and just a little care.

Roses in the Landscape

Roses are frequently grown singly as specimen plants to showcase their beautiful flowers. But long-blooming types with handsome disease-resistant foliage can also serve a variety of landscaping purposes. You can edge walkways or garden beds with miniatures and smaller bush roses and use larger bushes and climbers to form hedges, screens, or a backdrop to a perennial border. Many of the species and heritage roses fit right into "natural" landscapes.

When considering where to put roses, remember that they grow best with six or more hours of sun a day; in hot desert climates, shady relief from midday heat is advantageous. Protect roses from strong winds, which can damage delicate blossoms and quickly dry out a plant. Keep the plant's mature size in mind to allow the free air circulation that helps prevent some common fungal diseases.

Climbing roses, above right, are easy to care for and add charm to any location. There are hundreds of good climbers, so you'll be able to select a species adapted to your climate.

Buying Roses

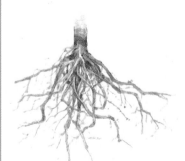

Bare roots allow you to check that root growth is healthy, well balanced around the stem, and spreading, with numerous young feeder roots.

Containerized roots should reach to the edges of the root-ball without circling the bottom or growing through drainage holes.

CHOOSING ROSES

Color, form, fragrance, bloom time, and whether blooms repeat all matter in rose choices. But don't forget about practical matters. A rose chosen with local conditions in mind—whether they be dry soils, high humidity, cold winters, or poor soil—is more likely to succeed and require less frequent care. If there's a group of rose enthusiasts in your area, seek them out for advice. Knowledgeable staff at a nursery or garden center can also offer valuable help.

Roses are sold *bare-root* or in containers. Bare-root plants are dormant, with leafless branches and roots bare of any soil. Most mail-order roses and many sold at nurseries are bare-root. Bare-root plants are generally sold or shipped in late winter or early spring, depending on where you live. It's best to plant a bare-root rose as soon as you can. If you have to wait a few days, keep it below 50°F so it won't break dormancy, and keep the roots moist. If you cannot plant it outside for a week or so, plant it in a large pot to keep it healthy.

Container-grown roses are typically more expensive than bare-root plants and come in a more limited selection of varieties. Look for healthy top growth. Roots growing on top of or out of the bottom of a container are a sign that the plant may have been in its pot too long. In general, you can plant container-grown roses anytime the ground isn't frozen, but fall or spring is usually preferred.

Roses add a touch of elegance to any garden. Despite their reputation, many, such as these David Austin shrub roses, are easy to grow, simple to prune, and resistant to diseases.

TYPES OF ROSES

Arose is a rose, but there are many different kinds, or classes, from which to choose. Rose classes take common features into account as well as ancestry and sometimes the length of time the plant has been cultivated. Many people grow and enjoy roses without knowing the classifications, but some familiarity with these groupings can help you choose the right plant for your purposes.

HYBRID TEA

This is the most popular rose, and the one that most people envision when they think of roses. Hybrid teas flower from late spring to fall and produce long stems, each usually bearing a single flower, ideal for cutting. Hybrid tea roses aren't all fragrant, so choose carefully if scent is important to you. Hybrid teas need well-drained soil, frequent fertilization, and heavy annual pruning, and often require regular spraying to control pests and diseases. Where winter temperatures drop below 10°F (Zone 7), they require winter protection. (See page 77.) Though the flowers are beautiful, the plants themselves are often sparsely covered with foliage and are difficult to integrate in landscape plantings.

'Double Delight'—bicolor red and creamy yellow, fragrant, *1977 AARS winner*

'Mister Lincoln'—deep red, fragrant, *1965 AARS winner*

'Peace'—pale yellow edged in pink, light fragrance, *1946 AARS winner*

'Pink Promise'—National Breast Cancer Foundation rose, pink, fragrant, *2009 AARS winner*

'Perfume Delight'—clear pink, fragrant, *1974 AARS winner*

'Pristine'—clear white, tipped with pink, light fragrance

'Love & Peace'—yellow-pink, fragrant, *2002 AARS winner*

'Tropicana'—salmon-red, fragrant, *1963 AARS winner*

AWARD-WINNING ROSES

All-America Rose Selection (AARS) winners have proved to be outstanding in trial gardens all around the country. Judges test them for many characteristics, including disease resistance, plant and flower form, and fragrance. In the lists on the following pages, AARS winners (and dates they won) are noted.

FLORIBUNDA

A cross between hybrid teas and polyanthas (next page), these bushy plants are larger than polyanthas but bear polyantha-like clusters of flowers in profusion throughout the growing season. ("Floribunda" means abundant flowers.) Floribundas fill a wide range of landscape uses—from containers for the smaller plants to hedges for the

'Peace'

'Betty Prior'

tallest, which can grow to 5 feet or more. The stems are shorter than hybrid teas, but the flowers are great for cutting because one stem can make a bouquet, and floribundas are less demanding and more disease resistant.

'Betty Boop'—yellow centers surrounded by ivory and tipped red, fruity fragrance, *1999 AARS winner*

'Betty Prior'—single, deep pink, very fragrant

'Europeana'—deep red, slightly fragrant, *1968 AARS winner*

'Iceberg'—white (sometimes with a pink tinge), slightly fragrant

'Walking on Sunshine'—bright yellow blooms, moderate fragrance, *2011 AARS winner*

'Rainbow Sorbet'—yellow-orange-red flowers, *2006 AARS winner*

POLYANTHA

Tidy low-growing plants, polyanthas bear large clusters of small flowers sporatically from late spring until frost. Because they grow only as high as 2 to 3 feet tall, they are an excellent choice for smaller yards. They also look good when placed at the edge of borders, in front of other shrubs or in containers. Polyanthas are very disease resistant and hardy.

'The Fairy'—pink, 1-inch blooms

'Red Fairy'—cherry-red

'Cécile Brunner'—light pink

GRANDIFLORA

These roses bear large flowers, usually in clusters, on long stems. Bushes are large and vigorous, ideal for hedges, screens, or backdrops for other plants. The large flowers are produced continuously from late spring to fall.

'Queen Elizabeth'—clear pink flowers 3 to 4 inches across, fragrant, *1955 AARS winner*

'Sunshine Daydream'—light yellow, *2012 AARS winner*

'Love'—double, red, slight fragrance

'Dick Clark'—double, cream tipped with red, moderate fragrance, *2011 AARS winner*

FRAGRANT FLOWERS

The most fragrant roses are heritage roses, but some modern roses have been bred with scent in mind. In addition to fragrant roses noted in this sidebar, the following have outstanding fragrance:

'Blanc Double de Coubert'—white rugosa

'Rosarie de l'Hay'—crimson hybrid rugosa

'Sutter's Gold'—orange-yellow hybrid tea

'Fragrant Cloud'—orange red hybrid tea

'Papa Meilland'—red hybrid tea

'Penelope'—pink hybrid musk

'Gertrude Jekyll'—pink David Austin hybrid

'The Fairy'

'Queen Elizabeth'

TYPES OF ROSES (Continued)

CLIMBERS

Few garden displays can match a rose-covered trellis in full bloom. These vigorous plants don't actually climb; the long canes (up to 20 feet) must be tied to a trellis or arbor. Climbing roses can also be trained into trees or over large shrubs. Most climbers bloom from early summer to fall; some do not repeat bloom (that is, they stop blooming after their early summer display). Hardiness varies among climbers; be sure to check before purchasing, as it's hard to provide winter protection for tall canes.

'Blaze'—scarlet clusters, grows to 12 feet

'Constance Spry'—clear pink blooms in early summer, fragrant, grows to 15 feet

'Fourth of July'—ruffled petals striped white and red, fragrant, grows 12 to 15 feet, *1999 AARS winner*

'Golden Showers'—golden yellow, fragrant, blooms all season, grows to 10 feet, *1957 AARS winner*

'Joseph's Coat'—red buds open to orange blooms changing to bright yellow, aging to red; all colors may be present, fragrant, grows to 10 feet

'New Dawn'—blush white, fragrant, grows to 15 feet

MINIATURES

These roses look like petite versions of larger roses, primarily hybrid teas and floribundas. Everything about the plant is small—flowers, leaves, and stature. They usually grow about 1 to 1½ feet high, but some cultivars can reach 4 feet. A few miniatures have longer canes and can be trained as climbers or used as ground covers. Use the others to edge a border, or brighten a rockery—or in containers, indoors or out. In the ground, miniatures bloom from early spring to fall. Container-grown miniatures can bloom almost year-round if overwintered indoors in bright light. (Supplemental lighting is usually necessary.)

Because most miniature roses are grown on their own roots, not grafted on a rootstock, they are very hardy. If the top growth dies back, they'll resprout—true-to-name—from the roots in spring. Nevertheless, it's wise to check winter protection requirements when purchasing. Miniatures grown outdoors in containers need winter protection; take them indoors and enjoy them through the cold months.

'Child's Play'—pink, 15 to 18 inches, *1993 AARS winner*

'Rainbow's End'—bicolored yellow and red, 12 inches plus—can be used as a climber

'Rise 'n' Shine'—clear yellow, 12 to 15 inches

'Sun Sprinkles'—double, bright-yellow 2-inch flowers, moderate, *2001 AARS winner*

SHRUB

If you love roses but dislike fuss, grow shrub roses. Vigorous, disease resistant, and hardy, these easy-care plants are so versatile that they're often called landscape roses. They range from 2 to 8 feet tall and can be sprawling, upright, or bushy. Shrub roses can make excellent hedges, specimen plants, or ground covers and work well in mixed borders. Many bloom for months. Some have been specially bred to survive northern winters with little protection. Others, such as the David Austin roses, are bred for fragrance and old-rose form.

'Golden Showers'

'Rainbow's End'

'Bonica'

'Royal Bonica'—deep pink, 4½ feet tall, 5 feet wide, *1987 AARS winner*

'Alba Meidiland'—tiny, pure white blooms in large clusters, 3½ to 4 feet tall, 6-foot spread

'Carefree Delight'—single, carmine-pink with white eye, 3 to 4 feet tall, 5-foot spread, *1996 AARS winner*

'Carefree Wonder'—deep pink with white reverse, light fragrance, 4 feet or more tall, 3 feet wide, *1991 AARS winner*

'Graham Thomas'—A David Austin rose with apricot-pink buds, yellow blooms, fragrant, 4 to 8 feet tall, 5 feet wide

'Flower Carpet Appleblossom'—clusters of small, rose pink blooms, 2 to 3 feet tall, 3 to 4 feet wide

'Lady Elise Mae'—semi-double coral blooms, mid-size, slight fragrance, *2005 AARS winner*

HERITAGE ROSES

Rose cultivars that existed before the 1867 introduction of the hybrid teas are called heritage, or old, roses. Originating in Europe and Asia, these roses may have histories spanning thousands of years of cultivation. Heritage roses are diverse and include plants across the spectrum of growth habits and size, hardiness, disease resistance, and bloom times and durations. While not as widely available as the roses discussed previously (called modern roses), these roses can be handsome elements in a garden as well as interesting to grow. Many are exquisitely scented.

Heritage roses include several classes. The following are among the best known.

Gallicas are considered to be the oldest of all garden roses, dating back 3,000 years. The 3- to 5-foot-tall plants bear fragrant flowers in late spring or early summer and large red hips (seedpods) in fall.

Alba roses date to the Middle Ages and are one of the hardiest and most disease resistant of old-garden roses. The fragrant flowers may be semidouble or fully double in shades of pink and white; they appear for about a month in early summer on plants 4 to 6 feet tall and 4 to 5 feet wide.

Damask roses were known as early as the fifth century bc. They produce fragrant white and pink flowers in bunches on plants reaching 6 feet tall and 8 feet wide. Most bloom once in late spring or early summer; several are repeat bloomers.

Bourbon roses trace their ancestry to China. Bearing double, highly fragrant flowers in white, pink, rose, or striped with crimson or red, plants can be shrubs or climbers.

SPECIES ROSES

Nature, not hybridizers, provides most of these roses, which growers have selected and propagated for garden use. They come in a variety of sizes and growth habits, including climbers, and a range of flower forms in shades of red, pink, white, or yellow.

Rugosa roses (*R. rugosa*) are real warhorses. They're hardy and grow well under extreme conditions, including windy sites, dry spells, sea spray, and road salt. Bushes up to 8 feet tall feature handsome, crinkled, disease-resistant leaves and large, fragrant flowers in white, pale yellow, pink, or deep red that repeat throughout the season. Plants spread by suckers; with numerous, large, sharp thorns they make impenetrable hedges.

'Apothecary' (Gallica rose)

'Felicite Parmentier' (Alba rose)

'Rose de Rescht' (Damask rose)

'Grootendorst' (Rugosa hybrid)

Growing Roses

Roses are as easy to grow as any other shrub, as long as you take their particular needs into account. If you grow climbing roses, for example, you'll have to provide a suitable trellis and keep up with tying canes in place. Most roses require annual pruning, and in cold climates, winter protection. Insects and diseases are particularly fond of roses, so prevention, monitoring, and control are essential. The following sections give a good foundation for growing any rose suitable to your conditions.

PREPARING THE SOIL

Roses may be grown individually or in beds with other plants. They grow best in fertile soil that drains well but doesn't dry out too fast. If you're making a new bed, prepare the soil as described in Chapter 2, pages 28–31. Drainage is particularly important for roses. Test for drainage as described in Chapter 2, page 24. If even a small amount of water remains in your test hole after 24 hours, plant elsewhere or build a raised bed for your plants. If you test the soil for pH and nutrients, tell the lab you're growing roses so that their recommendations will be appropriate.

If your soil is generally good, any organic matter you can add will make it better for roses. Experts often recommend amending even fertile soil with up to an equal amount of

ROSE HARDINESS

Roses can be damaged or killed by cold temperatures. Different types and cultivars of roses have different degrees of cold hardiness. Hybrid teas, floribundas, grandifloras, and climbers, for example, are generally hardy to between 10° and 20°F, while some rugosa roses are hardy to –35°F. With adequate winter protection, however, roses such as hybrid teas can be grown where temperatures drop to –10°F or lower. Because a rose's hardiness has so much to do with how well it is protected, nurseries and mail-order catalogs may not provide hardiness zone ratings. For the same reason, this book does not give hardiness ratings. Plants sold at local nurseries and garden centers should be hardy in your area, but be sure to check with knowledgeable staff or with local rose growers to see whether these roses require winter protection.

compost, leaf mulch, well-rotted manure, or peat moss. Work the amendments in to a depth of 12 to 15 inches. Poor soil can be improved with an even greater quantity of organic matter.

FLORAL DEFINITIONS

Single roses such as this 'Sally Holmes' have one row of 5 petals and up to 4 smaller interior petals.

Semidouble roses such as this 'Blanc Double de Courbet' have 8-20 petals.

Double roses such as this 'Madame Hardy' have more than 20 petals growing in several rows.

PLANTING

Roses are as easy to plant as any other perennial. It's important to make certain that the roots are in close contact with the soil and that they are thoroughly moistened after the plant is in place.

The only challenge in planting roses may lie in determining the height at which to position the bud union on a grafted rose. Rose suppliers often graft popular rose cultivars onto rootstocks that provide necessary characteristics such as robust growth, disease resistance, or hardiness. The bud union, where the rootstock joins the top growth, looks like a bump on the stem.

Experts disagree on the bud union positioning. Some recommend placing the bud union 2 inches below the soil line in areas where winter temperatures fall below −10°F, at the soil level where winter lows are between −10° and 10°F, and 2 inches above soil level where lows are above 10°F. Others recommend setting the bud union even with the soil surface in all climates. Confer with local rose experts or nursery staff to see which method seems to work best in your area. Plants grown on their own roots—typically species, miniature, and shrub roses—should be planted at the same depth they grew in the field, and that's usually apparent from a ring of discoloration at the base of the plant stem.

Planting Roses

BARE-ROOT ROSES

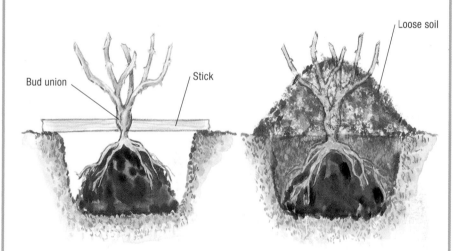

Bud union | Stick | Loose soil

CONTAINER-GROWN ROSES

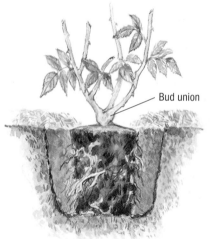

Bud union

Soak the roots for a few hours, and trim off any damaged or dead growth. Some people use a solution of liquid seaweed for soaking because of the growth stimulants it contains. Dig a wide hole at the correct depth to properly position the bud union. Work a few tablespoons of superphosphate or ½ to ¾ cup of rock phosphate into the bottom of the hole. Make a mound of soil in the hole bottom; pat it to make it firm; spread the roots over it; and position the bud union at the desired height. Place a straight stick across the hole to check the bud union position.

Spread the roots over the soil mound, and work additional soil around them. When the hole is two-thirds full, drench it with water. Let it drain before adding soil up to ground level. Tamp firmly, and water again. Mound 8 to 12 inches of loose soil around the stems to protect them from wind and sun. When new shoots are several inches long, gradually wash the soil mound away, and mulch with shredded bark or rough compost, allowing several inches of bare soil around the stems. A soil moat, built a few inches high around the perimeter of the planting hole, will also help retain water.

Water container bushes thoroughly before removing their pots and planting. Dig a hole about twice as wide as the root-ball and about the same depth. Work several tablespoons of superphosphate or ½ to ¾ cup rock phosphate into the bottom of the hole. Carefully place the plant in the hole, spreading the roots so that they don't encircle the ball. Check that the bud union is at the proper depth. Fill the hole halfway with soil, add water, and proceed as described for bare-root roses. Because container plants may have leaves, don't mound soil over the aboveground portion.

Rose Anatomy

The anatomy of a rose is useful to learn. Pay particular attention to elements such as the bud union and hips, and notice that a leaf is composed of three to five leaflets.

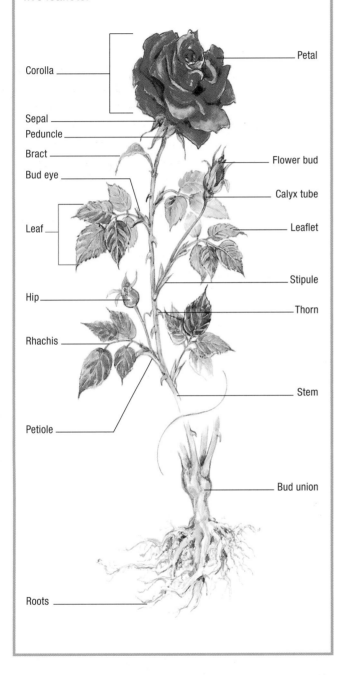

Corolla

Petal

Sepal
Peduncle
Bract
Bud eye

Flower bud

Calyx tube

Leaf

Leaflet

Stipule

Hip

Thorn

Rhachis

Stem

Petiole

Bud union

Roots

Pruning Guidelines

Few aspects of rose growing are more daunting to novices than pruning. There are a great many different kinds of roses, and experts may prune each one slightly differ-ently—and disagree with each other about the proper method. The best way to learn how to prune is to watch an experienced rosarian prune plants similar to yours. Follow these guidelines to get off to a sound start.

■ Do most pruning with a good pair of bypass pruning shears. Bypass pruners work like scissors; anvil pruners can crush the canes. Heavy loppers and a small pruning saw are useful for older thick, woody bushes.

■ Remove dead, diseased, or damaged wood and weak, spindly canes any time you see them. Damage may extend into wood that looks healthy on the outside; keep cutting until the pith at the center of the cane is white to light green. When

For all roses, remove dead, damaged, diseased, and weak canes, and canes that cross the center of the bush. Shorten healthy canes on shrub roses by about one-third, and shorten hybrid tea canes by one-half.

removing diseased canes, sterilize the shears by dipping them in rubbing alcohol between each cut.

- Annual pruning is best done toward the end of the dormant (winter) season, when the leaf buds are beginning to swell. Note that some once-blooming roses produce flowers on the previous year's growth—prune these after they bloom.

- In general, prune to promote new growth and to create a pleasing, healthy shape. Light to moderate pruning can produce good-looking garden plants and ample flowers.

- Remove canes that cross the center of the bush to help open the bush to air movement and sun. When possible, choose older canes to cut out.

- To promote growth away from the center of the plant, place your cuts just above an outward-facing bud. Make the cut at about a 45-degree angle, so the lower point is roughly even with the top of the bud. Rainwater runs off cuts that are slanted correctly, helping the plant to resist diseases caused by excess moisture.

- Many species and heritage roses thrive when pruned as described above. However, to keep them dense and free-blooming, these roses are often just lightly sheared back with hedge shears. For hybrid teas, grandifloras, and floribundas, cut back the previous season's growth during their dormant period. Cut hybrid teas back by one-half and the others by one-third to promote increased branching and blooms.

- Remove spent flowers, or deadhead, to encourage new blooms. Cut back to the first leaf with five leaflets. If an entire shrub or landscape rose has finished blooming, use hedge shears to remove dead flowers, cutting the plant back by about one-third. Then fertilize.

- Climbers have special pruning requirements, as shown in the illustrations.

- When cutting flowers for display, sever the stem just above the first leaf with five leaflets.

Repeat blooming climbers are pruned while they are dormant. After removing dead, weak, and diseased growth, prune out the oldest canes. In early spring, trim them back and tie them to horizontal supports to encourage blooming.

Ramblers and once-blooming climbers are pruned just after they bloom. Remove old canes just above the bud union and remove weak or diseased canes. Prune flowering shoots back to four or five sets of leaves.

CARE AND FEEDING

Roses are thirsty and hungry plants. They need plenty of nourishment and constant moisture in well-drained soil. How much and how often you need to water and feed plants depends on your soil and climate, the size of the plant, and the time of year. Be vigilant; check your roses regularly for signs of water or nutrient deficiency—yellowing or wilting leaves, no new growth, weak stems, or buds that fail to open.

When you irrigate, water deeply, wetting the entire root zone to a depth of 16 to 18 inches. (See Chapter 3, page 34 for monitoring soil moisture levels.)

Fertilize Roses Regularly. Fertilize your roses according to their class. Use either a rose or general-purpose fertilizer, but follow the recommended dosages—too much can cause problems.

Species roses, heritage roses, and climbers can do with a single application of fertilizer in early spring when leaf buds are about to burst forth. Use a fertilizer containing the same amount of nitrogen, phosphorus, and potassium or one with higher amounts of phosphorus, such as 18-24-16. In nutrient-rich soil, many of these roses thrive with no additional fertilizer. Repeat bloomers usually benefit from additional fertilizer after their first bloom.

Care and feeding of heritage roses is usually less demanding than that for hybrid tea roses.

Hybrid teas, grandifloras, and other modern roses need periodic feeding during the growing season. Fertilize new rose plants about a month after planting. Start feeding established plants after pruning—when new foliage begins to appear—then every four to six weeks, until mid- to late summer, in the amounts recommended.

Gardeners in cold-winter areas should stop applying fertilizers that contain nitrogen six to eight weeks before the average first fall frost. Nitrogen encourages the growth of succulent cold-sensitive new shoots. You can continue with phosphorus and potassium to strengthen roots and shoots for the winter.

Pest and Disease Control

Hybrid tea roses seem almost as attractive to pests and diseases as they are to people, and therein lies much of roses' reputation as difficult plants. But you don't need to fuss a great deal unless you're planning to enter a rose in a flower show competition or you're growing only hybrid teas. Most of the new shrub and landscape roses are quite disease-resistant. Some species and heritage roses seldom require intervention, giving all the more reason to seek out those that do well in your area. Healthy, well-watered, well-fed, and well-spaced plants are far less likely to sustain threatening damage from pests and diseases than unhealthy plants are. Don't crowd plants close together, because poor air circulation encourages disease. Good hygiene discourages many problems; clean gardens tend to be healthy gardens.

Various insects attack roses. Some insects, such as aphids and mites, can be controlled simply by washing them off leaf surfaces. Others, such as Japanese beetles, can be hand-

picked, but some require a biological control or insecticide. It can be difficult to identify the culprit because the bug you find at the scene of the damage may not be the one that caused it. And choosing the right control can be baffling. Often your best bet is to consult local rose experts or your Cooperative Extension Service about specific pests. And practice prevention: take a good look at your roses every day, and you'll be more likely to spot a pest problem before it becomes an invasion.

Rose Diseases Can Be Troublesome. The biggest problems are fungal—black spot, powdery mildew, and, in the West and Southwest, rust. Powdery mildew and rust disfigure but seldom kill plants, but black spot can completely defoliate and kill a rose. Good hygiene and air circulation help prevent all three diseases. Keep the ground beneath and around the plants clean of debris, and prune to allow free air movement. To control mildew, rust, and black spot, spray plants with horticultural oil after pruning and just after new growth begins. Use wettable sulfur every two weeks thereafter. A homemade spray can prevent powdery mildew. (See opposite.) Consult with local rose experts about combating diseases prevalent in your area. As a last resort, if your rose bed looks like a disaster zone toward the middle of summer, get out your pruners and cut back the canes as if it were spring. The plants will sprout new, though rather weaker, stems and flowers.

smart tip

CONTROLLING PESTS AND DISEASES

- Water in the morning so leaves and canes dry during the day. This helps prevent fungal diseases. Try to avoid getting water on the leaves, unless you're knocking pests such as aphids off the plants with a jet of water.
- Remove diseased or damaged leaves and canes as soon as you see them, and discard them in the trash—don't put them in your compost pile.
- Clean up for winter by stripping leaves off the plant after a hard frost in fall and removing debris, including old mulch, from underneath it. Spread new mulch for winter protection.
- After pruning and before new growth emerges, apply a dormant spray (lime-sulfur or horticultural oil) to kill overwintering insect eggs and disease organisms.

WINTER PROTECTION

Roses can be successfully grown outside their normal hardiness range if you protect the roots and canes from winter's drying winds, low temperatures, and freeze-thaw cycles. Where winter temperatures drop below 10°F, protect hybrid teas and a variety of other roses. The following procedures work for many roses; check with local experts to find out which roses in your area need protection and for recommended methods of protecting them.

- When nighttime temperatures drop consistently below freezing, cover the base of the plant with loose soil mounded about 1 foot high.
- Tie canes loosely together with soft twine. Cut long canes back, if necessary, to 2 to 4 feet long.
- When the soil mound is frozen, cover it with pine boughs or other insulation to keep it from experiencing cycles of freezing and thawing. You can enclose the plant in a wire cage about 4 feet tall and fill it with leaves or straw; this material will protect much of the length of the canes it encloses. Instead of mounding and caging roses, you can use polystyrene foam cones (available at nurseries and garden centers), but you'll have to prune the canes to fit the cone. Throw soil around the base of the cone to seal

it, and remember to weight it down so that it doesn't blow around.

- In spring, after the last hard frost, remove caged leaves, straw, or cones. Gradually remove the soil mound as it thaws. (Don't "chip" it away, or you may damage new growth under the mound.) By the time the weather has settled, the mound will be gone.

The coming winter is signaled by ripe rose hips. Rosa rugosa and other heritage roses make the largest hips. If you don't make tea or jelly from them, leave them for the birds.

CHAPTER 6

Spring-Flowering Bulbs

From the last days of winter to the first days of summer, few elements in the home landscape are appreciated as much as spring-flowering bulbs. This is particularly true in cold-winter areas where early bulbs such as windflowers, crocuses, and daffodils mark the changing of the seasons. In warm-winter gardens, freesias and paperwhite narcissus provide a fragrant accompaniment to less dramatic but no less welcome seasonal changes. With little effort, gardeners everywhere can sprinkle spring color near an entryway, through a woodland garden, or across a grassy hillside. And spring-flowering bulbs are undemanding. Some go years after planting without attention. Others need just a bit of fertilizer each year and, when a clump gets too crowded, division of the increased cache of bulbs and distribution of this bounty elsewhere on the property.

What a Bulb Is ... and Isn't

What we commonly call bulbs are actually several different kinds of plant structures. Some are true bulbs (daffodils, tulips), others are corms (crocuses, freesias) or tubers (windflowers, winter aconites). All three are fleshy structures that store food for the production of roots, leaves, stems, and flowers. Botanists note a variety of differences between bulbs, corms, and tubers, and they don't always agree about classification. Fortunately, these differences aren't important when it comes to choosing and growing the plants. For simplicity's sake, we'll refer to all three as bulbs in the general discussions that follow. For gardeners, it's helpful to know that all the food the plant needs to grow roots and shoots is stored in the bulb, corm, or tuber, and that plants

Landscaping with spring-flowering bulbs adds needed color and dimension when perennials are just emerging, above.

Spring-flowering bulbs, opposite, are truly easy-care plants that can brighten any landscape.

need to replenish this supply each year after flowering. In addition, each year most bulbs, corms, and tubers reproduce themselves, so that over time a single plant will form a small patch.

LANDSCAPING WITH BULBS

Bulbs can create almost any atmosphere, from formal to casual. Choose colors and forms carefully, and follow the guidelines below.

■ Create a visual bouquet by planting bulbs in bunches (groups of 6 to 15 or more), rather than in single-file straight rows. To make the planting look more natural, group the bunches in free-form drifts that intersect each other.

■ Plant some early-blooming bulbs, such as snowdrops, crocus, and glory-of-the-snow, in sunny spots by entrances or in view of windows so that you can enjoy them when it's still too chilly for leisurely strolls around the garden.

■ Don't be bashful about color. There's not a lot of competition for attention in the spring garden, so plant reds, yellows, oranges, soft peaches, pinks, and lavenders to enliven the scene. If you're ambitious, you can coordinate colors in different parts of the season, changing the look of your garden in the space of a few months—for example, from pale blue, yellow, and white through lavender, pink, and peach to hot red and orange.

BULBS IN WARM-WINTER CLIMATES

Many spring-flowering bulbs (crocuses, tulips, and hyacinths, for example) require a period of cool temperatures to grow and bloom well. In areas where winter temperatures don't fall below 45°F for extended periods of time, these bulbs can be a disappointment. Some warm-winter gardeners grow these plants as annuals, buying fresh bulbs each year from suppliers that prechill them before shipping in the fall. Gardeners wishing to recycle their own bulbs must dig them up and prechill them for a number of weeks in the refrigerator, a considerable task if you have many bulbs. Fortunately, there are many fine winter- and spring-blooming bulbs that warm-winter gardeners can grow without the prechilling fuss—freesias, paperwhite narcissus, ranunculus, cyclamens, and alliums. If you're uncertain about which bulbs grow well in your climate, ask at a local nursery or contact the local Cooperative Extension Service.

Bulb Bloom Times

Plant bulbs with a diversity of bloom times—early, midseason or late—for continuous spring color. Select some from each group and, as in this garden, plant in color-coordinated drifts. Plant annuals in the same space when the last of the bulbs have finished.

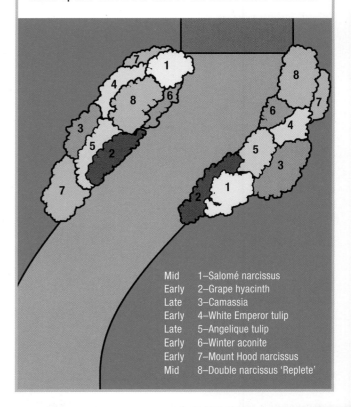

Mid	1–Salomé narcissus
Early	2–Grape hyacinth
Late	3–Camassia
Early	4–White Emperor tulip
Late	5–Angelique tulip
Early	6–Winter aconite
Early	7–Mount Hood narcissus
Mid	8–Double narcissus 'Replete'

Landscaping with bulbs involves planning for bloom time, color, and size.

Planting and Care

Like most garden plants, spring-flowering bulbs perform best in fertile, well-drained soil. Bulbs often share garden beds with other plants and benefit from the care you gave to preparing their soil. When you naturalize bulbs such as daffodils and crocuses in a lawn or woodland, extensive soil preparation is usually out of the question. You need to rely on the fertility of the native soil, but you can add fertilizers when you plant and, in subsequent years, just after the bulbs bloom.

When choosing beds or sites for naturalizing bulbs, bear in mind that poorly drained, soggy soil rots bulbs. Spring-flowering bulbs are sun-loving plants, but you can grow them beneath deciduous trees and shrubs that don't produce a sun-blocking canopy until after the bulbs have finished flowering.

Planting Bulbs. If you can dig a hole, you can plant a bulb. Plant spring-blooming bulbs in early fall. If you're planting clusters of a few bulbs each, use a trowel to dig small holes for each group. If you're planting a large number of bulbs in the same spot, use a shovel to excavate the entire area. You should plant most bulbs at a depth equal to two or three times the height of the bulb. (Suppliers usually provide planting guidelines for bulbs.) Though some bulbs will work their way to an optimal depth in a few years, it's worth the effort to plant them at the correct depth. Use a ruler if necessary; most gardeners plant bulbs too shallow.

After digging to the appropriate depth, loosen several inches of soil at the bottom of the hole for good drainage and root growth. Mix a handful of a complete, all-purpose fertilizer into the soil at the bottom of the hole. When applying fertilizer to a large bulb-planting area, follow label directions for application rates, and mix it into the soil. Set the bulbs on the soil surface, pointed end up and flattened side down, and cover them with soil. Space daffodils and other big bulbs 6 to 8 inches apart, and smaller bulbs closer. At this spacing they'll reproduce to form a satisfying clump in several years. To produce clumps more quickly, you can space bulbs closer, but you'll have to dig and divide them sooner to alleviate overcrowding. Gophers, voles, and other small animals find some bulbs, notably crocuses and tulips, a tasty treat. Protect bulbs by planting them in wire-mesh cages or, if you're planting a large number all at once, sandwich the bulbs between layers of chicken wire. Overlap at least two layers of the chicken wire to make the holes smaller, and place the layers on the soil surface. Cover the wire with an inch or so of soil, and set the bulbs in place. To protect the bulbs from the sharp wire, cover them with at least an inch of soil. Over this, place two more overlapping layers of chicken wire, bending it down at the edges to enclose all the bulbs. Add enough soil to bury the bulbs to the correct depth.

Water newly planted bulbs thoroughly and, if the winter is dry, periodically until the new leaves appear in spring. Keep the soil moist but not soggy while plants grow and bloom. After the flowers have faded, bulb foliage continues to produce food that's stored in the bulb for the next year's growth. Don't cut off the foliage until it has browned or completely yellowed and dried.

Planting large swaths of bulbs is easy if you clear and excavate the entire area.

MAINTAINING BULBS

Many perennial bulbs produce lovely displays for years with little care. Every spring when the foliage begins to appear, feed plants with a balanced fertilizer. When clumps become crowded, dig up the bulbs after the foliage has died back, and replant them promptly. If you want to wait until fall to replant, you can try storing the bulbs in a cool, dry spot. But because they're liable to rot or dry out over the summer, it's better to replant them right after digging.

Plantings of tulips and hyacinths sometimes deteriorate after a year or two, producing smaller and fewer blooms. Many gardeners treat these plants as annuals, digging and discarding bulbs after the growing season and planting new ones in the fall.

Bulbs in the Landscape

You can dress up areas in your yard with spring-flowering bulbs. Here are some landscaping suggestions.

IN MIXED BEDS AND BORDERS

Spring-flowering bulbs brighten any garden bed. Snowdrops and crocuses peeking out from under a light snow are a heartening sight after a long winter. They begin a months-long parade of bulbs, adding color to the awakening spring garden and complementing early-blooming perennials, shrubs, and trees.

Try one or more of several strategies for choosing bulbs. You can create a riot of color, select bulbs that complement or harmonize with other early-bloomers, or plant large swaths of bulbs in one or more colors. When you plant bulbs among perennials, keep plant heights in mind. Position bulbs where the foliage of perennials will hide the yellowing bulb leaves later in the season.

Spring bulbs are also effective in plantings of shrubs. They stand out handsomely against the dark greens of yews or the textured leaves of rhododendrons and other broad-leaved evergreens. Try a mixed planting of Darwin tulips and double-flowered tulips with a ground cover of lily-of-the-valley against a backdrop of green shrubs. Bulbs can also be striking accents with deciduous shrubs—contrast them with bare branches, such as the colorful stems of red-twig dogwood, or choose bulbs to complement spring-blooming shrubs such as star magnolia or forsythia.

SOME FRAGRANT BULBS

Plant bulbs with scented flowers for outdoor or indoor enjoyment.

Daffodils: 'Actaea' (Poet's narcissus), 'Carlton', 'Cheerfulness', 'Yellow Cheerfulness', 'Quail', 'Suzy', 'Geranium', and 'Thalia'

Tulips: 'Christmas Marvel', 'Union Jack', 'Ruby Red', 'Monte Carlo', 'Apricot Beauty', and 'Ad Rem'

Hyacinths: All common hyacinths and grape hyacinths

Plant bulbs in mixed beds, above left, so that the foliage of other plants will hide their fading leaves.

Bulbs planted under deciduous trees, above, receive enough sunlight to stay healthy and reproduce each year. For these sites, choose early to midseason plants such as snowdrops, crocus, and grape hyacinth.

POCKET PLANTINGS

Plantings of spring bulbs can enhance certain spots in the landscape where you might not have thought of putting a flower bed. Don't stint on the bulbs for these sites— a robust planting is much more eye-catching than a skimpy one. When the bulbs have faded, you can let them die back or dig them up and plant annuals. Here are a few ideas:

Surround a lamppost, mailbox, or even a fire alarm box with spring-flowering bulbs such as daffodils.

Place pots of hyacinths, daffodils, pansies, and wax begonias by the front and back doors.

Add springtime beauty around your trees with a collection of colorful bulbs.

Edge the front walk with a narrow border of tulips, daffodils, hyacinths, and grape hyacinths.

Showcase pastel or brightly colored tulips against the textured gray of stone-faced garden beds.

IN NATURALIZED SETTINGS

*I wandered lonely as a cloud
That floats on high o'er vales and hills,
When all at once I saw a crowd,
A host, of golden daffodils...
Ten thousand saw I at a glance,
Tossing their heads in sprightly dance.*

Few of us have space to plant the expanse of bulbs that so moved English poet William Wordsworth. But we can create a similar, if more modest, effect by naturalizing spring-flowering bulbs in a portion of the lawn, in a bed carpeted with ground cover, in a field, at the edge of a wooded area, or at the foot of a grove of deciduous trees.

Naturalizing is simply random planting—setting bulbs in the ground so that they look as if nature, not you, had placed them there. Crocuses and daffodils are frequently naturalized and make impressive displays; winter aconites, anemones, glory-of-the-snow, lily-of-the-valley, and snowdrops are also good candidates for naturalization. Use a mix of bulbs or stick to one kind. You can naturalize bulbs in a small area or a large one, but don't skimp on the number of bulbs—a few randomly spaced daffodils look forlorn in even a small expanse of lawn, and you won't notice smaller bulbs

like crocuses unless there are quite a few of them. When you consider sites, remember that after blooming, a bulb's foliage needs to replenish the food supply for the following year. Pick spots where you can allow grass or other plants to grow undisturbed until the bulb foliage has died back.

You can design a naturalized planting by placing bulbs so that they look "natural." Or simply scatter the bulbs on the ground without thought to a pattern, and dig holes where the bulbs land. You can dig individual holes for one or two bulbs with a special bulb-planting tool (available at nurseries and garden centers) that cuts a plug of soil 2 or 3 inches in diameter and 5 or 6 inches deep. This tool works well if the soil is not compacted. Plant larger groups of bulbs, as discussed on page 81, by excavating the area with a shovel or spade. If you skim off lawn turf with an inch or more of soil attached to the roots, you can replace it after planting the bulbs. Work granular fertilizer or compost into the soil at the bottom of the holes or planting areas. Make sure the granules are mixed with the soil or covered with a layer of sand so that they don't contact the bulb directly and "burn" it. If bulbs naturalized in a lawn aren't performing as well as you'd like, check to see that they aren't crowded. Use a high-potassium fertilizer, or amend the soil with greensand to encourage bloom. High-nitrogen fertilizer may cause the grass to grow more vigorously and compete with the bulbs.

Scatter tulips, left, through a woodland planting for unexpected drama through the spring.

Naturalized bulbs, above, take care of themselves in moderately fertile but well-drained soils. Divide crowded clumps as necessary.

IN GROUND COVERS

Naturalizing bulbs among the greenery adds spring color to an expanse of ground cover. Larger crocus, daffodils, and tulips planted in bunches have a pleasing look emerging through a ground cover. Choose the combination of ground cover and bulbs carefully. Evergreen ground covers such as vinca or pachysandra can hide smaller bulbs, while the leaves of larger bulbs may smother and kill the foliage of surrounding ground covers. Avoid these problems by planting bulbs among deciduous ground covers such as ajuga and sweet woodruff, because their foliage develops later in the season. Planting bulbs in established ground covers requires some tenacity. Pull the foliage out of the way, and make a hole with a trowel or bulb-planting tool. If you want to plant a group of bulbs, skim a shovel several inches under the ground cover, and lift or fold back the foliage, roots, and soil. Dig down to plant the bulbs at the correct depth, fill in with the soil you removed, and press the layer of skimmed ground cover firmly back in place. Water well, and the patch of ground cover should recover easily.

Ground covers have an extra dimension if bulbs such as these 'Angelique' tulips grow with them.

Bulbs in Containers

Containers of spring-flowering bulbs can create colorful focal points at your front door, along a walk, or on a patio or deck. They also look pretty set here and there in a perennial border. Because spring bulbs have a relatively short bloom period, they are often planted in containers on their own. If combined with other plants, spring-bloomers such as pansies or primroses are a better choice than those that bloom in summer. When all the bulbs have finished blooming, discard or relocate the annuals.

Plant spring bulbs in containers in the fall. Bulbs will do well in the same kinds of containers and potting soil as annuals and perennials. (See the discussion in Chapter 4, on page 52.) You can plant spring bulbs in single or multiple layers. The bulbs can be placed almost touching each other to produce a dense, rich effect. Bulbs don't need to be planted as deeply in containers as they are in the ground—hyacinths and paperwhite narcissus, for instance, are frequently grown indoors resting on a layer of gravel, the bulbs covered by a layer of damp moss. Outdoors, bulbs need more soil to hold greater amounts of water, provide nutrients,

and insulate them from temperature extremes. A container must be deep enough to allow 1 or 2 inches of soil under the bulbs. You can bury the tops of the bulbs or leave their growing tips exposed. Remember that the less soil there is in a pot, the more vigilant you'll need to be about watering. To make watering easier, the soil level in a container should be between ½ to 1 inch below the rim. You can mix in slow-release fertilizer at plant-ing time. Check the label to learn how much to use and how long it will be effective.

Maintaining Container Bulbs. After planting, water the soil thoroughly. If you live in an area with freezing winters, place the containers in a garage, tool shed, or other cool, frost-free location to keep the bulbs from freezing. Allow the bulbs to remain at temperatures between 35–40°F for 10 to 16 weeks to satisfy their chilling requirement.

In mild climates where it doesn't freeze, you can leave the containers outdoors. In marginal areas, where freezing temperatures are relatively rare, plunge the pots to their rims in loose soil or containers of sand.

Water the bulb pots through the winter to keep the soil from drying out. Do not let the soil remain soggy; bulbs in poorly drained soil are vulnerable to rot. When shoots appear, move pots to a warm area; when flower buds appear in late winter, move the pots to a sunny spot. Check the soil moisture once a day, and water as necessary. Plants packed tightly in a small amount of soil use a lot of water, and hot or windy weather can quickly dry the soil. When blooms have faded, discard the bulbs, or transplant them into soil so they have time to make and store adequate nutrients for the coming year. Even so, they may need another year to build enough food reserves to bloom.

Pots of hyacinths, left, can add a formal note to any garden scene.

Bulbs in containers, such as these Darwin tulips, below left, can add a stately note to a formal area.

Containers are ideal for tulips because they prevent rodents from eating the bulbs, below. Shown here are 'Angelique' tulips.

Layer-Plant a Container

DIFFICULTY LEVEL: EASY

Tools and Materials: plant container, crockery or nylon screening, potting soil, bulbs, water, fertilizer

1 Select a container at least 6 to 8 inches deep and 12 to 14 inches in diameter. Make sure it has holes in the bottom for drainage. Cover the drainage holes with broken crockery or coarse screening to keep the soil in the pot.

2 Spread about 2 inches of potting soil in the container, and set larger bulbs, such as tulips or daffodils, on top of the soil. Space the bulbs closely but not touching. Cover them with 2 to 3 inches of soil.

3 Set smaller bulbs on this soil layer. Cover them with about 2 inches of soil, filling the container to ½ to 1 inch below the rim. Water thoroughly. Over the winter, protect the pot from freezing, and keep the soil moist.

4 Set the container out in spring. Water as necessary, and fertilize according to guidelines given on the fertilizer packet. First foliage and then flower stems will find their way into the sun. Place the pot where you can enjoy the show.

Gallery of Bulbs

Following is a select list of popular, easy-to-grow spring-flowering bulbs.

Allium giganteum

'Blue Danube' camass
(*Camassia leichtlinii*)

Crocus (*Crocus
scardicus*)

ALLIUM (*Allium* species and cultivars)
The common onion has a number of attractive relatives that produce clumps of straplike leaves and striking clusters of tiny flowers on long, thin stems. Flowers may be sweetly scented. They cut and dry well. There are several spring-flowering species. Blooming in early to mid-spring are Turkestan allium (*A. karataviense,* Zone 4), with large pink to reddish clusters, and Naples onion (*A. neapolitanum,* Zone 7), with fragrant spreading clusters of white flowers on 1-foot stems that make wonderful cut flowers. Following in late spring are Star of Persia (*A. christophii*), with globes up to 10 inches across of purple flowers on stalks up to 30 inches tall, and blue allium (*A. caeruleum*), which produces 2-inch clusters on stems about 1 foot tall. Plant a clump of chives (*A. schoenoprasum*), and cut the pretty little lilac purple flowers for bouquets and the onion-flavored leaves for salads. Alliums require **full sun.** Planting depth varies according to the size of the bulb. Unless otherwise noted, flowering alliums are hardy to Zone 3.

CAMASS (*Camassia* species and cultivars)
Indigenous to the Americas, camass produces exquisite racemes of blue or white star-shaped flowers in late spring. The flowers open from the bottom to the top and are excellent for cutting as well as for enjoying in the garden. Leaves are narrow and grassy looking. Plants grow from 2 to 3 feet tall and should be massed in the garden or naturalized in a field or by a stream; small numbers aren't impressive. Camass requires **sun or light shade.** Plant bulbs 4 inches deep in well-drained soil that remains moist during the summer months. *C. cusickii* has pale-blue flowers and blooms in early summer; cultivars are deeper blue. Cultivars of *C. leichtlinii* (often sold as *C. plena*) have semidouble deep purple flowers. *C. quamash* has deep- to pale-blue or white flowers, depending on the subspecies or cultivar, and is very easy to grow. Zone 4.

CROCUS (*Crocus* species, cultivars, and hybrids)
Crocuses are delightful little plants. Although not quite the earliest flowers to bloom, they're often called the heralds of spring. There are both large- and small-flowered crocus in various shades of purple, pink, yellow, white, or bicolors. The tallest crocuses rise to about 8 inches; the shortest, about 4 inches. All have sparse grassy foliage. Most commonly grown are the large-flowered Dutch hybrids. The species *Crocus chrysanthus,* sometimes called snow crocus, has smaller flowers that bloom earlier. For the longest flowering period, plant some of each. Actually, plant a lot of each. Even though crocuses increase rapidly, they're small plants and need to be seen in quantity to look their best. Autumn crocus (*C. speciosus*) blooms in the fall. Plant in early fall and they'll bloom the same season. Crocuses require **sun or partial shade.** Plant about 4 inches deep in soil that drains well. Crocuses couldn't be easier to grow, except that squirrels and other rodents love them. When you plant, figure you'll lose some for their dinners. Zone 4.

DAFFODIL (*Narcissus* species and hybrids)
When people think of spring bulbs, chances are that daffodils come first to mind. Even young children are familiar with their cheerful, often fragrant flowers rising on leafless stalks from clumps of narrow, upright leaves. There are hundreds of different daffodils. Plants range in size from 6 to 18 inches tall, and a single stalk may bear from 1 to as many as 20 flowers. Flower colors are mostly whites and yellows (with orange, red, and pink highlights), but flower shape and size is interestingly varied. Daffodils are classified into 12 groups, or divisions, according to the flower form. The most popular group is the trumpet daffodils, with the familiar trumpet-shaped flower. You don't need to know the divisions, but if you get bitten by the daffodil bug, you can have fun for years growing the various kinds.

In addition to daffodil bulbs, nurseries and garden centers often sell bulbs identified as jonquils or narcissus. Both are daffodils—or more properly, all three are *Narcissus,* the botanical classification. Those known as jonquils produce clusters of small, very fragrant flowers in mid- to late spring. Narcissus isn't used with great precision as a common name; some people call all daffodils narcissus. Others use the term only to refer to small-flowered, fragrant, usually white daffodils with multiple blooms per stem, such as the pungent paperwhite narcissus forced into early bloom indoors. There are so many cultivars and natural hybrids that beginners shouldn't worry about names. You'll find more than enough

'Ascot' daffodil

daffodils at your local garden center to get you started. And if you become enthusiastic, you can turn to numerous mail-order bulb specialists.

Daffodils prefer **full sun.** For the best, longest-lasting display, plant early, midseason, and late-blooming cultivars. Plant the bulbs with the tops 4 to 6 inches below the soil surface. Warn children that daffodil bulbs, leaves, and flowers are poisonous when eaten. Most daffodils are hardy to Zone 4.

GLORY-OF-THE-SNOW (*Chionodoxa* species)
An early spring treat, these little bulbs produce spikes of white, blue, or pink flowers on stems up to 6 inches tall. For contrast, plant in drifts near plants with yellow or white flowers. These plants prefer **sun in spring and partial shade in summer.** Plant 3 inches deep and 3 inches apart. Plants will self-sow to form a patch and won't need division for years. Zone 4.

Glory-of-the-snow

A SELECTION OF DAFFODILS

Unless otherwise noted, all plants grow 14 to 20 inches high and bear single flowers, one to a stem.

Very Early
'Peeping Tom'—yellow,
    6 to 10 inches tall
'Tête à Tête'—yellow,
    6 to 10 inches tall

Early to Midseason
'Carlton'—yellow
'Mount Hood'—white
'Dutch Master'—yellow
'Ice Follies'—white

'Ice Follies' daffodil

Late
'Actaea' (Poet's narcissus)—white; center or eye yellow, red, or greenish
'Geranium'—white with orange cup, several flowers per stem
'Hawera'—yellow, 8 inches tall, several flowers per stem
'Cheerfulness'—white with pale yellow center, double flowers
'Yellow Cheerfulness'—yellow, double flowers

GRAPE HYACINTH (*Muscari* species)

These sweetly scented, grapelike clusters of purple or white flowers last for several weeks in mid-spring. The grassy foliage appears in fall, survives until spring, and dies down by early summer. Growing only 8 inches high, they're good plants for edging a bed, mixing with taller bulbs such as tulips, or for naturalizing. Plant in **full sun or partial shade.** 'Blue Spike' is a double-flowered form; *M. botryoides* 'Album' is white-flowered. Zone 4. 'Album' is hardy to Zone 3.

'Blue Spike' grape hyacinth
(*Muscari armeniacum*)

HYACINTH (*Hyacinthus orientalis*)

The fragrant blooms of hyacinths are available in blue, pink, rose, yellow, white, apricot, or lilac. Stately little plants growing 8 to 12 inches tall, their stiff upright blooms and pointed leaves lend a formal appearance to border and container plantings. They also look good in small groups in front of shrubs or hedges and combine particularly well with early tulips. Flower clusters tend to be looser in the second and subsequent years.

The size of the bulb and of the flower spike are related—bigger bulbs produce bigger spikes. Bulbs multiply slowly. Hyacinths require **full sun.** Plant in fall, with bulbs almost touching each other. Plant larger bulbs about 6 inches deep, smaller bulbs 4 inches deep. Excellent cultivars are 'Pink Perfection', 'City of Haarlem' (soft yellow), 'Carnegie' (white), 'Ben Nevis' (double, white), and 'Delft Blue'. Zone 5 (sometimes 4 with a thick winter mulch).

SNOWDROP (*Galanthus nivalis*)

One of the earliest-blooming bulbs, snowdrops survive frosty weather; their bell-shaped white flowers are frequently seen pushing through the snow. Because they are small (3 to 5 inches tall), you'll need scores for a good show. They multiply rapidly and are excellent for naturalizing under trees and shrubs. *G. nivalis* 'Flore Pleno' is a double-flowered form. Plant in **full sun or partial shade.** They prefer well-drained soil and can tolerate dry conditions in summer. Plant the small bulbs 3 inches deep and about 3 inches apart; they'll quickly fill in. Zone 3.

SQUILL (*Scilla* species and cultivars)

These little bulbs bloom after snowdrops in early spring, producing star-shaped flowers in a lovely shade of blue; white and light pink forms are also available. Up to four stalks rise from each bulb, and each 4- to 8-inch stalk bears several flowers. The grassy foliage is sparse. Plant squill in drifts—the more bulbs the better. The **spring sunlight and summer shade** found beneath deciduous trees suits them fine. Set bulbs 3 inches deep and 3 inches apart. Squill spread quickly and naturalize well because the bulbs multiply fast and new plants also grow from seed. Zone 3.

Hyacinth   Snowdrop

Squill

TULIP (*Tulipa* species and hybrids)

Tulips, like daffodils, are synonymous with spring. They appear with other plants in beds and borders, on their own in mass plantings, and in containers. The familiar garden tulips are seldom naturalized: the bulbs are a favorite food of burrowing animals, plus the stiff, upright flower is too formal to look natural dotted about a field. Species tulips, which often have more relaxed foliage and cheerful star-shaped flowers, look very much at home in naturalized plantings. Unlike most tulips, which die out after a few years, they return for years. Species tulips usually bloom earlier than garden types.

There's a vast selection of hybrid, or garden, tulips. Ranging in height from 6 to 30 inches, they come in every color, including one so dark red that it's often sold as a "black" tulip. Like daffodils, tulips are classified into classes or divisions by flower type, ancestry, and bloom time. A few of these classifications are worth noting because you'll see the names at garden centers. Darwin hybrid tulips are among the largest of all types; they flower in late spring. Lily-flowered tulips have flowers that flare out at the tips (resembling lilies). Peony-flowered tulips are double, with many petals. Rembrandt tulips have large flowers with stripes or streaks in a contrasting color. Tulips require **full sun.** Planted too shallowly they often perform poorly. Plant full-size bulbs with the tops 8 to 10 inches deep. In mild-winter regions, grow tulips as annuals, using prechilled bulbs. Zone 4.

WINDFLOWER (*Anemone blanda*)

With small daisylike blue, pink, or white blooms, windflowers spread to form charming carpets of early spring color under deciduous trees or in the lawn. The plants are small (3 to 6 inches tall), but the flowers are up to 2 inches wide. Windflowers require **partial shade** and prefer cool, moist (but not soggy), soil. Windflowers don't thrive in hot climates. Plant tubers 2 inches deep after soaking them in water overnight. Plants self-sow and spread rapidly. The wild species is on the international endangered plant list, so buy only nursery-propagated tubers or cultivars such as 'White Splendor' or 'Blue Star'. Zone 4.

WINTER ACONITE (*Eranthis hyemalis*)

These early spring-bloomers appear at least two weeks before the crocuses. Like snowdrops, they'll bloom through a shallow cover of snow; the species are delightful companions for each other. Winter aconite bears bright yellow flowers on stems 3 to 6 inches tall. Foliage appears after the flowers and is gone by summer. Grow in **sun or partial shade.** Purchased tubers are usually too dried out to grow well. The best way to introduce winter aconite to your garden is by transplanting a start from a friend's garden immediately after the plants bloom. The plants are easy to move at this point; once established they persist for decades and multiply by spreading and by self-sowing. Zone 4.

'Golden Emperor' tulip

Rembrant tulip

Windflower

Winter aconite

CHAPTER 7

Herbs

Herbs are a fascinating group of plants with a history of cultivation stretching back to the dawn of civilization. Once the herb garden was a practical project, necessary for supplying flavorings for the kitchen and medicines for the family. Today, gardeners are less likely to grow herbs for medicinal purposes than for their attractive looks, pleasing fragrances, and tasty flavors. Whether your interest is kindled by taste, aroma, beauty, or history, you'll find herbs a satisfying addition to your garden.

What Are Herbs?

Traditionally, herbs have been defined as plants that are useful to people. The oregano and thyme on your pizza are herbs just as the ornamental foxglove, from which we once extracted the medicine digitalis, is an herb. The insecticide pyrethrin is derived from the painted daisy, making it an herb as well. The list goes on and on; we use herbs and herb products every day.

Ordinarily, gardeners consider herbs to be the plants used as food seasonings, teas or home remedies, those with noteworthy fragrances, and—increasingly—those that please the eye. We grow basil, chives, marjoram, rosemary, tarragon, and thyme for their flavorful leaves. Coriander and dill provide tasty leaves and seeds. For fragrance, we plant scented geraniums, mints, sages, and sweet woodruff. And we grow lamb's ears for its soft silver leaves; bee balm for its fiery flowers; and germander for its compact form, ideal for an herbal hedge.

Herbs include plants that are used for seasoning, fragrance, medicinal qualities, and appearance, right.

Herbs are so easy to grow and maintain, opposite, that you can create a magnificent herb garden in only a year or two.

Choosing Herbs

In addition to an herb's taste, aroma, and appearance, consider its preferred growing conditions when choosing what to grow. Herbs are such a diverse group of plants that broad generalizations are often misleading. Most herbs thrive in moderately fertile, well-drained soil in a sunny location; some do well in poor soil or partial shade, and a few tolerate soggy soil. Despite a reputation as carefree plants, some herbs may be affected by insects and diseases just as other plants are. A few herbs, such as dill and basil, are annuals. Most, though, are perennials; these must be able to tolerate the extremes of winter cold and summer heat in your climate. If you live in a cold-winter climate and want to grow an herb that's too tender for your winters—rosemary, for instance—you can grow it in a pot and overwinter it indoors. Plants adapted to the conditions of your area (soil, temperatures, rainfall, and so on) are more likely to succeed for you and to require less regular care. The table on page 94 and the Herb Gallery at the end of this chapter will help you choose plants for various uses and growing conditions.

Herbs in the Home Landscape

With such a wide variety of flowers, foliage, and forms to choose from, you can consider an herb for a spot in a flower bed or border just as you would any other annual, perennial, or shrub. Take advantage of aromatic herbs such as lavender, clary sage, and dianthus, which have scents that waft through the air, by placing them near seating or upwind of open windows. Place herbs with leaves or flowers that must be crushed to release their fragrance, such as mints and sage, within easy reach. If herbs can withstand light foot traffic, as do chamomile, pennyroyal, and oregano, plant them between flagstones on a path or patio. Plant herbs such as creeping thyme in soil that fills the spaces between stones in a wall or rocky outcrop. Use santolina or creeping thyme as a sunny ground cover. The small stature, leaves, and flowers of a number of herbs fit nicely with the diminutive alpine plants traditional in rock gardens.

SOME FAVORITE HERBS

FOR COOKING

Anise	Dill	Mustard
Basil	Fennel	Oregano
Bay	Garlic	Parsley
Caraway	Lemon balm	Rosemary
Chervil	Lemon grass	Sage (various)
Chives	Lovage	Sorrel
Coriander	Marjoram	Tarragon
Cumin	Mint (various)	Thymes (various)

FOR EDIBLE FLOWERS

Borage	Nasturtium	Violet
Calendula	Rosemary	Sage (garden)
Chives	Viola	Sage (pineapple)

FOR FRAGRANCE

* indicates herbs with fragrant flowers

Basil	Lemon thyme	Scented geranium
Bee balm	Lemon verbena	Sweet marjoram
Chamomile	Mint	Sweet woodruff
Catnip	Oregano	Tansy
*Dianthus (some)	*Rose (some)	Tarragon
Lavender	Rosemary	Thyme
Lemon balm	Santolina	Southernwood

FOR BEAUTY

Artemisia	Hyssop	Rose
Bee balm	Lady's Mantle	Rue
Calendula	Lamb's Ears	Sage (various)
Chives	Lavender	Santolina
Feverfew	Nasturtium	Sweet woodruff
Foxglove	Purple Basil	Thyme (various)
Germander	Purple Coneflower	Violet

Herbs can make home landscapes varied and interesting. As pictured above, foxglove, valarian, lamb's ears, and poppies complement a bed of ornamentals.

KITCHEN HERB GARDEN

If your interests are culinary, grow herbs used for food and flavoring where they'll be handy—near the kitchen door. Such gardens are often small and laid out geometrically, but they can also be planted as a border along the back walk or around a patio. Divide the plantings into beds with narrow paths of wood chips or brick to emphasize the geometry and provide easy access.

Suggested Plants. You'll undoubtedly have favorite herbs you'll want to plant, but consider including oregano, sage, chives, thyme, and tarragon. These perennials can form the foundation of the garden. Plan spaces for them first because they will remain in the garden for years and will spread considerably while they're there. When they're young, fill in spaces between them with annuals. (Place tall annuals where they won't shade or crowd the young perennials.) Chives and oregano will self-sow everywhere if you let the flowers go to seed; instead, cut the flower stems when blooms are half-open, and hang them upside down to dry for use in indoor bouquets.

Must-have annuals for any herb garden are green- or purple-leaved basil, fern-like parsley, tall and airy dill, and leafy coriander, which is known as cilantro when grown for its leaves. Plant the annuals where you can clean them up in the fall with- out disturbing your perennials.

Several indispensable herbs are woody. Rosemary and lemon verbena are shrubs, though they're usually referred to as tender perennials. Sweet bay grows slowly into a tree. With the exception of a hardy rosemary named 'Arp', which survives in sheltered sites in Zones 7 or 6, none of the three overwinters in areas colder than Zone 8. If you live in a cold-winter region, plant these tender herbs in containers, or pot them up at the end of the season. Bring them indoors for the winter months. You'll need to repot both rosemary and sweet bay every two to three years because they get quite large as they mature.

Small herbs grow well in the tight quarters that this wagon-wheel planter provides.

Kitchen herb gardens can grow on a windowsill as easily as in a backyard.

KNOT GARDEN

If you're ambitious, consider an herbal knot garden. Knot gardens can be spectacular additions to your landscape, but they are time-consuming to make and can be tedious to maintain. If you're interested in creating a knot garden, it's worthwhile to visit one and talk with the gardener to find out what's involved. A local nursery or garden club may be able to refer you to someone in your town who has a knot garden.

Knot refers to the intertwining pattern of low-growing, neatly trimmed hedges that form interlocking geometric shapes—circles or diamonds, for example. The hedges appear to twine together, one over or under the other, like the strands in a knot. This is an illusion enhanced by careful planting and clipping where one hedge intersects another. In an herbal knot garden, the outline is usually made with low-growing evergreen herbs, such as germander or santolina. The spaces they create are filled with other herbs, often with foliage or flowers in contrasting colors. You can make an herbal knot garden for purely decorative purposes or get double duty from it, planting the interior spaces with culinary or fragrant herbs. Remember that the appearance may suffer when leaves, flowers, or whole plants are harvested for use. Instead of herbs, you can also plant spring bulbs followed by annual flowers as fillers.

Knot gardens are traditionally formed by low-growing hedges. Plants can fill interior spaces or, as shown here, colored stones and other mulches can be used.

Making a Knot Garden. First prepare the soil as you would for a new garden bed. (See Chapter 2, pages 28–31.) Lay out the lines of the hedges using garden lime as "chalk" to draw the pattern on the soil surface. Create circles or arcs with string and a stake (the stake at the center, the string forming the radius). Use straight pieces of wood or flexible garden hose to lay out other shapes. Plant the hedge plants first; then fill in the centers. The hedge plants may take a season or two to grow together. Prune by cutting back the stem tips to encourage bushy growth. Pruning time and amount depends on the plants. A knowledgeable nursery staff member or herb gardener can help you select appropriate herbs for the hedges in your knot garden, as well as teach you the best pruning times and techniques.

CONTAINER GARDENS

Many herbs make excellent container plants. If your gardening is restricted to a patio or balcony, you can easily grow mints, chives, basil, parsley, and many other herbs in pots. Container planting also allows gardeners in cold-winter climates to move tender herbs such as sweet bay and rosemary inside for the winter. You can have fun combining plants in single pots, arranging groups of containers for best effect, and placing potted herbs in garden settings to provide added interest. As long as they have the same sun and moisture requirements, you can combine different herbs (as well as other plants) in the same container. Try creeping thyme or chamomile as a ground cover for a sweet bay tree. Edge a pot of geraniums with curly-leaved parsley. Combine chives, parsley, and thyme in a window box or deck-railing box.

Annual and tender perennial herbs are grown the same way as other container plants. (See Chapter 4, page 52.) Remember that containers must have drainage holes, the soil must drain well, the plants will need periodic fertilizing, and the containers may need watering as often as twice a day, especially in sun.

Perennial herbs and those that are shrubs or trees can be grown in pots, too. These plants need special care to keep them healthy from year to year. Overwintering herbs indoors in pots or growing them indoors year-round is problematic because light levels, even in south-facing windows, are seldom sufficient. Plants may survive, but growth and flavor will be weak and shoots and stems will be "leggy" (elongated with leaves spaced too far apart).

To ensure robust health in overwintered herbs, grow them under fluorescent lights. Place them so thattheir top leaves are a few inches below the tubes, and keep the lights on for 16 to 18 hours a day. Make sure the soil doesn't dry out. Fertilize plants that continue growing every month, but don't fertilize plants that normally go dormant during the winter. As the plants grow, they'll need to be pruned and repotted in the same or larger pots.

Container gardens of herbs make practical and decorative additions to any space, indoors or out.

Getting Started with Herbs

Herbs comprise annuals, perennials, shrubs, and trees, and are grown and cared for like other members of their respective groups. You can buy plants from a nursery, or you can start many annual and perennial herbs from seeds, as described in Chapter 4, pages 52–55. Nursery-bought plants are your only option for true French tarragon, particular mints, and oregano, which need to be grown from cuttings or divisions to produce the desired characteristics. Depending on the herb, you can increase your supply of plants by dividing clumps in your garden or rooting cuttings. Planted in moderately fertile, well-drained soil, many herbs require little routine care after they've become established. Poor drainage is the bane of many herbs because soggy soil readily rots their roots (especially over winter) or harbors fungal diseases. If your soil doesn't drain well, consider growing herbs in raised beds or containers.

Combining raised beds and containers, above, makes it possible to grow a wide variety of herbs in a small area.

Dried seeds, below, drop from the plant. To keep them, enclose the seedheads in paper bags before they are completely brown.

HARVESTING HERBS

Herb leaves can be harvested throughout the growing season. Depending on the plant and your needs, you may gather just a few leaves or cut away half or more of its foliage. For some herbs, picking stimulates new growth and provides a long season of harvest. Harvest in the morning, when the dew has dried off the leaves but before the heat of the day has driven off some of the plant's flavorful oils. Descriptions in the Herb Gallery offer specific information on harvesting certain herbs.

Herbs that you wish to use fresh will keep for a short time in a vase of water. Leaves can also be dried and stored for long periods. Bind small bundles of stems together with rubber bands, and place the bundles in a dry, well-ventilated place, out of direct sun. You can hang the bundles or place them on screens (for air movement). Turn the bundles regularly to ensure uniform drying (and to check for mildew and mold). When the leaves are brittle, strip them off the stems, and put them in lidded jars. Don't crush the leaves until you use them; crushing releases their oils.

To collect herb seeds, harvest when the seeds begin to turn brown. Band seed stalks together in small bundles, and put the bundles inside a paper bag tied around the stem. As they dry, the seeds will drop into the bag.

For other methods of preserving herbs, including oven drying, microwave drying, and freezing, contact your Cooperative Extension Service or consult one of the many books devoted to herbs.

GETTING STARTED WITH HERBS

Buy Plants

French tarragon	Lavender	Rosemary
Germander	Mints	Sage
Lemon thyme	Oregano	Sweet bay
Lemon verbena	Parsley	Thyme
		Winter savory

Direct Seed Outside in Spring

Coriander	Chervil	Dill
Chamomile	Chives	Lemon balm
		Summer savory

Start Early Indoors

Basil	Parsley	Sweet marjoram

Gallery of Herbs

Unless otherwise stated, plants all grow best in fertile, well-drained garden soil in full sun or light shade.

ANNUALS

BASIL (*Ocimum basilicum*)

Prized as a flavoring for pesto and as a tasty companion to tomato in all its forms, basil also has a long medicinal history. It was once a folk remedy for fever and snakebite but was also used for more mundane purposes of settling the stomach and aiding digestion. Basil is an attractive plant. Lustrous, deliciously fragrant leaves grow on a sturdy, many-branched plant that can reach 2 or 3 feet tall. Sweet basil is the most common culinary basil, but a variety of cultivars provide different leaf sizes, colors, flavors, and fragrances. Purple-leaved forms, such as 'Purple Ruffles' and 'Opal', are attractive in combination with other plants in the garden or containers. You can direct-seed basil into the garden after the frost-free date, but for earlier harvest, buy plants or start seeds indoors. Plant seeds indoors about 6 to 8 weeks before the last frost. Plants remain productive for months if you pinch off the flower spikes before the tiny white flowers open and harvest leaves and branches rather than the whole plant.

Genovese basil

Chervil

CHERVIL (*Anthriscus cerifolium*)

Chervil's ferny, finely cut leaves resemble and are used like parsley, though their flavor is more like lemony licorice. It is a common seasoning for salads and fish and is one of the ingredients of the French *fines herbes* seasoning. Plants grow 1 to 2 feet high and bear umbels of white flowers in midsummer. They bolt to seed quite quickly and do not tolerate hot weather, so plant seeds in early spring and late summer.

CORIANDER (*Coriandrum sativum*)

A must for the kitchen garden, coriander, also called cilantro, quickly produces a crop of ferny leaves, followed by clusters of pale flowers on 1- to 3-foot stalks. Use fresh-cut leaves to flavor salads and soups or in Mexican and Oriental dishes. The scented seeds are crushed and used to season a variety of foods. Direct-seed in early spring, adding small patches at 2- to 4-week intervals until late summer to ensure a continual supply. Thin seedlings to 6 inches apart. Because the plant grows and is harvested so quickly, it's not a good candidate for ornamental plantings.

DILL (*Anethum graveolens*)

Well known to many as a seasoning in pickles and vinegar, dill seeds are also used in some breads. The ferny leaves are used to flavor fish, lamb, and salads. Fragrant, finely divided leaves form quickly, followed in mid-summer by 3- to 4-foot-tall branching stalks topped with umbels of small yellow flowers. Freshly cut flowering stalks and dried seed heads make attractive fillers in flower arrangements. Sow seeds in the garden in early spring and, for a fall crop, in midsummer. Thin to 18 inches apart if you want seeds, 4 inches apart if you want only leaves. Dill self-seeds readily.

Cilantro

Dill

PARSLEY (*Petroselinum crispum*)

Two kinds of parsley are commonly grown. Both form foot-tall rosettes of finely cut leaves. Italian parsley has flat leaves and a stronger flavor than the curly leaf types that are familiar as a garnish. Both are rich in vitamins A and C. Plants are biennial, forming a tall flowering stalk in the second year, but most people grow them as annuals. Buy plants, or start seeds indoors, 8 to 10 weeks before the last frost. Plant seedlings 8 to 12 inches apart. Keep the transplants moist. Harvest stems on the outside edges of the plant, and new growth in the center will provide a long-lasting supply of leaves.

SWEET MARJORAM (*Origanum majorana*)

The tiny gray-green leaves of this bushy little plant are used fresh or dried to flavor meats and vinegars and as a scent in perfumes. It bears inconspicuous white flowers for much of the summer. Sweet majoram is perennial in Zone 9. In colder climates, grow as an annual in pots or garden beds, where it makes a fine edging. Start indoors from seed sown 8 weeks before the last frost, or buy plants. A slightly alkaline to neutral pH gives the best results.

SCENTED GERANIUM (*Pelargonium* species and hybrids)

Tender perennials grown as annuals, the many types of scented geraniums all have strongly scented leaves and form mounds 1 to 3 feet high. Most have sparse but attractive little flowers in white, pink, or lavender. Leaves are used for flavoring and in sachets and potpourris. The range of scents includes lemon, lime, apple, rose, nutmeg, coconut, ginger, and peppermint. Your local nursery probably won't carry them all, but they might order plants for you. Buy plants for use in the garden or in containers. Wait until after the last frost to move them outside. Pinch back the growing tips to keep the plants bushy. They become extremely leggy in shady conditions. Container plants overwinter well indoors. Put them in a bright window or under lights, and don't give them as much water as they had outdoors.

PERENNIALS

BEE BALM (*Monarda didyma*)

Bee balm is grown today chiefly for its ornamental qualities, but its minty leaves also make fine tea and have been used for relieving fevers, colds, and intestinal gas. In early summer, slender, straight, leafy stems from 2 to 4 feet tall are topped for weeks with shaggy clusters of small tubular flowers in shades of red, pink, purple, or white. Bee balm is a good plant for a perennial border, and bird lovers grow it to attract hummingbirds. Bee balm thrives in **full sun,** except in hot climates where it does best with some afternoon shade. Buy plants to be assured of getting particular flower colors. Bee balm tolerates heat if grown in fertile, moist soil, but never tolerates dry conditions. Plants spread to form large patches. The center tends to die out once a plant reaches four to five years old; divide and replant the young vigorous growth to keep the planting looking good. Older cultivars are susceptible to powdery mildew. This fungus destroys the leaves and looks terrible, but it seldom kills the plant. Zone 4.

Curlyleaf parsley

Italian parsley

Rose-scented geranium

Sweet marjoram

Bee balm

German chamomile

Chives, standard

Garlic chives

English lavender

CHAMOMILE, ROMAN (*Chamaemelum nobile*)

Known to children as Peter Rabbit's favorite tea, Roman (or English) chamomile is also used as an herbal ground cover. It tolerates light foot traffic and releases a pungent aroma when stepped on or mowed. Branches of finely dissected leaves form a low spreading mat about 6 inches tall. Chamomile requires **full sun,** tolerates heat, and grows best in slightly dry soil. Zone 4.

German chamomile (*Matricaria recutita*) has similar leaves and flowers but is an annual that grows up to 30 inches high. This is the chamomile of choice for making tea. Sow seeds directly in the garden. Give it more moisture than its perennial cousin.

CHIVES (*Allium schoenoprasum*)

Enjoy the scent of this little onion's lavender flowers in late spring, and snip the mildly onion-flavored leaves for salads and soups from spring until hard frost. Slender, hollow leaves grow 1 to 1½ foot long. Garlic chives (*A. tuberosum*) have solid, flat garlic-flavored leaves and edible white flowers on 2- to 3-foot stalks in late summer. Chives are vigorous self seeders; prevent invasive growth by snipping flowers before they form seeds. Chives are easy to grow from seed sown in the garden or started indoors, but it's faster to divide a clump from a friend's garden. Zone 3.

French tarragon

ENGLISH LAVENDER (*Lavandula angustifolia*)

Few plants are as striking in the landscape as a hedge of lavender in full early-summer bloom. And lavender smells as good as it looks. When not in flower, the neat, rounded 2-foot-tall mounds of narrow gray leaves are also attractive. Cultivars offer a range of heights and flowers in pink, white, or lavender-blue, as well as the purple of the species. Lavender is used as a flavoring and in perfume and cosmetics; it has been used as an antiseptic treatment for fever, burns, and eczema. Home gardeners can easily dry lavender flowers for use in sachets and potpourri—pick the flower stalks as soon as the flowers open, and hang them upside down in a cool, shady, well-ventilated room to dry. Buy plants unless you're growing the new annual, 'Lavender Lady', which can be started from seed early indoors and transplanted to the garden. Lavender needs well-drained soil and will tolerate drought once established. It usually does poorly in hot, humid climates. Lavender is evergreen in mild-winter climates (Zone 8). In cold-winter areas, prune winter-damaged shoots back to healthy growth in late spring. Zone 5.

FRENCH TARRAGON (*Artemisia dracunculus* var. *sativa*)

Tarragon is grown for its deliciously flavored leaves rather than its nondescript appearance. The plant is a mass of stems 2 feet or more in length, covered with shiny, narrow, dark green and strongly aromatic leaves. A single plant slowly spreads by creeping rhizomes to form a patch. The anise-flavored leaves are used in salad dressings, vinegar, and in egg, fish, and chicken dishes. Tarragon tolerates poor soil but not drought. True French tarragon seldom flowers and is sterile, so you'll need to buy plants or get divisions from a friend. Cut the plant back to maintain the size you want. Avoid Russian tarragon, which lacks flavor and good looks and is commonly sold as "tarragon." Zone 3.

GERMANDER (*Teucrium chamaedrys*)

Once used as a tea to treat throat ailments and fevers (a practice not recommended due to its ability to cause liver damage if ingested), germander is a shrubby perennial that's grown for its attractive flowers and evergreen or semievergreen foliage. Plants form neat bushy clumps about 1 foot tall and wide. The upright stems bear small shiny aromatic leaves. Germander makes a tidy edging or hedge that can be sheared for a more formal look. Clusters of small purple flowers line the stems in midsummer and attract bees. There is also a white-flowered form. 'Prostratum' grows just 4 to 6 inches high and spreads over several feet; 'Variegatum' offers leaves with white, cream, or yellow markings. Germander tolerates heat, poor soil, and drought, but needs good drainage. Buy plants. Shear plants in spring to create a full, dense bush, and shear again after flowering to maintain a tidy form. Zone 5.

GREEK OREGANO (*Origanum vulgare* subsp. *hirtum*)

If you're fond of Mediterranean cookery, grow Greek oregano—a particularly pungent form of this popular herb that makes a patch of leafy stems about 2 feet tall. If you grow this plant from seed, select only the white-flowered plants. But even among white-flowered selections, you'll find that both fragrance and flavor will vary from plant to plant. To guarantee good flavor, choose plants in person. A subspecies, 'Aureum', reaches just 12 inches tall; its leaves are bland tasting but are a lovely yellow-green color that looks good as a ground cover in beds or containers. Oregano tolerates heat and dry soil. Zone 5.

LAMB'S EARS (*Stachys byzantina*)

Once used to stop bleeding in minor wounds, lamb's ears' only therapeutic value today comes from the pleasure of stroking the soft woolly surfaces of its thick, silver gray leaves. The plant's low mound of foliage makes it ideal as an informal edging for flower beds, paths, and patios, and the woolly leaves make lamb's ears indispensable for children's gardens. In late spring or early summer, most cultivars produce foot-tall stalks of small

leaves and pink or purple flowers. Some people find the flowers attractive; others cut off the stalks. 'Silver Carpet' is a nonflowering cultivar. All cultivars tolerate heat but not high humidity, which rots the leaves. Buy plants, and set them 12 to 18 inches apart as an edging. Increase your supply by dividing mature plants in spring or fall. Zone 5.

LEMON BALM (*Melissa officinalis*)

The heavily veined leaves of this herb have a delicious, lemony flavor and aroma. They're used fresh to flavor drinks, salads, and fish dishes. Sheared regularly, the upright stems will form a bushy mound about 2 feet high. Shearing also removes the insignificant flowers and keeps the plant from invasive self-seeding. Although it is a mint, its rootstock spreads slowly, so lemon balm can be used in mixed plantings. Buy plants, or grow them from seed; you can sow lemon balm directly in the garden. Zone 5.

LEMON VERBENA (*Aloysia triphylla*)

Grown for the lemon fragrance of its leaves, this tender shrub bears clusters of tiny lilac or white flowers in summer. Grown in the ground in mild-winter climates, it will reach 10 feet tall. Pinch off the growing tips of the stems to encourage a bushier habit. Gardeners in cold-winter areas grow lemon verbena as an annual in the garden or in containers, where the plant's growth is stunted and it usually doesn't flower. Use fresh or dried; it adds a lemony scent to sachets and potpourri. Buy plants, and grow them in well-drained soil. Overwinter container plants under lights in a cool, dry spot. Zone 8.

Greek oregano

Lamb's ears

Lemon balm

Germander

Lemon verbena

MINT (*Mentha* species)

Gardeners can choose among numerous types of mints, each with a different fragrance and flavor. In addition to the familiar spearmint and peppermint, there are chocolate, orange, apple, and pineapple-scented mints. If you're willing to police the group's invasive tendencies, you can have fun growing and comparing the different types.

Spearmint (*M. spicata*) has dark green leaves and grows to 3 feet tall. It forms whorls of tiny pink, lilac, or white flowers in summer. The leaves of peppermint (*M.* x *peperita*) can be green, purple, or green marked with white. Both species are very invasive. Pineapple mint (*M. suaveolens* 'Variegata') is less invasive and offers lovely, variegated bright green and white leaves. Buy all mints as plants; they don't come true from seed. Plant them in an out-of-the-way place where it's okay if they spread, or be prepared to monitor their growth and uproot shoots that stray too far. You can also plant mints in pots and sink the pots into garden beds. To eliminate control problems completely, grow them in containers.

ROSEMARY (*Rosmarinus officinalis*)

Used as a flavoring, infused as tea, and dried for aromatic sachets, rosemary is a handsome addition to the landscape in warm-winter climates or, where winters are cold, to a container garden. Upright forms grow from 4 to 6 feet tall and can be grown as hedges or specimen plants, either trained and sheared or left "natural." Low, spreading forms make fine ground covers or look good trailing over a wall. All rosemary plants have aromatic, needlelike leaves and bear small flowers for weeks in winter and spring. Flowers can be blue, lavender-pink, or white. Buy plants because this herb grows so slowly. Rosemary requires well-drained soil and does well in hot, dry conditions. Prune in spring to control size and shape of the plants. Cold-climate gardeners grow rosemary in containers, overwintering it in a cool but sunny room or under lights. Most rosemaries are hardy to Zone 8; 'Arp' survives in Zone 6 on well-drained sites protected from cold winter winds.

SAGE (*Salvia* species)

There are numerous sages for the landscape and kitchen garden. Annual sages are popular plants for flower beds and containers, but perennial sages outnumber the annual types. Perennial sages include both herbaceous and shrubby types. Sages have long been used for culinary and medicinal purposes, although modern gardeners are often more attracted to their ornamental qualities.

Garden sage (*S. officinalis,* Zone 5) is a bushy perennial growing about 2 feet high and wide with woody growth at its base. The small, elongated, fragrant, gray-green leaves are used in seasonings and in teas. In early summer, the plant bears eye-catching spikes of small, blue-purple flowers. The plant is evergreen in warm-winter climates, but the foliage dies back to the base in colder areas. Grow sage in containers, as a specimen, or in massed plantings in well-drained garden soil. Cultivars offer gold, purple, or variegated leaves.

Several other sages are cold hardy. Meadow sage (*S. pratensis,* Zone 3) is a smaller bush that forms a rosette of fragrant dark green leaves and bears blue, violet, rosy, or white flowers. Clary sage (*S. sclarea,* Zone 4) is a biennial. It produces a clump of large gray-green leaves the first year and branching flower stalks the second. The flowers are small and white, but the colorful bracts are ornamental. You can maintain clary sage in your garden by transplanting the self-sown seedlings in midsummer.

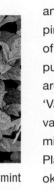

Spearmint

Peppermint

Rosemary   Culinary sages

Many sages are tender perennials or shrubs that are evergreen within their zones and are grown in pots elsewhere. Cleveland sage (*S. clevelandii,* Zone 8 or 9) forms a rounded mass of gray-green foliage with tall spires of fragrant lavender flowers from spring to summer. Pineapple sage (*S. elegans,* Zone 9) is a fast-growing perennial with deep green leaves that smell and taste like pineapple. Hummingbirds are attracted to the red flowers that bloom from late summer to frost.

SAVORY (*Satureja* species)

Two savories, one perennial and the other annual, are grown as flavorings for vegetables and soups and for use in medicinal teas. Winter savory (*S. montana,* Zone 5) is a shrubby perennial with small flowers in late summer. Forming a mound of glossy evergreen leaves about 1 foot tall and 2 feet wide, it makes an attractive low hedge for an herb garden. Grow in well-drained soil. Winter savory tolerates some drought. Harvest leaves before bloom.

Summer savory (*S. hortensis*) is an annual that's not much to look at—a loose collection of slender, gray-green leaves on 18-inch stalks, topped by a smattering of tiny flowers. But because its leaves and stems are milder in taste and aroma than those of its perennial relative, this plant is often grown in pots for kitchen use.

SWEET BAY (*Laurus nobilis*)

This small tree provides the bay leaves widely used in cooking. It is also a versatile landscape and container plant. In warm-winter climates, sweet bay's dense, dark evergreen foliage makes an excellent backdrop for other plants. It can be trained and clipped as a formal hedge or shaped into topiary forms. Left on its own, sweet bay grows slowly to form a roughly conical tree, 10 to 40 feet tall. Sweet bay is an excellent container plant, and can be cut back to control its size. Grown in the ground, sweet bay needs good drainage but, once established, tolerates a range of soil conditions, including drought. In cold-winter areas, container-grown sweet bays must be moved into a cool, well-lighted room before temperatures drop below 20°F. Zone 8.

SWEET WOODRUFF (*Galium odoratum*)

Known today primarily as a tough perennial ground cover for shady areas, sweet woodruff has a history of use as a flavoring. Traditionally, May Day revelers in Europe added fresh shoots to their white wine, but today we know that an excess of this herb can be mildly toxic. The dried leaves bring a clean, fresh scent to potpourri and sachets. Plants grow 6 inches high, spreading to form a thick mat of aromatic deep green leaves topped in late spring with clusters of small white flowers. Sweet woodruff can be evergreen in warm-winter areas. Grow this herb in **partial or full shade.** Plants spaced 1 foot apart will soon fill in, spreading by runners and self-seeding. In rich moist soil, it can be invasive. Zone 4.

THYME (*Thymus* species)

A variety of thymes are grown as culinary or landscape plants. All are low-growing perennials. Common thyme (*T. vulgaris*) forms a foot-tall, upright clump of wiry stems and narrow gray-green leaves. In summer, it's covered with tiny lilac flowers. Lemon thyme (*T. x citriodorus*) has lemon-scented leaves and a spreading habit. Woolly thyme (*T. pseudolanuginosus*) and mother-of-thyme (*T. serpyllum*) make excellent ground covers. Fragrance varies among seedlings, so choose the most aromatic plants at the nursery. You can also grow thymes from seed started indoors about six to eight weeks before the last frost. Thyme tolerates drought once established, but soggy soil readily kills it. In cold-winter areas, drying winds kill shoots. If you lack a consistent snow cover, cover plants with pine boughs or straw mulch over the winter. Zone 4.

Sweet bay

Sweet woodruff

Summer savory

Lemon thyme

Ground Covers

Ground covers—plants that produce stems, branches, and foliage in sufficient density to cover the ground and prevent other plants from growing beneath them—are expanding their place in American home landscapes. For many people, a flawless carpet of rich green lawn continues to be the symbol of a well-maintained prop-erty. But increasing numbers of homeowners are discovering the useful and attractive qualities of other ground covers. In areas where lawn grasses struggle to survive because of heavy shade, steep slopes, or a dry climate, a variety of other ground-covering plants will thrive. Because they often need less water, fewer nutrients, and minimal care, these alternatives to grass can save you time and money. Homeowners are also using alternative ground covers to add variety and interest to the landscape. With attractive colors and textures of their own, ground covers are effective as complements to the house, patio, deck, and entryway, and as living carpets beneath plantings of trees and shrubs or woven through flower beds and borders.

Introducing Ground Covers

A wide range of perennials and shrubs grow densely enough to make good ground covers. Some initially require large numbers of small plants, but these often multiply rapidly. Others, including larger perennials and low shrubs, cover the ground with fewer plants but wider-spreading leaves and branches.

Ground covers can be less than an inch to several feet tall and are valued primarily for their foliage, which can be as thin as a blade of grass or as broad as a dinner plate. They come in every green imaginable as well as in silvers, grays, bronzes, yellows, and more. Many ground covers offer lovely blooms as well, from the blizzard of tiny white blossoms that cover snow-in-summer to the elegant flowers of daylilies. Evergreen ground covers supply a welcome dose of color in the winter landscape. Other perennial ground covers are deciduous, meaning they drop their leaves or die back to the ground in the fall. But even these may continue to please the eye with attractive bark or branching patterns or by providing shelter for overwintering birds or other wildlife.

The discussions that follow provide suggestions for taking advantage of the diversity of ground cover plants to deal with difficult sites—shady, sloped, or dry. But choosing a ground cover depends on more than matching plants to growing conditions. Think about how you use the site.

Does your yard cater to games such as touch football, volleyball, badminton, or crocquet, or to overspill from par-

Perennial evergreen ground covers, such as these heathers at left, look good through the year with their variously colored foliage.

Ground covers can add unexpected beauty to a landscape, opposite. Here, they supply color and a textured background.

ties on the deck or patio? Few ground covers are as well suited to sports and other active entertainments as lawn grass, so you'll want to maintain enough turf for them.

But there may be substantial portions of the yard that don't require the durability of grass. For places that are adjacent to areas of activity or high traffic, such as patios and entrances, consider ground covers that will withstand occasional forays by ball-chasing children or wandering visitors. For more out-of-the-way spots, select a ground cover for its looks or its easy maintenance.

Year-Round Considerations. Imagine how a ground cover will look and function throughout the year, particularly in winter. Evergreen ground covers are preferred by many because of their year-round foliage. The bare branches of deciduous shrubs and the dried leaves and stems of ornamental grasses and other deciduous perennials can also be striking through the winter. But you might appreciate these qualities more at a distance than up close. Deciduous shrub and perennial ground covers don't cover the soil as well when dormant as they do when in full growth, and some perennials disappear altogether for at least part of the year. Deciduous ground covers can be effective in beds and borders, but their appearance (and disappearance) may be less practical or satisfying in other areas. Vines can be effective ground covers, but establishing a dense, weed-suppressing cover can take time and persistent weeding and pruning. Once established, the aggressive growth of the vines may overpower the space allotted to them. Annuals last only part of the year, so they are primarily used as temporary cover between slow-growing perennials and shrubs.

GROUND COVERS FOR SHADY PLACES

Most lawn grasses suffer in dense shade. If they're growing under trees, this difficulty is usually compounded by the tree's competition for water and nutrients. Many favorite flowering plants also suffer in shade. In these situations, shade-loving ground covers provide attractive substitutes.

Common shade-loving, evergreen vining or creeping ground covers include creeping Jenny, English ivy, lamium, pachysandra, vinca, and winter creeper. For a grassy look, there's lilyturf, which tolerates root competition. Taller deciduous plants include a wide range of hostas and some ferns. Hostas with variegated or light-colored leaves can brighten a shade garden. Ajuga, astilbe, lily-of-the-valley, and sweet woodruff provide colorful flowers, and astilbe has attractive seed heads in late summer and fall. Ground covers that can become a nuisance in a sunny spot (for example, variegated goutweed) grow more slowly and are less problematic in the shade.

Shade-tolerant ground covers, such as this periwinkle, or myrtle, provide a wonderful carpet under trees.

GROUND COVERS FOR SLOPES

Slopes often pose difficult growing conditions, including poor soil, hot sun, and drying winds. Steep slopes also can be a chore to mow. Instead of struggling to grow or mow grass on a slope greater than about 20 degrees, plant a ground cover more suitable to the site's conditions.

Valued ground covers for slopes include Asian jasmine (*Trachelospermum calycinum*), ivies, winter creeper, and pachysandra, all of which are evergreen. Junipers and cotoneasters are useful shrubs, as are several forms of bearberry (also called kinnikinick). Various ice plants, which flower in blazing colors, are widely used in California and mild-winter areas of the Southwest. The prostrate form of rosemary also makes an attractive cover in mild-winter areas, with evergreen leaves and pale lavender flowers in winter and spring. Other possibilities include verbena, vinca, honeysuckle, daylily, evening primrose, mahonia, crown vetch, various sedums, and Aaron's-beard (*Hypericum calycinum*). Once established, these ground covers check erosion by creating a network of soil-retaining roots and protect soil from driving rain and wind.

Ground covers for slopes, such as this creeping juniper, must often tolerate thin soils, hot sun, and drying winds.

GROUND COVERS FOR DRY SOILS

Americans are increasingly conscious of the amount of water required to maintain residential plantings, particularly the lawn. Drought-tolerant ground covers can help reduce water use while adding variety to the landscape. Plants tolerant of dry conditions are particularly valuable for slopes, which are likely to be drier than nearby areas and more difficult to water artificially.

Good plants for dry sites include blue fescue, fragrant sumac, kinnikinick, cotoneaster, and junipers. Candytuft, evening primrose, and verbena provide colorful flowers, as do many of the low-growing sedums, which have distinctive fleshy leaves that show to advantage after the flowers have gone. Ceanothus, lantana, and African daisy are useful for warm areas. In the north, the vining stems of winter creeper and vinca cover dry sites quickly.

Ground covers for dry soils, such as this gazania, can add a spot of bright color to the landscape for a portion of the year.

GROUND COVERS TO WALK ON

Few ground covers are as durable as lawn grass, but some can stand up to occasional or light foot traffic. Grow these sturdy plants in low-traffic areas, as outdoor "area rugs," or insert them between flagstones, bricks, or other pavers in paths and patios.

Thyme forms a low woody mat covered with tiny, fragrant leaves. The strawberry-like foliage of spring cinquefoil (*Potentilla tabernaemontani*) is perhaps a bit more durable and is covered with numerous yellow flowers in spring and summer. Try either between the flagstones of a path or patio. Other ground covers that take some foot-traffic include ajuga, chamomile, common thrift, Himalayan fleece flower (or knotweed), moss pink, sweet alyssum, and sweet woodruff.

Ground covers to walk on include baby's tears (Soleirolia soleirolii). Most tolerate light foot traffic but aren't as sturdy as lawn grass.

EYE-CATCHING GROUND COVERS

Planted in broad swaths, as free-form islands, or as an edging to a walkway or a drive, ground covers can be primarily decorative elements, adding color and texture to the scene. A massed planting of low shrubs, such as prostrate juniper, or ornamental grasses, such as blue fescue, creates an attractive, undulating contrast to a nearby lawn. Large patches of hostas, astilbes, violets, or ferns provide a transition to a woodland garden. A meadow-like planting of grasses and wildflowers can brighten even a small backyard. Annuals such as creeping zinnia, gazania, and nasturtium can be used as fillers while slow-growing plants mature, and will burst with colorful flowers or foliage for a season—or longer in mild-winter areas. Perenni-

Eye-catching ground covers, such as these coleus and impatiens, can add color and texture to a landscape.

als that you usually think of planting in a garden border—but form lovely, carefree ground covers on their own—include daylilies, hardy geraniums, and sundrops.

Growing Ground Covers

Growing healthy ground covers depends to a large extent on plant selection. As always, plants adapted to conditions in your area require less site preparation and less long-term care than plants that are marginal in your area. Ground covers are usually planted in large areas. Rather than attempting to correct soil that is too moist or dry with amendments, choose plants that tolerate your soil conditions. That said, prepare the soil as well as possible—good soil benefits any plant. Keep in mind that ground-cover plantings can be difficult to weed, so be thorough when eradicating weeds prior to planting.

Where many small plants are needed, prepare the site as you would for a garden bed. (See Chapter 2, pages 28–31.) For large, ground-covering shrubs, it is more efficient to prepare individual planting holes. Make the holes slightly larger than the plants' root-balls. If you're planting in native soil or around a new house, dig wide, shallow holes and loosen the remaining soil. Work compost, dried manure, or other amendments into the bottom and sides to encourage plant roots to extend both out and down.

Planting under shallow-rooted trees requires some care. Do not excavate the entire area. If you are starting small ground-cover plants such as pachysandra, spread a 4- to 6-inch layer of topsoil over the area, and transplant into that. This depth will give the plants a good start. Do not add more than 6 inches of topsoil, because you'll run the risk of suffocating the tree's roots. For larger plants such as hostas, dig individual holes, avoiding the trees' roots as much

as possible. Because the new plants will be competing with the trees for nutrients, mix in extra compost, dried manure, or other amendments to give the plants a sure start.

START WITH PLANTS

Ground covers are really no different from other plants—you just plant more of them over larger areas, so the discussions of planting and care on pages 32–39 apply. The summary here highlights the more important points.

Purchase your ground covers as plants. There are few perennial ground covers that an average homeowner can easily grow indoors from seed and few, if any, that are easily established by direct seeding. The number of plants you'll

ORNAMENTAL GRASSES

Many ornamental grasses make fine ground covers, but the larger species require considerable space to fulfill that function. On a residential lot, a few large grasses planted together will take up a lot of space, but they're more likely to function as accents or focal points, not ground covers. Smaller ornamental grasses make practical ground covers for modest home landscapes. The two grasses covered in the Ground Cover Gallery, pages 110–15, are widely available and tolerate a range of growing conditions.

Start ground covers with plants rather than seeds. The larger and more sturdy the plants, the faster they will cover the area.

Transplant ground covers in staggered rows to guarantee more even coverage when the plants mature.

Expand your ground covers by dividing the plants you have.

need depends on the type of ground cover you are using as well as the size of the area you're planting. Take a site plan, drawn to a measured scale, to your nursery or garden center, and they can calculate how many plants will be required for the ground cover you've chosen.

Planting Ground Covers. Transplant young plants in staggered rows, spaced according to their mature size. Even though plants that are more closely spaced will fill in more quickly, crowded conditions as they mature can make them unhealthy or ungainly. Be sure to water young plants—even drought-tolerant ones—regularly during the first season. Mulch with compost, bark chips, or grass clippings to conserve moisture and keep weeds down. When planting large numbers of plants, spread the mulch first and dig through it to place each plant. Pull the mulch away from the plant's crown to avoid disease problems. If you're using large, slow-growing ground covers, consider planting annual ground covers between them for several seasons. Use annuals that won't shade the young ground-cover plants by growing taller than they are.

Planting on a Slope. Slopes pose special problems of erosion from wind or rain. On mildly sloped sites, you can construct small "terraces" by mounding earth on the downhill side to hold young plants in place until their roots are anchored. On steeper sites, you can push a wooden shingle into the ground below each plant or pile up a few rocks. Planting in staggered rows helps avoid erosion by keeping water from running off in a straight line. Heavy mulch also breaks the force of driving rain or wind on a slope. If the site is particularly steep and conditions are windy or rainy, consider

Planting on a slope gives better results if you terrace. Build it up with rock walls, or mound soil in place.

covering the soil with water-permeable landscape fabric or netting. Spread the fabric or netting, and cut an "X" through the material to set each plant in place. Landscape netting and fabric are available at nurseries and garden centers.

EXPANDING GROUND COVERS

Once you've gotten a ground cover started, you can expand your patch or start a new one from the plants already there.

Some plants reproduce from aboveground stems, called runners, or stolons. To aid this process, pin several stems to the ground at a node—a swelling on the stem where a leaf or branch can develop—but don't sever them from the parent plant. Regularly moisten the surrounding soil. Roots will form at the nodes. When the stems offer some resistance to a gentle tug on the node, sever these new plants from the parent, dig them up, and transplant them.

Some ground covers spread by underground runners called rhizomes. Dig up the offspring of these plants with some roots attached, cut the connection to the parent plant, and transplant. Clump-forming plants, such as daylilies and hostas, can be divided as shown in Chapter 4 (page 57), and the divisions set out to enlarge the patch.

Gallery of Ground Covers

Following is a list of easy-to-grow ground-cover plants.

Ajuga

AJUGA (*Ajuga reptans*)

A low-growing, mat-forming perennial, ajuga has glossy leaves that are evergreen in mild winters. Erect, 6-inch spikes densely packed with small flowers are very showy for a few weeks in May. 'Alba' has green foliage and white flowers; 'Bronze Beauty' has dark, purplish bronze foliage and blue flowers. Grows in **sun or shade.** Plant 8 to 12 inches apart. Shear off the flowers after they fade (in a large planting, a mower works well). Ajuga spreads quickly and can invade your lawn unless you keep cutting along the edge or install an edging. It's easy to start new plants from rooted runners. Zone 3.

BERGENIA (*Bergenia cordifolia*)

A perennial used as a specimen plant or ground cover, bergenia forms a clump up to 18 inches tall and 2 feet wide of large, glossy, tropical-looking leaves. Summer foliage is green but turns bright red in the fall. In mild-winter areas, the foliage looks good through the winter. Clusters of white or rosy red flowers are held just above the foliage in late spring. Cultivars include 'Bressingham

Bergenia

White', with white flowers, and 'Bressingham Ruby', with reddish flowers and leaves that are maroon on the undersides. Berginia prefers **partial shade or, in cool-summer areas, full sun.** Water during dry spells. Plant rhizomes about 15 inches apart and increase by dividing crowded clumps. Zone 3.

BLUE FESCUE (*Festuca glauca,* also sold as *F. ovina* and *F. ovina* var. *glauca*)

A neat, compact perennial grass, blue fescue forms a dense tuft of thin, blue-green leaves about a foot tall and a foot wide. It presents an undulating expanse of small mounds when massed as a ground cover. Slender flower spikes appear in early summer and soon turn tan. 'Sea Urchin' is a popular cultivar with especially blue foliage. Blue fescue requires **full sun** and well-drained soil. It tolerates dry conditions. Plant 12 inches apart. Cut old foliage to the ground in late winter. Divide clumps only when plants become crowded. Zone 4.

COMMON THRIFT (*Armeria maritima*)

An evergreen perennial, thrift forms cushions of narrow, grasslike foliage. In spring, small ball-shaped, rosy pink flowers rise above the foliage on long wiry stems. Plants grow about 6 inches tall and spread slowly to about 1½ feet. This plant requires **full sun** and good drainage but little fertilizing or watering. Space individual plants about 1 foot apart. Thrift is also called sea pink, so it's no surprise that it grows wonderfully at the shore. When the center of a clump begins to die, divide plants in either spring or fall. Zone 3.

Blue fescue

Common thrift

COTONEASTER (*Cotoneaster* species and cultivars)

Several of these shrubs make effective and attractive ground covers. Bearbeary cotoneaster (*C. dammeri*) grows less than a foot tall but spreads rapidly to cover an area up to 10 feet wide. It sports bright, glossy evergreen leaves that turn purple in cold weather, white flowers in spring, and red berries in fall. Cotoneaster does well in **full or partial sun** and tolerates dry conditions. It's excellent for slopes. Space plants 3 to 4 feet apart, and prune as necessary to restrict spread. Zone 5.

Two deciduous relatives, cranberry cotoneaster (*C. apiculatus*), hardy to Zone 4, and rockspray cotoneaster (*C. horizontalis*), hardy to Zone 5, are taller (1 to 3 feet) and bear striking red foliage in fall. Several compact cultivars of the evergreen willowleaf cotoneaster (*C. salicifolius*) are planted as ground covers in Zone 6 and warmer areas. These include 'Emerald Carpet', 'Repens', and 'Scarlet Leader', all of which are less than 2 feet tall and spread up to 8 feet wide.

CREEPING JENNY, OR MONEYWORT

(*Lysimachia nummularia*)

This creeping perennial forms a carpet of round, green leaves. Cheerful yellow flowers last for a month or so in early summer. 'Aurea' has yellow leaves. This plant grows well in **full or partial shade.** Space about 8 inches apart. Creeping Jenny prefers moist soil that is well-drained. It spreads rapidly by stems that root where they touch the soil. Zone 3.

ENGLISH IVY (*Hedera helix* selected cultivars)

This evergreen vine is an excellent ground cover if you're willing to control its aggressive growth. There are many ivies, so be sure to buy cultivars recommended as ground covers. Some ivies, such as 'Thorndale', have large leaves, 2 to 4 inches long. 'Baltica' and others have smaller leaves. Some ivies with small or miniature leaves grow more slowly and are more suitable for smaller areas. Ivies grow in **full sun in cool-summer areas and full to partial shade in hot climates.** Plant 8 to 12 inches apart and

water regularly during the first year. You'll need to trim back established plantings several times a year to keep them in bounds. With some cultivars, you can mow large areas. Zone 4 or 5 (depending on cultivar). Algerian ivy (*H. algeriensis,* Zone 9) and Persian ivy (*H. colchica,* Zone 7) are used as ground covers in warmer climates.

EVENING PRIMROSE, SUNDROPS

(*Oenothera speciosa* and *O. fruticosa*)

These fast-spreading plants form a dense patch of thin leafy stems topped by cheerful flowers all summer. Stems die back after bloom, and plants form a new mat of low-growing red-tinged leaves in fall. *O. fruticosa* is taller (to 2 feet), and hardier (Zone 4), and it has yellow flowers. *O. speciosa* reaches about 1 foot, is hardy to Zone 5, and has white or pink flowers. Both bloom during the day and require **full sun.** Space 1 to 2 feet apart. They tolerate heat and dry soil. To prevent either of these plants from taking over a flower bed, particularly one with rich, moist soil, surround them with a barrier that reaches 8 inches below the soil surface. Zone 4.

Cotoneaster

Creeping Jenny

Sundrops

English ivy

Candytuft

Maidenhair fern

Fountain grass

CANDYTUFT (*Iberis sempervirens*)

This bushy perennial forms a mound of slender, glossy evergreen foliage, topped for several weeks in spring with clusters of bright white flowers. Cultivars range in height from 4 to 12 inches and spread up to 3 feet. Several rebloom in the fall. Candytuft requires **full or partial sun** and well-drained soil. Plant 2 feet apart. Shear off the top half of the plants after they bloom. They need no other care. Zone 3 or 4.

FERNS (Various genera)

These carefree, long-lived perennials are excellent ground covers for shady sites. They form broad patches of distinctive, finely cut fronds in one or another of an attractive range of greens. Evergreen ferns include Christmas fern (*Polystichum acrostichoides,* Zone 3) and marginal shield fern (*Dryopteris marginalis,* Zone 3), both with glossy fronds about 2 feet tall. Deciduous ferns include maidenhair fern (*Adiantum pedatum,* Zone 3), and New York fern (*Thelypteris noveboracensis,* Zone 4), which reach 2 feet tall, and hay-scented fern (*Dennstaedtia punctilobula,* Zone 4), a vigorous spreader that grows 2 feet tall with fronds that give off a vanilla-like fragrance when mowed. Ferns require **shade** and prefer soil with lots of organic matter. Consult knowledgeable gardeners or your local garden center to learn which other ferns do well in your area.

FOUNTAIN GRASS, DWARF (*Pennisetum alopecuroides* dwarf cultivars)

This perennial grass forms a hassocklike clump of arching leaves that are green in summer and gold or reddish tan in fall. Fluffy pink, white, black, or cream-colored flower spikes bloom on arching stems from midsummer to fall. They turn tan or golden in fall. The foliage of dwarf cultivars such as 'Hameln' and 'Cassian' is 1 to 2 feet high and about as wide, and the flower stalks rise 3 feet. 'Little Bunny' forms a clump less than a foot tall. Fountain grass requires **full sun, or partial shade in hot climates,** and good garden soil. Space 18 to 24 inches apart. It tolerates dry soil. Foliage and seed heads look good through the winter. Cut the clumps to the ground in late winter. Zone 5.

JUNIPERS (*Juniperus* selected species and cultivars)

The low-growing forms of these tough shrubs make excellent ground covers. The dozens of species range from 4 inches to about 3 feet tall. Many spread 6 to 10 feet wide or creep indefinitely, putting down roots where shoots touch the ground. Prickly needlelike or scaly foliage clings to the twigs. Colors range from bright green to blue to silvery gray; some are almost gold. Most junipers need **full sun; a few tolerate partial sun.** Many low-growing junipers tolerate heat, drought, and poor soil, but they vary in their tolerance as well as in rate of growth and hardiness. Both shore juniper (*J. conferta*) and cultivars of creeping juniper (*J. horizontalis*) such as 'Bar Harbour' and 'Wiltonii' are particularly versatile, but check plant labels, or consult with staff at your local nursery to determine which junipers perform best in your area. Zones 2–6 (depending on species).

Creeping juniper 'Blue Rug'

LAMIUM, OR SPOTTED DEAD NETTLE (*Lamium maculatum* cultivars)

Despite its forbidding common name, this perennial makes an attractive ground cover from early spring until late fall. 'Beacon Silver' forms low mats of heart-shaped silver leaves edged with green. Clusters of lilac-pink flowers bloom in early summer. 'White Nancy' has similar leaves and white flowers. 'Chequers' offers pink flowers and green leaves with a white stripe down the center. All grow under 1 foot tall and spread by rhizomes, or runners, to form a patch. Provide **partial shade** and moist soil. Space 8 to 12 inches apart. If the plants become shabby, cut the foliage back, and new leaves will appear. Zone 4.

LILY-OF-THE-VALLEY (*Convallaria majalis*)

An old-fashioned favorite, lily-of-the-valley produces sprays of wonderfully fragrant, bell-shaped white or pale pink flowers for several weeks in midspring. Foliage grows about 8 inches tall and looks good all summer. Red berries appear in fall. Lily-of-the-valley is a fine ground cover under shrubs and trees. Though the flowers are small, their scent makes them worth clipping and bringing inside; cut blooms when a quarter of the spray has opened. *C. majalis* 'Rosea' has pink flowers. Lily-of-the-valley thrives in **partial sun or shade** and grows in ordinary unamended soils. It tolerates dry conditions, but if the site is too dry plants may go dormant early, dying down as soon as midsummer. Plant the small rhizomes, called *pips,* in the fall. It spreads readily, and you can lift and transplant clumps easily. Lily-of-the-valley can be invasive in colder climates; hot or dry conditions check its invasiveness. All parts of the plant are poisonous. Zone 2.

LILYTURF (*Liriope muscari*)

Lilyturf forms clumps or mats of grasslike, evergreen leaves and bears spikes of small flowers in late summer. Foliage grows 1 to 2 feet tall. 'Big Blue' (blue flowers) and 'Majestic' (purple flowers) both reach 2 feet and have dark green foliage. 'Variegata' has lilac flowers and leaves edged with narrow stripes that start out golden yellow and fade to creamy white. Lilyturf grows best in **partial sun but tolerates full shade.** Plant sprigs 4 to 6 inches apart; set container-grown plants about 1 foot apart. Plants tolerate dry soil for short periods. Mow or shear off the old foliage in early spring. Zone 6.

Creeping lilyturf (*L. spicata*) is smaller, to 18 inches, with less conspicuous flowers. It spreads by runners to form a dense mat of foliage. An invasive plant, it isn't ideal for use in beds, but it works well under trees where lawn grass struggles. Zone 5.

MOSS PHLOX (*Phlox subulata*)

A delightful, spreading perennial with evergreen needlelike foliage, moss phlox is covered in spring with tiny blooms in pink, white, or lavender blue. It forms a dense mat about 6 inches high. It tolerates some foot traffic and spreads slowly around stones in a patio or walk. This plant is also good for a slope or hillside, or where it can spill over rocks, displaying the dazzling color of its flowers to full advantage. Moss phlox requires **full sun** and sandy or other well-drained soil. Space about 1 foot apart. It's easy to divide and transplant, so you can expand the area that it covers. Zone 3.

Two other phlox make fine ground covers under the light shade of deciduous trees. Wild sweet William (*P. divaricata*) grows 8 to 12 inches high and bears pale blue to white flowers for several weeks in spring. Creeping phlox (*P. stolonifera*) has narrower leaves and flowers in blue, pink, or white, depending on cultivar. Both prefer **light shade** and moist soil. Zone 3.

Lily-of-the-valley

Lily Turf

Lamium

Moss Phlox

PACHYSANDRA (*Pachysandra terminalis*)
This classic ground cover has glossy evergreen leaves and creeps slowly to form dense patches about 8 inches tall. In spring, small white flowers provide a brief dash of color. Plants do well under and around trees and shrubs. 'Silver Edge' is a lovely cultivar with light green leaves edged in silver-white; it requires **full or partial shade** and well-drained soil. Plant in spring or fall. Prepare the soil and then spread 2 inches of mulch over the area. Plant four plants per square foot through the mulch. Hand-weed for the first year or two. After that, you'll never have to tend it again. Zone 5. (It survives on sites sheltered from winter sun and winds in Zone 4.)

SEDUM (*Sedum,* selected species and cultivars)
Low-growing sprawling or spreading forms of these perennials make fine ground covers. Sedums have distinctive fleshy leaves that are often evergreen, pretty little flowers, and sometimes attractive seed heads. Leaf colors range from light greenish yellow to purple or bronze.

Some evergreen sedum leaves turn color in winter. Popular *S. spurium* (Zone 3) spreads by creeping stems to form a patch of 6-inch tall, semievergreen foliage, and several cultivars offer different-colored leaves. 'Dragon's Blood' has purple leaves and pink flowers. *S. kamtschaticum* (Zone 3) has yellow 1- to 2-inch-wide flower clusters in late summer. Growing conditions and spacing vary according to species and cultivar; check plant labels. Ground-cover types are generally easy to grow and trouble free.

SWEET VIOLET (*Viola odorata*)
A long-time garden favorite for its lovely fragrance, sweet violet spreads by runners and seeds to make a patch or ground cover about 4 inches high. Dark green, heart-shaped leaves are evergreen in mild winters. Flowers are white, deep violet, or blue, and they bloom in early spring and, often, again in fall. Provide **full sun or shade where summers are hot.** Violets adapt to most soils. In mild climates, sweet violets can be an invasive nuisance. Zone 4.

Sedum

Pachysandra terminalis 'Variegata'

Sweet violet

VERBENA (*Verbena* species and cultivars)
Evergreen and deciduous forms of verbena make excellent ground covers, particularly in hot, dry areas where they grow wild. Their sprawling stems are covered with clusters of lavender, purple, or red flowers from early summer to frost. *V. canadensis* (Zone 6) reaches 1½ feet tall, has rosy pink flowers and is a good choice for dry sunny slopes. The hybrid cultivar 'Homestead Purple' stays under 1 foot tall and does well in hot, humid climates. Check at your nursery or garden center for new hybrid verbenas that make good ground covers for Zones 6 and warmer. Garden verbena (*V. hybrida*) is grown everywhere as an annual and can be used as a temporary ground cover. Reaching less than a foot tall, it's available with flowers in a range of bright colors. All verbenas require **full sun** and well-drained soil.

VINCA (*Vinca minor*)
One of the most versatile ground covers, vinca (also called common or dwarf periwinkle) grows well in **shade or partial shade,** in hot climates and dry soil, and is excellent for slopes. Its leathery, evergreen leaves are small and glossy and reach about 6 inches tall. Lilac flowers appear for several weeks in late spring. A range of cultivars offers variations in flower and leaf color. Once established, it needs absolutely no care, only control. Vinca can spread 2 to 3 feet per year. Greater periwinkle (*Vinca major*) is hardy only to Zone 7, is taller with larger leaves and flowers, prefers moist soil, and is even more invasive. Plant both types about 6 inches apart. Both are easy to expand by division. Zone 4.

WILD GINGER (*Asarum* species)
Two wild ginger species make good ground covers for **full or partial shade.** Eastern wild ginger (*A. canadense,* Zone 2) is deciduous; its wide heart-shaped leaves seem to float about 6 inches above the ground at the end of long thin stems. European wild ginger (*A. europaeum,* Zone 4) is evergreen, with smaller glossy green leaves. Both have inconspicuous flowers (hidden beneath the leaves), and both spread slowly—years will pass before they fill in, so be prepared to police for weeds in the planting. They require constantly moist but well-drained soil. Space 12 inches apart. After they're established, they require no routine care.

WINTER CREEPER (*Euonymus fortunei* cultivars)
In both its shrub and vine forms, winter creeper has many cultivars that make fine ground covers. Its glossy evergreen leaves come in a variety of colors. Some notable choices include: 'Canadale Gold', with compact growth and green leaves edged with a broad yellow stripe; 'Coloratus', a sprawling plant with dark purple leaves in fall and winter; and 'Ivory Jade', which is low and spreading and has leaves trimmed with white edges that shade to pink in winter. Common winter creeper (*E. f.* var. *radicans*) has a remarkably varied growth habit—it can sprawl, climb walls, or grow as a bushy shrub and can be invasive. Winter creeper isn't fussy about conditions. It will grow in **full sun and shade,** tolerates dry spells, and does well on slopes. It does require well-drained soil. Scale insects can cause damage or death; control them with horticultural oil sprays. In cold-winter areas, leaves and stems may freeze. In this case, trim off any damaged shoots in spring, and new growth will follow. Shear as needed to maintain desired form. Zone 5.

Vinca minor

Wild ginger

Verbena

Winter creeper

CHAPTER 9

Trees and Shrubs

Trees and shrubs have a special place in the home landscape. They are useful plants. They shelter us from wind, rain, and snow, create privacy, obscure nearby eyesores, and provide food and protection for birds and other wildlife. But they are also something more. As children, we create secret hideaways in a mass of forsythia and swing on ropes suspended from a towering oak. Later in life, we anticipate the first blossoms of azaleas in spring and enjoy the fiery leaves of burning bush in fall. We welcome the cool shade beneath a maple on a sweltering summer's day. In winter, the vivid evergreen foliage of spruce, arborvitae, and yew provide relief from the snowy monotony in northern climes. Spring is signaled in many areas by the fragrant blooms of flowering trees. Trees and shrubs often become life-long companions—all the more reason to choose them carefully.

Deciduous or Evergreen?

The most common—and useful—categories into which trees and shrubs are grouped concern their foliage. Plants that shed all of their leaves at the end of a growing season are called *deciduous.* Maple, ash, birch, horse chestnut, oak, and crab apple are a few of the many common deciduous trees. Lilac, forsythia, hydrangea, mock orange, sumac, flowering quince, and spirea are among the many handsome deciduous shrubs.

Plants that retain their leaves year-round are called *evergreens.* These plants drop and replace leaves, but usually a few at a time. When Northerners say "evergreen," they're probably thinking of plants such as pines and spruces which are *conifers*—plants with evergreen leaves that are thin, like needles, or tiny and layered like scales on a fish. Some conifers produce seeds in woody *cones;* others such as yews and gingkos make fleshy fruit, while junipers produce waxy berries. There are also many *broad-leaved* evergreens, which are especially popular where winters are mild. Their leaves come in a great variety of sizes and shapes. Broad-leaved evergreens include rhododendrons, most hollies, some oaks, citrus, and camellias.

The distinction between evergreen and deciduous, although helpful, isn't clear-cut. In many groups of shrubs and trees, there are both deciduous and evergreen species. Also, many shrubs that are evergreen in mild climates lose some or all of their leaves where winters are cold; these are called semievergreen.

Deciduous trees, such as this sugar maple at left, drop all their leaves in autumn.

Trees and shrubs create beauty in the home landscape, opposite, while providing practical benefits such as privacy, food, and habitat for wildlife, and relief from summer sun and winter wind.

TREE OR SHRUB?

There is no hard-and-fast dividing line between trees and shrubs. In general, trees have a single stem, or trunk, and grow taller than about 15 feet, while shrubs are shorter and have multiple stems. But there are exceptions. Yaupon holly, a small evergreen tree, can have numerous stems, while a low-growing "shrubby" juniper may have only one; a rhododendron can outgrow many small trees, while a shrub border of lilacs can tower over a diminutive flowering cherry tree. Some plants can serve either as trees or shrubs, depending on how they're trained and pruned. Fortunately, most of us "know" a shrub or a tree when we see one, based on a common-sense judgment involving height, growth habit, and landscape use.

Uses in the Landscape

Both evergreen and deciduous trees and shrubs are versatile plants. They often define the boundaries of our property and delineate spaces for recreation, entertaining, and other activities within those boundaries. And with a vast and delightful variety of foliage, flower, and form, trees and shrubs are grown for their beauty as well as their utility.

TREES FOR SHADE

Large Deciduous Trees	**Smaller Deciduous Trees**
Green ash	Dogwood
Lacebark elm	Redbud
Honey locust	Silverbell
Red maple	Crab apple
Gingko	Bradford pear
Scarlet oak	

Large Broad-Leaved Evergreen Trees	**Smaller Broad-Leaved Evergreen Trees**
Blue gum	Silver wattle
American holly	Olive
Live oak	Evergreen ash
Southern magnolia	Yaupon holly

CREATING SHADE

Of all the practical services trees render, none is more appreciated than shading us from the sun. A leafy canopy can lower temperatures beneath it by 15°F. Properly placed in relation to morning, midday, or afternoon sun, a tree can make your patio or deck a welcome haven even in the heat of summer. Morning and early afternoon shade can prevent the buildup of heat inside your house too, saving you money on air conditioning. In cold-winter areas, deciduous trees are ideal—after shading your house in summer, they drop their leaves and allow the sun to warm the house in winter. You can also plant trees and shrubs to shelter favorite shade-loving plants.

Consider the kind of shade you desire when selecting trees. Spreading trees with low branches and lots of leaves—such as the deciduous beech and Norway maple and the evergreen Southern magnolia—cast a deep shade conducive to solitary musings, but few plants will grow there. The smaller leaves, upright forms, and deep roots found in red oak, honey locust, Kentucky coffee tree, green ash, and some acacias and eucalyptuses provide a more cheerful atmosphere. The dappled sunlight they create encourages convivial gatherings and allows a wider range of plants to grow under them.

We don't usually think of conifers as shade trees. Many lack a spreading crown and (with the exception of some mature pines) adequate headroom beneath for lounging. Their dense foliage often casts deep shade that is inhospitable to many understory plants. However, by making use of the shade cast *beside* these plants, rather than under them, you can effectively cool a patio or decrease heat buildup in parts of the house with eastern or southern exposures.

Shade trees help to cool the house during summer, and once their leaves drop in fall, allow it to warm in the winter.

PLANTING UNDER TREES

Homeowners with large shade trees or wooded stands on their property often find it difficult to grow grass in these areas. However, these spots are perfect for small woodland or wild gardens. With the addition of a comfortable bench, they can become a "secret" garden. If the shade is created by deciduous trees, you can turn the area into a special spring garden. Grow spring-flowering bulbs and early-blooming perennials, which will thrive in the early-season warmth and sun under the bare branches and will finish flowering before the trees fully leaf out. In areas that are shady throughout much or all of the growing season, plant shade-tolerant shrubs, perennials, and ground covers. (See Chapters 4 and 8, pages 58–65 and 110–15.) Shade-tolerant annuals such as impatiens and begonias can brighten a shady spot, but plant them in containers rather than disturb the tree's surface roots with yearly digging. When you plan a shade garden:

- Observe the area over a growing season, and note the extent of the shade and how long it lasts. Note also the quality of the shade—light, deep, or dappled.
- Remember that practically nothing will grow without some sun, whether it's dappled throughout the day or occurs seasonally (under the bare branches of deciduous trees in spring, for instance).
- To lighten deep shade, prune off the lowest limbs, and thin the upper limbs of deciduous or evergreen trees.
- Choose plants that need less than six hours of direct sun for healthy growth.
- Check with a knowledgeable gardener or nursery staff member to make sure that the tree beneath which you wish to plant is one that won't be damaged if you disturb surface roots. Also determine whether your tree has shallow roots, as maples and birches do, that make it difficult for understory plants to compete for water and nutrients. Dig carefully around tree roots when planting a large plant.

Planting under trees allows you to grow lovely shade-loving plants such as hostas, ferns, and pachysandras.

- If you're planting lots of smaller perennials or annuals, you can add up to 6 inches of topsoil under a shallow-rooted tree. If your plans call for substantial grade changes beneath an established tree, consult a certified arborist before proceeding. Adding or removing large volumes of soil under an established tree can severely damage or kill it.
- Some established native trees, such as madrone and certain oaks in California, are sensitive to the root disturbance and watering that often accompany new plantings under their canopies. Consult with an arborist before planting beneath such trees.
- Provide extra fertilizer and water to help the plants compete with the roots of established trees and shrubs.

SCREENING AND PRIVACY

Trees and shrubs can provide privacy, block unwanted views, frame a desirable vista, create "outdoor rooms" on your property, or form a backdrop or enclosure for flower gardens. With their dense year-round foliage and regular forms, conifers are ideal for many of these purposes, as are broad-leaved evergreen shrubs. While more limited for these uses, deciduous screens are common; they can offer more color with their flowers and autumn foliage than many evergreens can.

Hedges are uniform plantings of trees or shrubs that have been selected for dense branching and foliage. They are frequently used for screens and living fences as well as for delineating "outdoor rooms." Formal hedges are trained and shaped or sheared into geometric shapes; they range in height from less than a foot to over 20 feet. Plants for formal, sheared hedges should retain leaf-covered branches near the ground and have leaves that are small and closely spaced on the stem. Good plants for formal hedges include deciduous shrubs such as burning bush, coniferous trees and shrubs such as hemlock and yew, and broad-leaved evergreens such as boxwood. Avoid cypresses and pines,

which don't sprout new growth on old wood; you won't be able to prune them back hard if they get out of hand.

Informal hedges are more natural-looking barriers that are pruned lightly, if at all. A natural hedge of plants with a uniform growth habit, such as Japanese holly or Japanese spirea, can present a neat, tidy appearance. More unruly plants make wilder looking but no less effective hedges. Taller plants, such as those listed in the table opposite, make effective natural screens.

Singly or in groups, trees and shrubs can screen unwanted views or protect you from wind and driving rain and snow. In an informal massed planting they can do double duty, providing a screen as well as a pleasing composition on their own. A row of columnar trees, such as Japanese privet or incense cedars, will effectively camouflage nearby objects that are tall or large, such as a neighbor's house. By placing a single tree in the line of sight, you can block a view of a distant object from a picture window, patio, or other specific vantage point. Wind can be annoying to people and damaging to plants. Carefully placed trees and shrubs planted singly, in groups, or as hedges, can break the force of prevailing winds.

Formal hedges, left, are composed of small-leaved shrubs that retain branches close to the ground, such as this California privet.

Screening and privacy are easy to achieve, above, with conifers such as these American arborvitae.

PLANTING FOR PLEASURE

Homeowners often plant trees and shrubs simply for the pleasure they will give. Flowers can be prominent among those pleasures. They can be exotic, such as those of the star magnolia or deciduous azalea; simple, such as pussy willow or winter jasmine flowers; or fragrant, such as viburnums, sweet pepperbush, or winter honeysuckle blooms. Broad-leaved evergreens, including rhododendrons, gardenias, and citrus, can provide spectacular, sometimes fragrant, floral displays.

But flowers are so fleeting that you should consider other qualities, too. The leaves of deciduous trees and shrubs provide color for months. They offer greens of every hue as well as the shimmering two-tone foliage of aspens, the deep purple of copper beech, and the reddish new growth of Japanese pieris. Maples, birches, tupelo (*Nyssa sylvatica*), ashes, and others earn their place with spectacular fall foliage colors. Fruits, nuts, and seedpods—both edible and ornamental—recommend deciduous trees and bushes such as crab apples and plums to both humans and wildlife. In winter the striking bark of sycamores and crape myrtle catch the eye, as do the wispy shoots of weeping cherries or willows.

Choosing for Form. Deciduous trees and shrubs come in a wide variety of shapes and sizes, from ground-hugging to towering. Some trees have a spreading shape; others form rounded crowns or rise in a pyramid. Unusual forms, often specially selected and propagated, are popular—there are columnar English oaks and gingkos, or weeping cherries, beeches, and willows. Deciduous shrubs provide virtually any shape you wish, either by growing that way naturally or by being trained to do so.

Trees and shrubs have long been used to complement, accent, or mask architecture. Most common of these uses is the foundation planting, traditionally an arrangement of sheared shrubs at both sides of the front door. Today's foundation plantings are often more imaginative, incorporating trees and shrubs that provide flowers, a range of foliage colors and textures, and interesting natural forms.

Choosing for Beauty. While many evergreens, and conifers in particular, are generally less flamboyant than deciduous trees and shrubs, they are no less beautiful. Evergreen foliage ranges across yellow, blue, and reddish hues as well as greens. Some provide striking cones or colorful berries; Scotch pine and lacebark pine have attractive bark. Evergreens also exhibit a variety of shapes and sizes. Sprawling junipers are ideal for ground covers, whereas a majestic spruce can anchor a large-scale composition. Coniferous trees tend to be conical when young, but with age a number become strikingly picturesque, their branches gnarled, their profiles irregular. There are also conifers with weeping forms. Both broad-leaved and coniferous evergreen shrubs can be trained to almost any shape. Yew, for example, can be a dense, closely cropped hedge or a 40-foot tree.

Shrubs and smaller trees are valuable elements in beds and borders. Mix them among perennials with an eye to combining shapes, colors, and textures for greatest effect. Use one or more as focal points in a bed. A group of taller shrubs or small trees can provide an excellent backdrop and foil for other plants in a bed. Dwarf forms allow you to manipulate the perception of scale in a garden bed or to produce a diminuitive grove of container-grown shrubs and trees on a patio.

Trees and shrubs add a pleasurable dimension to a garden—their architectural shapes stand out in every season.

The vivid color of new leaves makes Japanese pieris, or lily-of-the-valley bush, a prominent feature in any environment.

Textured bark adds to the beauty of the London plane tree.

The Right Plant for the Site

Because trees and shrubs are long-lived and often expensive, make sure your choices are well-suited for the site conditions. Consider their preferences for temperature, sunlight, water, and soil. If you live with sweltering summers, cold winters, drying winds, high humidity, or drought, take those conditions into account. If you choose well, your plants will be more likely to succeed and will require less attention. The local Cooperative Extension Service or arborist can be a good source of information.

Given the large amounts of water required by many trees and shrubs, it makes sense to select those that thrive with the normal rainfall in your area. It is difficult, if not impossible, to alter large areas of soil for the extensive root systems of many trees and shrubs. Similarly, it's best to match soil pH to the plant's requirements. If you have alkaline conditions, for example, trying to grow acid-loving rhododendrons or azaleas will be disappointing unless you create raised beds with specially prepared acid soil for them.

Also consider the *mature* size of the plant. A full-grown sugar maple, Norway spruce, or eucalyptus can overwhelm a small lot. Shrubs such as junipers that tuck in nicely beneath a picture window when young can block the view in a few years. Choose plants whose mature size will suit their place in your garden or landscape.

SHRUB CHOICES

Shrubs for Shaped, or Formal, Hedges

Barberry	Willowleaf cotoneaster
Boxwood	Pittosporum
Cherry laurel	Privet
Flowering quince	Sweet olive
Hollies	

Shrubs for Natural Screens

Abelia	Mahonia
Barberry	Red-twig dogwood
Burning bush	Rugosa rose
Camellia	Sweet olive
Euonymus	Sweet pepperbush
Highbush blueberry	Wax myrtle
Nandina	Lilac

Planting

Trees and shrubs are sold in several ways. Deciduous trees are sometimes sold *bare-root;* the plants are dormant, with leafless branches and roots bare of any soil. Larger evergreen and deciduous trees are offered *balled-and-burlapped* (B&B); these are dug from a growing field while dormant, and the mass of roots and attached soil (the "ball") are wrapped in burlap. An increasing number of trees and shrubs are grown and sold in plastic, cardboard, or metal *containers*. Bare root stock is only sold during times of the year when the plants are dormant—early winter to spring, depending on where you live. Plant them as soon after purchase as possible, before they break dormancy. Balled-and-burlapped and container-grown plants can be planted from spring to fall in cold-winter areas and from fall to spring where winters are mild.

When you select a tree or shrub at a nursery, examine it carefully. Avoid plants with damaged bark or branches. If the plant has leaves, check to see that they are healthy looking—not wilted or discolored—and that the soil in the container or root-ball is moist. Soil in containers should be snug against the sides of the pot. Roots growing on top of or out of the bottom of a container are signs that the plant has been in the pot too long.

You can plant small trees and shrubs with little difficulty, but large balled-and-burlapped plants pose daunting transporting and planting challenges. Nurseries selling these large plants usually offer planting services or can recommend capable professionals.

Avoid buying pot-bound plants—roots growing on top or out of the bottom of a container are a tip-off that the roots are crowded.

PREPARING TO PLANT

Digging is your first step in planting a tree or shrub. The hole must be large enough to accommodate the root ball easily. Depth is critical; the tree or shrub should be planted no deeper than it has been growing. This is easy to determine on container-grown plants. On balled-and-burlapped and bare-root plants, look for a change of color near the juncture of stem and roots. Don't disturb the soil at the very bottom of the hole; loose soil will settle after the tree or shrub has been planted, and the tree will sink. But use a rake or garden fork to loosen the soil on the sides of the hole and encourage root penetration out to the sides of the surrounding soil.

Place the soil you dig on a tarp nearby, and remove rocks and other debris. When you are planting trees and large shrubs you don't need to amend the soil. Research shows that they do best when planted in unamended sites. However, small shrubs and trees planted in the same beds as perennials will do fine in amended soil.

Poor drainage can doom a plant. To check the soil, fill the hole with water, as directed in Chapter 2, page 24. Plant in another spot if standing water remains in the hole 24 hours after the second filling.

PLANTING CONTAINER-GROWN TREES AND SHRUBS

Container-grown trees and shrubs are planted the same way that you plant other container-grown plants. (See Chapter 5, page 73.) After digging the hole and thoroughly watering the plant (several hours before planting), remove it from the container, and untangle any circling roots. When you place it in the hole, make certain that the soil line on the trunk or stems lines up with the top of the hole. Fill the hole about halfway with the soil you removed, and water thoroughly. After the water is absorbed, finish filling the hole, and tamp the soil down firmly. As shown below, build a small berm of soil around the circumference of the planting hole. Water again before spreading 2 to 3 inches of bark chips, compost, or another organic mulch. Keep the mulch at least 6 inches away from the trunk.

Don't stake newly planted trees unless you live in a very windy area. In that case, drive two sturdy stakes on opposite sides of the planting hole and a foot or so outside its perimeter. Secure the trunk of the tree to the stakes with strong twine or wire threaded through a section of old garden hose to protect the trunk from abrasion. The fastenings should allow movement. Remove the stakes within one to two years so the tree can strengthen.

EYE-CATCHING TREES AND SHRUBS

The following are attractive in at least two seasons:

Deciduous Trees

Beech	Redbud
Crape myrtle	Scarlet oak
Dogwood	Shagbark hickory
(tree and shrub forms)	Serviceberry
Hawthorne	Sour gum
'Heritage' river birch	Sourwood
Lacebark elm	Sycamore
Paper birch	Tree lilac
Poplar	Yellowwood

Evergreen Trees

Bottlebrush	Lacebark pine
Eucalyptus	Loquat
Holly	Scotch pine
(tree and shrub forms)	Southern magnolia
Japanese black pine	Madrone
Incense cedar	

Deciduous Shrubs / **Evergreen Shrubs**

Deciduous Shrubs	Evergreen Shrubs
Blueberry	California lilac
Chokeberry	Camellia
Mock orange	Heather
Red-twig dogwood	Japanese pieris
Shrub roses	Oregon grape
Viburnum	Rhododendron

Make a berm around the planting hole to help hold water. The crown of the plant should be slightly higher than the surrounding moat so that it remains dry when you water.

PLANTING BARE-ROOT TREES AND SHRUBS

Plant bare-root trees or shrubs much as you do bare-root roses. (See Chapter 5, page 73.) Soak the roots for 12 to 24 hours in a weak solution of liquid fertilizer and prune off any broken roots or stems. Place the tree or shrub in the hole and spread out the roots to prevent circling. Fill the hole with soil, gently working it in around the roots. As you work, make certain that the plant is at the correct depth. Water and fill again as described in Chapter 5, page 73.

PLANTING BALLED-AND-BURLAPPED TREES AND SHRUBS

In some ways, a balled-and-burlapped plant can be thought of as growing in a large flexible container. Before planting, keep the root-ball moist at all times. Always carry and move B&B plants by the root-ball, not the stem.

Dig a wide, saucer-shaped planting hole that is a couple of inches shallower than the height of the root-ball. Loosen the soil on the sides of the hole to encourage the roots to spread into the surrounding soil. Once the tree or shrub is placed in the hole, cut the twine and pull the burlap away, folding it down over the sides of the ball. Roots will grow through the burlap, which will eventually decompose. If the wrapping is plastic or another nonbiodegradable material, use a lever to pull it out from under the root-ball.

Fold back the burlap on a B&B plant after lowering it into the planting hole. Completely remove nonbiodegradable materials such as plastic.

Giving a Good Start

Water newly planted trees and shrubs regularly, especially during the first year. Dry winters are particularly hard on evergreens. Trees usually don't need fertilizer in the first year. In the second and subsequent years, sprinkle a light dressing of a balanced granular fertilizer on the soil around them in early spring. Trees planted in a lawn usually get all the supplemental nutrients they need from fertilizers applied to the lawn.

New trees and shrubs don't need pruning other than trimming branches damaged in transport or planting. If you're plagued with bark-gnawing rabbits or mice, protect the trunk by wrapping it with tree wrap from the garden center, or with aluminum foil extended at least a foot above the height of the anticipated snow cover. A reflective tree wrap covering also protects young tree trunks from sunscald—damage induced in some areas of the country by exposure to intense summer sun or sun reflected off snow in winter.

Pruning Pointers

Pruning helps keep plants healthy, enhances their appearance, and helps control the extent and form of their growth. It can also be one of the most daunting tasks for beginners. Having invested considerable time and money in shrubs and trees, a novice is understandably reluctant to begin lopping off pieces of them. Fortunately, basic pruning is neither difficult nor demanding.

Pruning to maintain a plant's health is, for the most part, based on common sense. Removing dead, damaged, and diseased branches improves both health and appearance. So does thinning out plants that have grown too dense to admit light and air. And by doing some drastic pruning, you can reinvigorate plants that have simply grown old and tired.

Pruning for appearance is more subjective. Your idea of an attractively shaped shrub and your neighbor's idea may differ completely. Some people train, trim, and shear shrubs and trees into all sorts of shapes. Others try to maintain or enhance the shape nature provides. In either case, you'll need to prune to encourage compact growth or to direct a branch into an area.

The point of pruning is not simply to end up with less than you had. Good pruning actually encourages growth. A little elementary plant physiology will help you understand why. All plants produce growth hormones, or *auxins,* in the tips of growing shoots. These hormones stimulate growth at the tip and suppress it along the sides of the shoot. Removing the growing tip and its supply of hormones releases some of the buds along the shoot, called *lateral buds,* from dormancy, allowing them to grow into side shoots. (See right.) Thus, whether the plant is a rose, spirea, or yew, pruning off the growing tips of shoots and branches produces a bushier plant.

Cutting off more than just the growing tip is called *heading back.* Stems are usually headed back to a lateral (side) bud. Cutting whole stems back to the plant's crown, or severing lateral branches at the crotch where they arise, is called *thinning.* Thinning directs a plant's energy to producing vigorous new shoots.

PRUNING SHRUBS AND TREES

Shrubs and trees come in a wide range of shapes and sizes. When you purchase a plant, ask how to prune it. If possible, watch an expert work on the same species. Fortunately, there are a few general pruning principles and practices.

When to Prune. Remove dead, damaged, or diseased growth as soon as you see it to minimize diseases and insects. Cut back to healthy wood. Although you can snip off a healthy stem or branch almost anytime, extensive pruning of healthy growth is best done at specific times of the year.

When flowers aren't a consideration, you have greater flexibility in pruning time. The structure of deciduous plants is easiest to see before they leaf out. Thus winter or early spring is a good time to prune them. Prune in the spring to encourage a bushy habit or to stimulate or direct growth. In cold-winter climates, be wary of pruning in the fall. Pruning always stimulates new growth; if it forms too late in the year to properly harden, it will be more susceptible to damage from cold, wind, and snow.

Light pruning. Many shrubs and trees thrive for years with a minimum of pruning. Even so, they can benefit from some of the following techniques:

- To force shrubs into bushier, more compact forms, pinch or cut off growing tips in the spring.
- Deadhead spent flowers to direct the energy that would otherwise be spent on forming seeds toward roots and shoots. Deadhead rhododendrons and azaleas as soon as possible after flowers fade because seed formation greatly reduces the number of flowers these plants produce the following year.

Pruning Cuts

Pruning growing tips stimulates lateral buds to develop. When cutting stems with alternate buds, prune at a 45-degree angle just above the bud you want to stimulate. If buds are opposite, cut across the stem in a straight line.

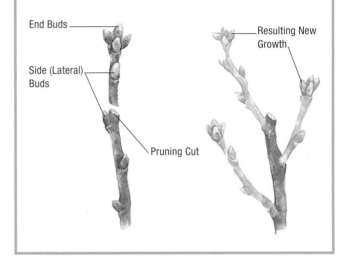

End Buds

Side (Lateral) Buds

Pruning Cut

Resulting New Growth

- Head back or thin out stems or branches that cross the center of a bush to reduce the incidence of diseases that breed in the humid conditions of dense growth. Similarly, remove stems that rub on neighboring growth; the damage they cause can open the tree to many diseases.
- Encourage branching into a particular area by finding a bud facing the direction you want a branch to grow and cutting just above it. Remember to cut at an angle close to a bud.
- New shoots that arise at the base of stems or from roots are called *suckers.* A few may be desirable; too many can produce a thicket. Cut them off flush with the stem base; pull up those sprouting from roots.

smart tip

PRUNING FLOWERING SHRUBS

- Spring-flowering shrubs (forsythia, lilacs, etc.) usually bloom on growth formed the previous year, so prune them right after they bloom.
- Plants that flower later, such as potentilla and crape myrtle, bloom on the current season's growth, so prune them in late winter or early spring before growth begins.

Heavy pruning. A few shrubs can be pruned heavily each year to produce robust new growth the following growing season. Spirea, red-twig dogwood, and shrub willows are often cut back almost to the ground. Other shrubs may be cut back to old wood or to just a few buds on new wood. Shrubs that die back to the ground in colder climates and renew themselves each spring, such as butterfly bush and caryopteris, should be cut close to the ground in late winter or early spring.

Heavy pruning can bring new life to overgrown or tired shrubs. Some, such as mahonia, respond well if cut almost to the ground. But lilacs and cotoneaster respond when stems are headed back to several feet above the crown. Renew a rhododendron in stages—cut one-third of the stems back hard one year, another third the next year, and the remainder in the third year. Sometimes you can nurture selected suckers as replacement stems.

Heavy pruning can be risky. Most conifers, along with many broadleaved evergreens and deciduous shrubs, will not sprout from old leafless wood. They don't have latent buds below the foliage area; if you cut a branch past that area, it will die. If you're uncertain about a shrub's ability to rejuvenate, ask a local expert before making any cuts.

Tips for Pruning Trees

A well-formed tree, planted and cared for correctly, should require little pruning when young and even less as it matures. This is particularly true of conifers, which may not need the attention of a pruning saw for years.

Pruning techniques are the same as for shrubs but size complicates matters—removing a 6-inch-diameter branch growing 30 feet above the ground can be both difficult and dangerous and should be done by a professional arborist. But you can do a great deal while standing firmly on the ground.

- Open a tree to air and sun by thinning crowded branches and removing those that cross the center.
- Sometimes mature branches or trunks develop unatractive, slender, vertical shoots called watersprouts. Remove these by cutting flush with the parent branch.
- Don't use wound dressings; research shows they cause as many problems as they prevent. A healthy tree can protect itself from disease, particularly if you prune whole branches just beyond the collar.

- Some trees, such as maples and birches, "bleed" if pruned when sap is rising in early spring; these are best pruned when dormant.
- Trees with a columnar shape such as oaks, pines, and spruces often have a dominant central trunk, called a leader. If a young conifer has two leaders, trim the second leader back to its base. Do the same with deciduous trees, or cut the second leader back by half to ensure that the tree develops the desired shape.
- Do not cut off, or "top," the central leader of a columnar tree. The sad results of such pruning can be seen wherever power companies have "pruned" trees away from their lines. Better to remove the tree and plant one that won't grow so tall.

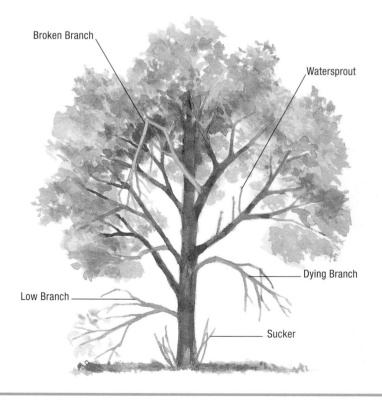

Broken Branch

Watersprout

Dying Branch

Low Branch

Sucker

Pruning Tools

Homeowners can take care of all their tree and shrub pruning needs with only a few tools. If you are on a tight budget, begin with a good pair of pruning shears and a small folding pruning saw. Add more tools as your plants grow over the years. Hedge shears or clippers are essential if you plant a hedge, and you'll need loppers to prune thick branches.

Bypass Shears   Anvil Shears

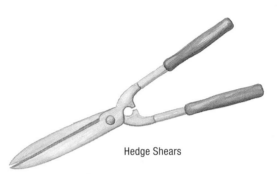

Hedge Shears

Pruning shears: For green twigs and branches up to about ½ inch thick. Bypass types are best; they have two curved blades that cut like scissors.

Folding Pull Saw

Electric Hedge Trimmer

Pruning saw: For branches up to 3 or 4 inches in diameter. Look for a folding saw with thin, hardened steel blades 8 to 12 inches long and long, thin teeth. Often advertised as "Japanese" saws, these are unsurpassed for efficiency and convenience.

Hedge shears: For trimming tender tip growth on hedges and shrubs. Essentially, these are heavy-duty scissors on long handles. If you have a lot of shearing and shaping to do, consider power hedge clippers.

Simple Bypass Lopper   Ratcheted Anvil Lopper

Loppers: For heavier branches and those out of reach of pruning shears. Loppers are available with bypass blades or an anvil design, where one straight blade cuts against the soft metal surface of the other blade.

Gallery of Trees and Shrubs

The following plant portraits introduce a selection of the most popular and useful species and cultivars from the vast range of trees and shrubs suitable for home landscapes. Cultural preferences vary within each genus and are mentioned only when particularly noteworthy. Check nursery tags for specific information on a particular plant, or consult with experienced gardeners and nursery staff to find plants that meet your needs and are proven performers in your area.

TREES

ASH (*Fraxinus* species)

These large, upright shade trees are familiar throughout much of North America. White, or American, ash (*F. americana,* Zone 3) and green ash (*F. pennsylvanica,* Zone 2) are two of the most commonly grown. Both are fast-growing deciduous trees that reach 50 feet or more in height, with distinctive compound leaves and bark that is divided by furrows into neat diamond shapes. Leaves of white ash turn yellow or purple in fall; green ash leaves turn yellow. White and green ashes are prone to insects and diseases, but any damage is often overcome by vigorous growth. However, homeowners should be vigilant.

Arizona ash (*F. velutina,* Zone 6) is a common deciduous street tree in the Southwest. Oregon ash (*F. latifolia,* Zone 6) is also deciduous and is used similarly in the Northwest.

BIRCH (*Betula* species)

Prized for their arresting bark and striking autumn foliage, these deciduous trees are frequently planted as eye-catching specimens or in groups as small groves. Fast-growing to 40 feet or so, often with multiple trunks, birches fit comfortably into most residential landscapes, where the leaves shimmer in the breeze and cast a dappled shade.

Birches suffer from a long list of insects and diseases, which is one of the reasons they're relatively short-lived trees. Before purchasing, it pays to research which birches do best in your area.

European white birch (*B. pendula,* Zone 2) offers attractive white bark and drooping branchlets covered in fall with golden leaves, but is a poor choice because it is extremely prone to insects and diseases. Paper birch (*B. papyrifera,* Zone 2) also has lovely white bark, and is more insect resistant but less graceful than European white birch. Neither of these birches thrives in hot, humid weather. *B. nigra* 'Heritage' (Zone 4) is an exceptional tree that has good fall color and peeling pinkish or reddish bark. It tolerates heat and wet soil and is resistant to bronze birch borers, the bane of many white-barked birches. Whitespire birch (*B. platyphylla* var. *japonica* 'Whitespire', Zone 4) is an excellent single-trunked specimen with white bark, yellow fall foliage, and resistance to the bronze birch borer. Sweet birch (*B. lenta,* Zone 3) has reddish-brown or black bark and exceptional fall color.

Ash   Paper birch

CRAB APPLE (*Malus* species)

Spring wouldn't be nearly so uplifting without crab apples covered with appealing pink buds and then clouds of white, pink, or red flowers. They're not just one-season wonders, either. Summer foliage mixes rich greens with hints of red and purple. In late summer and fall, red and yellow foliage complements glossy fruit in shades of red, orange, and purple. The handsome branching patterns and long-lasting fruit of some crab apple cultivars extends their attraction through early winter.

When you choose a cultivar, you can select for the overall growth habit (weeping, upright, vase-shaped, or spreading), the color and fragrance of the flowers, and the size and character of the fruit (long-lasting on the tree, for example). The fruit can be as small as ³/₈ inch in diameter or as large as 2 inches. They are a mixed blessing. Though attractive to the eye and useful for jams and jellies, they can become a lumpy mess on the ground. Resistance to pests and diseases is equally important. Some recently introduced hybrids, including Japanese flowering crabapple (*M. floribunda,* Zone 4) and tea crabapple (*M. hupehensis,* Zone 4), are resistant to scab, rust, and powdery mildew. Though these common diseases disfigure the leaves they seldom kill the tree.

There are crab apples for any size property. Sargent crab apple (*M. sargentii,* zone 5) grows only 6 to 10 feet tall and spreads half again as wide. It bears small fragrant white flowers and small fruit. Japanese crab apple and a wide range of hybrid crab apples (Zone 4) grow into handsome spreading trees between 20 and 30 feet tall and wide. Hybrid cultivars include 'Adams', with reddish pink flowers; 'Donald Wyman', with red buds, white flowers, and small fruits that cling to the tree until spring; and 'Prairiefire', which offers reddish-purple flowers, red-orange fall foliage, and eye-catching red twigs through the winter.

CRAPE MYRTLE (*Lagerstroemia indica*)

A small deciduous tree or shrub, crape myrtle produces large, eye-catching clusters of flowers from midsummer until early autumn. Grown with single or multiple trunks, planted individually or in small groves, crape myrtles are versatile landscape plants for properties of any size. The tree's flowers are rivaled by its colorful peeling bark. Leaves turn from yellow-bronze in spring to green in summer and to yellow, orange, or light red in fall.

There are dozens of cultivars. They range in size from 3 to 25 feet and offer flowers colored white to pink to dark red. A series of cultivars with American Indian names ('Hopi' and 'Sioux') are mildew- and disease-resistant, as well as lovely. 'Natchez' is one of the most popular, with white flowers, striking bark, and orange-red fall foliage. All cultivars are hardy to Zone 7.

DOGWOOD (*Cornus* species)

Spring flowers, bright autumn foliage, eye-catching berries, handsome bark, attractive form, convenient size—dogwoods supply just about everything you could want in an ornamental tree. Flowering dogwood (*C. florida,* Zone 5) reaches 25 feet or more. In early spring it produces cheerful white or pink flowers before the leaves appear. The "flowers" are actually bracts surrounding tiny true flowers. Dark green leaves turn red or maroon in fall, when they're joined by bright red berries. Kousa dogwoods (*C. kousa,* Zone 5) are Asian natives that resist insects and diseases now problematic for flowering dogwoods. About the same size as flowering dogwoods, their fruit and fall foliage are equally attractive. They bloom slightly later, after leaves have formed. Cornelian cherry dogwood (*C. mas*), a large shrub or small tree, is hardy to Zone 4. Its yellow flowers appear in very early spring. The bright red fruits attract birds and can be used for preserves. Fall foliage is colorful.

Crape myrtle

Pink flowering dogwood

Pygmy crab apple

HOLLY (*Ilex* species)

Prized for the spiny, glossy dark green leaves and bright red berries that are familiar holiday decorations, hollies are more varied than you might imagine. Hollies can be trees or shrubs, deciduous as well as evergreen, with large or small, spiny or smooth-edged leaves and fruit of orange, yellow, or deep blue-black as well as red. The hollies mentioned here are often grown as trees. (See the Holly entry under shrubs for discussion of smaller, more bushy hollies.)

American holly (*I. opaca,* Zone 5) grows 15 to 30 feet tall and is widely planted as a specimen tree in the East. It forms a pyramidal tree when young, but with age becomes more open, more irregular, and more picturesque. Evergreen leaves are dark green and spiny, the fruit a dull red.

Where summers are mild and not too humid, gardeners can grow the English holly (*I. aqui-folium*). Most cultivars are confined to Zone 6 or warmer. Its spiny evergreen leaves and bright red berries make classic holiday sprigs and wreaths. It grows into a pyramidal tree 30 feet or more in height and bears small, white, fragrant flowers in late spring.

Gardeners with small properties should consider possum haw (*I. decidua,* Zone 5), a small deciduous tree with showy red, orange, or yellow berries and smooth-edged leaves that turn gold in fall.

Several other small holly trees make attractive specimens. Lusterleaf holly (*I. latifolia,* Zone 7) is a narrow upright tree with unusually long evergreen leaves—up to 8 inches—as well as fragrant yellow flowers in spring and clusters of large red berries in fall. Long-stalked holly (*I. pedunculosa,* Zone 5) bears its berries on stalks, like cherries. It grows 15 to 20 feet tall with graceful branches and leaves that are dark green in summer and yellow-green in winter. Yaupon holly (*I. vomitoria,* Zone 7) can be trained as a multi-trunked tree up to 20 feet tall with eye-catching twisty branches, narrow evergreen leaves, and abundant red berries.

To produce berries, female hollies need to be pollinated by a male holly. Your nursery can tell you which plants to pair up. Carried by bees, pollen from a single male can pollinate female plants several hundred yards away; before you buy check to see if there's a suitable male plant within range.

English holly

Saucer magnolia

MAGNOLIA (*Magnolia* species)

Magnolias, with their large, fragrant, almost succulent flowers and broad canopy of thick, leathery, dark green leaves, evoke the American South for many people. But magnolias also come in smaller sizes and thrive as far north as Zones 5 and even 4. Both evergreen and deciduous magnolias grow in the South, but magnolias hardy enough for northern winters are all deciduous.

Star magnolia (*M. stellata,* Zone 4 or 5) is a delicate little deciduous tree, one of the hardiest magnolias and the earliest to bloom. It's an excellent tree for small gardens. The slightly fragrant flowers are small by magnolia standards, but they float prettily among the leafless branches for several weeks and can appear as early as February in warm-winter areas. The dark green leaves are attractive all summer. Cultivars of *M. x loebneri* (Zone 4) produce similar flowers on larger, hardier, more widely adapted deciduous trees.

At the other end of the spectrum is southern magnolia (*M. grandiflora,* Zone 7), the grande dame of southern gardens, a majestic tree rising up to 80 feet with a broad canopy of graceful horizontal branches. Its evergreen leaves are as long as a foot, glossy, thick, and dark green with fuzzy brown undersides. Flowers appear in late spring, peak in early summer, and continue sporadically through the summer. They are very large, up to 10 inches or more wide, and deliciously fragrant. Cultivars provide the same beauty in smaller trees.

Saucer magnolia (*M. x soulangiana,* Zone 5) is a versatile plant, widely grown as a small, multi-trunked deciduous tree or shrub. It grows 20 to 30 feet tall, spreads as wide, and is used as a specimen or in groups. White, pink, or reddish purple flowers appear in early to midspring and sporadically thereafter. Leaves are 6 inches long and may turn yellow in fall.

Oyama magnolia (*M. sieboldii,* Zone 7) is another fine tree for small, warm-winter gardens, reaching 15 feet tall and wide, with 3-inch-wide, white, very fragrant flowers in late spring and early summer.

MAPLE (*Acer* species)

One of the most popular residential trees in North America, maples provide pretty little flowers in the spring, cooling shade in the summer, and spectacular foliage color in the fall. Large maples are grown for the shade and commanding presence they provide. Red maple (*A. rubrum,* Zone 3) grows quickly, reaching 40 to 80 feet high and 30 to 40 feet or more wide, depending on the cultivar. It produces red flowers early in spring and breathtaking fall foliage colors—reds, yellows, oranges, and pinks. Cultivars provide some opportunity to choose among fall colors. Sugar maple (*A. saccharum,* Zone 3) has equally brilliant fall colors but is less suitable than red maple for most landscape uses because of its size—up to 90 feet—as well as its susceptibility to problems caused by heat, drought, and a variety of insects and diseases. Silver maple (*A. saccharinum,* Zone 3) provides shade quickly and grows in almost any conditions. However, its limbs are weak and prone to breaking in storms. Also, its extensive system of shallow roots makes growing anything under or near it difficult, and it's attacked by numerous insects and diseases.

Several smaller maples make fine shade trees more in keeping with the scale of ordinary city or suburban lots. Trident maple (*A. buergerianum,* Zone 4) reaches 25 to 30 feet tall and 20 feet wide. It has pretty flaking bark, red or yellow fall foliage, and less-competitive roots than most maples, making it easier to plant beneath. Amur maple (*A. tataricum* subspecies *ginnala,* Zone 3) is about the same size as trident maple but with multiple trunks, white spring flowers, and scarlet fall foliage.

Japanese maples (*A. palmatum,* Zone 5) are strikingly handsome small trees grown singly as specimens, or in large mixed borders. The foliage and form of the trees are equally compelling. Leaves are often deeply lobed, some to the point of laciness; leaf color ranges from green to red, bronze, or purple in summer, and most turn scarlet in fall. Branches are often twisted and strongly horizontal; some have particularly attractive bark. For striking bark, consider the paperbark maple (*A. griseum,* Zone 4), a slow-growing tree with curly, cinnamon-colored bark on its trunk and main limbs. Summer leaves are green; fall leaf color is variable, but can be striking.

Maples are often grown for their fall color, but you should be aware that this characteristic varies from region to region and from tree to tree; cultivars are likely to be more dependable. Consult with local arborists or nursery staff to learn which maples perform best in your area.

OAK (*Quercus* species)

Oaks are rich in folklore and history. In the landscape, their trunks of majestic girth and canopies of impressive height and spread make them a sort of royalty. Because most oaks eventually become huge, ordinary urban and suburban properties have room for one or two at most.

Northern red oak (*Q. rubra,* Zone 4) is a widely grown shade tree that reaches as high as 90 feet with a round crown of up to 50 feet across. Fast growing, it may reach 20 feet or more in 20 years. Leaves can be up to 9 inches long and may turn bright red in fall. Pin oaks (*Q. palustris,* Zone 5) are also widely used, fast-growing shade trees. They mature to a tall (to 100 feet) narrow (40 feet or less) form, with lower limbs that droop attractively to the ground. Leaves are deeply cut and can turn copper-red in fall. Scarlet oak (*Q. coccinea,* Zone 5) is similar, but tolerates drier conditions and holds its bottom branches higher.

Midwesterners will be familiar with the native bur oak (*Q. macrocarpa,* Zone 3), a very hardy shade tree reaching 80 feet tall with an almost equal spread. It doesn't put on much of a show in autumn, but it does tolerate a wide range of poor growing conditions.

(*Continued on next page*)

Japanese maples

White oak

(*Continued from previous page*)

Gardeners in mild-winter climates can grow several evergreen oaks. Aged specimens of coast live oak (*Q. agrifolia,* Zone 9) are revered in California, where they reach 100 feet tall and wide with splendidly gnarled branches. Young live oaks grow quickly and are sometimes planted and pruned to form hedges. Holly oak (*Q. ilex,* Zone 7) is smaller but equally fast-growing and versatile. Southeastern native evergreen oaks include the southern live oak (*Q. virginiana,* Zone 7), a tree with a short thick trunk and a very large, spreading crown that can reach 60 feet tall by 100 feet wide. Laurel oaks (*Q. laurifolia,* Zone 7) are taller than wide and drop their leaves before spring.

Oaks aren't all behemoths. Sawtooth oak (*Q. acutissima,* Zone 5) reaches just 35 to 50 feet with an equal spread. Its long, deciduous leaves have serrated edges and turn from yellow-green in spring to dark green in summer and gold or brown in fall. Gambel oak (*Q. gambelii,* Zone 5) is even smaller—15 to 30 feet tall—and is grown as a single or multi-trunked specimen or en masse as a shrubby screen. Ideal as a specimen or screen in small yards is upright English oak (*Q. robur* 'Fastigiata', Zone 6), a cultivar of the venerable English oak that grows 50 feet high but only 15 feet wide.

PINE (*Pinus* species)

Pines are such familiar trees that many people refer to all coniferous evergreen trees as "pines." They are, of course, distinct from other conifers, and are recognizable because their needles are gathered into clusters of two, three, or five. Many of the most popular species have long needles with the appealing look and feel of soft brushes. All pines bear cones and a few bear edible seeds (pine nuts). In the landscape, pines have a year-round presence as specimen or background plants. They range in size from dwarf plants only a few feet tall to stately 70- or 80-foot trees. Hedges and screens of pine are effective and attractive whether sheared or left natural. When young, many pines are upright, conical trees.

With age, some develop a more open or irregular picturesque form. Some pines drop their bottom branches and, when large, can provide headroom for strollers and shade for a bench. Pine species also include weeping, narrowly upright, or spreading forms.

Eastern white pine (*P. strobus,* Zone 3) is a fast-growing tree with soft blue-green needles. Grown as a specimen, it can reach 80 feet tall—or it can be trained and sheared as a hedge or tall screen. Scotch pine (*P. sylvestris,* Zone 3), with its stiff needles and conical form, is familiar to many as a Christmas tree. Growing to 70 feet, older trees are handsome focal points with open, irregular branches and colorful peeling bark. Austrian pine (*P. nigra,* Zone 4) is one of the best pines for city conditions; it tolerates a wide range of of environments. Lacebark pine (*P. bungeana,* Zone 5) is a 50-foot, often multi-trunked tree prized for its colorful flaking bark. Mugo pine (*P. mugo,* Zone 3), a bushy tree with dense dark green foliage, ranges from a few feet to 15 feet tall. Its cultivars are popular and versatile landscape plants used as specimens or mass-planted.

Gardeners in the South and West can choose from many excellent native pines. Check with your local nursery or garden center to find which are good performers in your area. Of the southern pines, spruce pine (*P. glabra*) has a twisting trunk and irregular branches even as a young tree. Longleaf pine (*P. palustris*) has distinctive needles up to 18 inches long. Growing to 80 feet, longleaf pines make fine shade trees, as do loblolly pines (*P. taeda*). Most southern pines are hardy to Zone 7, some to Zone 6, so check labels or ask about hardiness when you buy.

In the west, the bristlecone pine (*P. aristata*) is noteworthy for its picturesque presence and its longevity—some specimens are believed to be 4,000 years old. Ponderosa pine (*P. ponderosa*) is a majestic shade tree growing to 60 feet with an open habit and handsome orange-tinted, furrowed bark. Western pines are frequently small trees, generally cold-hardy (to Zones 4 or 5) and tolerant of wind, heat, and drought, as befits their mountain and desert origins.

Austrian pine

SHRUBS

BOXWOODS (*Buxus* species)

These evergreen shrubs are the quintessential plant for formal garden hedges. Their small, glossy leaves are packed densely on many branched twigs, making them ideal for shearing to precise shapes. Left on their own, boxwoods form tidy mounds. Various cultivars of littleleaf boxwood (*B. microphylla,* Zones 4 or 5) are widely available. Some grow faster than others; some are upright, others spread, and the leaves of some turn bronze in winter. Their mature size is about 3 to 4 feet tall and wide. In contrast, English boxwood (*B. sempervirens,* Zone 5) can grow much larger, to 20 feet tall and wide. Its cultivars are equally diverse, but all have the densely packed leaves that make them such good hedge plants.

Boxwoods grow slowly, so buy the largest plants you can afford. They thrive in **full sun to partial shade** but can be fussy about soil, water, heat, and pests—check with local nursery staff to find out which cultivars do best in your area.

BUTTERFLY BUSH (*Buddleia* species)

Weeks-long displays of lovely fragrant, butterfly-attracting flowers earn these deciduous shrubs their place in the garden. Elongated clusters of tiny flowers form at the ends of arching branches from midsummer to fall. Flowers are pink, white, violet, lilac, blue, or purple. *B. davidii* (Zone 5) and its cultivars are widely available; other less-hardy species are available in the South. Plants can grow to 10 feet tall and wide, and there are compact or dwarf cultivars. Butterfly bush requires **full sun.** Cut the woody stems to 1-foot stubs in early spring; new shoots can reach 5 feet or taller over the growing season. In cold-winter climates top growth may die back over the winter, but the plant will regrow from the roots.

CAMELLIA (*Camellia* species)

Camellias are the glory of many home landscapes in the South, West, and coastal areas where the climate is mild enough to support them (Zone 8, sometimes 7). There are small camellias for patio containers, camellias that can be

trained as espaliers, and camellias that form trees or bushes 15 feet tall and wide. All cultivars have attractive evergreen foliage and beautiful, sometimes spectacular flowers. The leaves are glossy, dark green, and leathery. Flowers can be single or double, from 3 to 9 inches across, in colors ranging from white to pink to red. Depending on cultivar and conditions, camellias begin blooming in fall, winter, or spring; they continue to flower for months. Cultivars of *C. japonica, C. sasanqua,* and *C. reticulata* are commonly available. *C. sasanqua* produces generally smaller plants and flowers than the others, and *C. reticulata* produces striking flowers on lanky plants. Camellias require **partial shade.**

Gardeners in colder climates may wish to search out oil-seed camellia (*C. oleifera*) and the Ackerman hybrids developed from it. These are hardy to Zone 6 and may survive in protected spots in Zone 5.

Boxwood

Camellia

Butterfly bush

COTONEASTER (*Cotoneaster* species)
These versatile plants include low-growing, spreading ground covers, upright shrubs with stiff branches, and tall plants with graceful arching limbs. Whether evergreen or deciduous, all bear spring flowers that are small, white or pink, and pretty if not spectacular. Colorful berries appear in fall and may last the winter.

Cotoneasters used for ground covers are discussed in Chapter 8, on page 111. Bigger shrubs used as specimens or in massed plantings include spreading cotoneaster (*C. divaricatus,* Zone 5), which forms a 10-foot-wide mound 5 or 6 feet tall. It has deciduous leaves that turn red in fall. Evergreen red clusterberry (*C. lacteus,* Zone 7) forms a dense mass of arching stems that are covered with large clusters of red berries for much of the winter. Willowleaf cotoneaster (*C. salicifolius,* Zone 6) has long narrow evergreen leaves that are green in summer, purple in winter. Cultivars include a low-growing ground cover as well as a shrub 10 feet tall and wide.

Cotoneasters grow in **full sun or partial shade** and tolerate a range of soils, heat, and drought. When stressed by hot weather or lack of water, they are susceptible to fire blight. Check with your local Cooperative Extension Service to learn whether fire blight-resistant cultivars are necessary in your area.

DOGWOOD (*Cornus stolonifera* and *C. alba*)
Several dogwoods are handsome and valuable landscaping shrubs. (Tree-form dogwoods are discussed on page 129.) Hardy to Zone 2, they have something to offer in every season. Siberian dogwood (*C. alba*), red-twig, and red-osier dogwood (*C. stolonifera*) are similar in many respects. All produce showy white or creamy flowers in spring and white or bluish white berries thatstand out against the good-looking summer foliage. Leaves turn red or purple in fall. Colorful red stems brighten the winter landscape. Siberian dogwood forms a small, somewhat compact bush growing 6 to 8 feet tall, while red-twig dogwood grows 10 feet tall and wide. Cultivars offer variegated foliage, dwarf forms, and twigs colored yellow, coral, or maroon.

Shrub dogwoods grow in **full sun to full shade.** Cut oldest stems to the ground every two or three years to stimulate new, more colorful growth.

EUONYMUS (*Euonymus* species)
Whether it's a low-growing, shrubby, or vining ground cover or a strikingly colorful fall accent, there's probably a place for at least one euonymus on your property. These tough plants grow in **full sun or full shade.** Burning bush (*E. alatus,* Zone 3) is prized for its blazing red fall foliage, but the transition of the deciduous leaves from dark green to pale pink to red spreads out the enjoyment over months. Burning bush grows 6 to 10 feet high and wide, depending on the cultivar. The distinctive ridged twigs are interesting in winter and are the source of the plant's other common name, winged euonymus.

Winter creeper (*E. fortunei,* Zone 5) is less flamboyant. Evergreen leaves and varied growth habits make winter creepers good plants for adding structure to a planting. Vining forms make dense ground covers that can be invasive or climbers for walls or fences. Upright, bushy forms are effective in foundation or mass plantings and as informal hedges. Cultivars offer leaves that are varie-gated with white, cream, or gold edges or that change color in fall and winter. Inconspicuous flowers produce orange fruits that may last all winter.

Japanese euonymus (*E. japonicus,* Zone 7 or 8) is frequently used in warm-winter areas. It can be grown as an individual specimen, massed in groups, or as a hedge or screen. This species grows to 10 feet tall and 6 feet wide. Cultivars with variegated leaves edged in gold, cream, or white make striking accents, particularly since the colors don't fade in full sun or hot weather.

Cotoneaster

Siberian dogwood

Euonymus

HOLLY (*Ilex* species)

In addition to handsome trees (see page 130), hollies include attractive shrubs for foundation plantings, mass plantings, hedges, or screens. Many can be used as formal, precisely sheared hedges; others look best in a more natural form. Evergreen hollies with spiny, shiny leaves and red berries are common. Chinese holly (*I. cornuta,* Zone 7) grows to 10 feet tall and wide. It thrives in the heat of the South and in the alkaline soils and hot, dry climate of the Southwest. Japanese holly (*I. crenata,* Zone 5 or 6) has small leaves and inconspicuous berries. The cultivars 'Compacta' and 'Helleri' make excellent natural hedges 4 to 6 feet tall. A number of hybrids developed by Mrs. Kathleen Meserve (*I. x meserveae,* Zone 4 or 5) are hardier plants, mostly with blue-green leaves and bright red berries. They include upright and mounded cultivars that grow 8 to 15 feet tall. Winterberry holly (*I. verticillata,* Zone 3) is a deciduous holly whose berry-covered stems are striking for months in the winter, or until appreciative birds harvest the fruit. Hollies require **full sun to partial shade.**

HYDRANGEA (*Hydrangea* species)

Gardeners have long valued hydrangeas for their large clusters of showy flowers. These deciduous plants grow as vines, shrubs, or small trees, with flat to spherical flower clusters up to a foot wide. Climbing hydrangea (*H. petiolaris,* Zone 5) is a vine reaching 60 feet or more in length. For several weeks in summer it bears flat flower clusters, 6 to 8 inches wide, that are white and slightly fragrant. The glossy dark-green foliage looks good through the summer and fall. The leaves drop to reveal pretty reddish- brown bark. This plant grows in **full sun to full shade.**

The familiar garden hydrangea (*H. macrophylla,* Zone 6) has large shiny leaves that make an attractive backdrop to the showy clusters of white, blue, pink, or red flowers. Flower color varies with the pH of your soil—acid soil produces blue flowers, neutral and alkaline soil make them pink or red. Flowers appear in summer and last until fall. The species reaches 4 to 8 feet tall and 6 to 10 feet wide, but much smaller cultivars are available. Garden hydrangeas prefer full sun to partial shade.

Gardeners in colder areas can grow *H. arborescens* 'Annabelle' or 'Grandiflora', which bloom on new growth and can be cut back to the ground each winter. Or they can grow PeeGee hydrangea (*H. paniculata* 'Grandiflora', Zone 3) whose 6- to 12-inch-wide flower clusters turn from white to pink to tan through the summer, fall, and into winter. Plants can reach 25 feet tall and wide, but are usually pruned to control the size.

Oakleaf hydrangea (*H. quercifolia,* Zone 5) is grown as much for its colorful oak-like leaves and shaggy red-brown bark as for the clusters of white flowers it produces in early summer. The dark green leaves turn red, orange, and purple in the fall. Oakleaf hydrangeas require partial sun or shade.

JUNIPER (*Juniperus* species)

Ubiquitous in the landscape, junipers come in a vast range of sizes and shapes suitable for just about every landscape purpose. The evergreen foliage is scaly or needlelike, varying from bright green to gray-green, blue-green, or even blue. Some cultivars turn purple or bronze in winter. The fleshy cones look like berries. For ground cover junipers (*J. horizontalis,* Zone 2), see Chapter 8, page 112. For foundation plant-ings, mass plantings, screens, and hedges, there are numerous shrubby forms, both spreading and upright. Most of these are cultivars of *J. x media* (Zone 4 or 5), shore juniper (*J. conferta,* Zone 6), savin juniper (*J. sabina,* Zone 3), eastern red cedar (*J. virginiana,* Zone 2), and Chinese juniper (*J. chinensis,* Zone 3). Use junipers with striking foliage, such as the bright-blue *J. squamata* 'Blue Star' as specimen plants. Junipers thrive in **full sun.**

Winterberry holly

Garden hydrangea

Chinese juniper

LILAC (*Syringa* species)

Lilacs, with their large clusters of sweetly fragrant flowers, are a traditional staple of the spring landscape and a background plant the rest of the year. Many cultivars of the common lilac (*S. vulgaris,* Zone 4) are available, offering violet, blue, magenta, purple, pink, white, or, of course, lilac-colored flowers in midspring. Plants form thickets of upright stems reaching 20 feet tall and wide; stems are clad in dark green deciduous leaves. Common lilacs flower only after receiving several weeks of cold temperatures. Gardeners in warm-winter climates can grow Descanso hybrids, which have no chilling requirement.

Several lilac species are smaller, more compact plants that suit small properties and mixed borders better than the rangy common lilac. Dwarf lilac (*S. meyeri* 'Palibin', Zone 4) reaches 6 to 8 feet tall and wide and produces fragrant lavender flowers in midspring and sometimes again in fall. Miss Kim lilac (*S. patula* 'Miss Kim', Zone 4) is about the same size and blooms in early summer with pale lavender-blue flowers. The foliage turns purple in fall. Both of these small lilacs resist mildew, which often infests common lilac.

Japanese tree lilac (*S. reticulata,* Zone 3) grows to 30 feet tall and is frequently trained as a single or multi-trunked tree. Its foot-long clusters of fragrant white flowers are a handsome accent in the early summer garden. Deciduous foliage and attractive bark provide interest at other times.

Lilacs grow well in **full or partial sun.** Prune them after flowering, removing spent flowers to encourage formation of new buds.

'Miss Kim' lilac

RHODODENDRON AND AZALEA

(*Rhododendron* species)

These shrubs are among the loveliest and best-loved garden plants. Prized above all for their splendid and distinctive clustered flowers, they also provide handsome evergreen or deciduous foliage on attractively formed plants. There are rhododendrons or azaleas suitable for almost every area of North America.

Deciduous azaleas produce flowers in a breathtaking range of colors—reds, pinks, yellows, lavenders, oranges, whites, numerous

Azalea

bicolors—and their fall foliage is often colorful, too. Many bloom in mid- to late spring, some bloom into early summer, and some are fragrant. Plant size varies among the numerous cultivars; many grow 4 to 6 feet tall and are either upright or spreading. Most are hardy to Zone 5 or 6. Northern gardeners should look for Northern Lights hybrids; these were developed at the University of Minnesota and are hardy to Zone 3.

Evergreen azaleas showcase trusses of bright spring flowers against rich green foliage that is attractive year-round. Plants can be low-growing spreaders or bushes, neat and rounded or upright. Flowers are seldom fragrant but can be very large, up to 5 inches across. Some evergreen azaleas are quite tender, surviving only in Zones 8 or 9, but others are hardy to Zone 6 or 7.

Rhododendrons come in just about any size and flower color you could possibly want. Plants less than a foot tall nestle comfortably in a rock garden, while giant rhododendrons up to 20 feet tall and wide are a commanding presence in the largest of landscapes. A vast selection suitable for foundation plantings, screens, or specimen plants are 3 to 8 feet tall and wide. Most rhododendrons bloom in midspring and are evergreen. Leaves are green but vary in hue as well as in shape. Take these characteristics into consideration since they're on view far longer than the flowers. Many rhododendrons are hardy to Zone 5 or 6, but hardier cultivars are available.

Rhododendrons and azaleas grow easily in the Northeast, Northwest, Mid-Atlantic, and Southern regions. Elsewhere they can be rather fussy. In general, they grow best in **light shade,** in constantly moist but well-drained and acid soil with abundant organic matter. Hot summers, cold winter temperatures, and drying winds can damage leaves and sometimes kill plants, as can a range of insects and diseases. That said, the popularity of rhododendrons and azaleas is attested to by the number of gardeners who go to great lengths to grow them in less-than-ideal conditions.

Where soil is insufficiently acid or poorly drained, for example, gardeners grow rhododendrons and azaleas in deep raised beds filled with a rich mix of pH-adjusted, organically amended soil. Where winters are cold and windy, they construct protective shelters. If conditions are too problematic to alter in the garden, you can grow rhododendrons and azaleas in containers.

If you're a beginner in a region where rhododendrons and azaleas are not common, the best course of action is to consult with an experienced rhodendron or azalea gardener in your area, or ask the local garden club. They'll know which species, cultivars, and cultural practices have proven themselves in local conditions.

SPIREA (*Spiraea* species)

Spring-blooming spireas, with long arching branches covered in tiny white flowers, are a long-time favorite. The most commonly planted spring-blooming spirea, *S.* x *vanhouttei* (Zone 4), grows 6 to 8 feet tall and wide and makes a formidable specimen or screen. During the summer, its deciduous leaves are a lovely, light blue-green color. *S. nipponica* 'Snowmound' (Zone 4) grows 2 to 4 feet tall and wide and has pure white flowers in late spring and early summer.

Gardeners with limited space and those who want a more dramatic plant can choose from a number of compact forms that offer flowers in summer and colorful leaves through the growing season. Japanese spirea (*S. japonica,* Zone 3) and the related *S.* x *bumalda* cultivars (Zone 3) grow up to 3 feet high and wide. The tidy, twiggy mounds are covered with clusters of tiny flowers in red, pink, or white for several weeks in summer; foliage is often attractive as well. 'Anthony Waterer' has rich pink-red flowers and pink-tinged green foliage. 'Goldflame' has deep pink flowers and golden leaves that are tinged in spring and fall with red and copper.

Spireas grow well in **full or partial sun.** They tolerate many soil types but do require good drainage.

VIBURNUM (*Viburnum* species)

Grown for their flowers, their foliage, and their berries, viburnums are excellent landscape and garden plants that can be evergreen or deciduous. All viburnums prefer **full or partial sun.**

Korean spice viburnum (*V. carlesii,* Zone 4) produces rounded clusters of very fragrant flowers in midspring, preceded by pretty pink buds. Plants grow to 5 feet tall and wide. The dull green, deciduous foliage may turn red in fall. *Viburnum* x *burkwoodii* (Zone 5) grows to 12 feet tall and also has fragrant flowers in spring. Double-file viburnum (*V. plicatum* var. *tomentosum,* Zone 6) is a large shrub with tiers of branches and deciduous leaves that are green in summer and red-purple in fall. Flat clusters of striking white flowers appear to float above the foliage in midspring. Bright red fruits follow, as do birds to feast on them.

European cranberry bush (*V. opulus,* Zone 3) features white flowers in May, red berries in fall and winter, and colorful fall foliage. This large species grows up to 12 to 15 feet tall and wide, but 'Compactum' is about half that size and 'Nanum' is tiny—just 2 feet tall and wide. Arrowwood viburnum (*V. dentatum,* Zone 3) stems were once harvested for arrow shafts. Today, gardeners are more likely to appreciate the patch of straight stems that can make an accent in an informal planting. Glossy, green deciduous leaves turn shades of red, purple, or orange in fall. Early summer's creamy white flowers produce blue berries that are much sought after by birds.

Evergreen viburnums include leatherleaf viburnum (*V. rhytidophyllum,* Zone 6), an upright shrub with shiny green leaves that drop in midwinter in colder areas. Large flat clusters of white flowers bloom in midspring, and the red berries darken to black. Laurustinus (*V. tinus,* Zone 7) is an erect shrub that can be pruned to form a hedge; its pink buds and clusters of slightly fragrant white flowers appear in late winter and early spring, followed by blue berries in summer. *V. davidii* (Zone 7) is a small shrub (3 feet tall and wide) with dark green leaves that show off scentless white flowers and pretty blue berries.

Spirea

Viburnum x *burkwoodii*

CHAPTER 10

Specialty Gardens

Pursuing special interests is one of the pleasures of gardening. The more experience you gain, the more likely you are to be drawn to particular types of gardens. Before long, you may find yourself developing a collection of particular plants such as daylilies or roses, installing a pond for water plants, or turning your entire yard into a miniature wildlife refuge to attract birds and butterflies. While much of the information presented in previous chapters can help you get started with particular plants, this chapter will help you delve a bit deeper into three of the most popular types of specialty gardens.

Gardens for the Birds

Of all the creatures around us, birds hold a valued spot in most people's hearts. Their songs brighten the mornings, and their plumage delights the eye. Their comings and goings herald the changing of the seasons. While most backyards are visited by at least a few birds, it's not difficult to entice many more to stop by, and even to set up housekeeping for a season.

Like all animals, birds require food, shelter, and water to survive. They are more likely to frequent places that provide all three elements rather than just one. You can grow plants that provide food and shelter, and to entice birds further, offer feeders, birdhouses, and a basin or pond for water.

Birds' specific needs vary greatly depending on the particular species, the place, and the time. Take food, for example. Blue jays eat a variety of insects, seeds, and fruits, but most birds have more limited diets. Finches and grosbeaks are primarily seed eaters; mockingbirds and waxwings prefer berries; wrens and woodpeckers eat mostly insects; and hummingbirds drink nectar. But bird diets often change with the seasons. Bluebirds eat moths and other flying insects in the summer but switch to berries in the winter when insects are scarce. And robins will even forsake earthworms when blue-berries begin to ripen.

Given this diversity, if you want to attract birds to your garden in greater numbers or wider variety, it's important to know which birds frequent your region and what their particular needs and preferences are. Nature centers and knowledgeable bird lovers familiar with your area are excellent sources of information, as is the local Cooperative Extension Service and library.

Gardens for the birds can be as beautiful as they are practical, left. Use a birdbath as a focal point, and plant a mixture of seed-bearing ornamentals and sheltering shrubs.

Specialty gardens, opposite, allow you to pursue particular interests and develop expertise in chosen plants or garden types while creating unique areas on your property.

DESIGNING FOR BIRDS

Gardening with the intention of attracting birds need not conflict with your other gardening ambitions. But you will face choices. Tidy, formal yards and those with a few kinds of plants provide less shelter and fewer food sources than do diverse landscapes that offer a smorgasbord of trees, shrubs, grasses, perennials, vines, and annuals. Natural landscapes, where hedges, screens, and other plants are pruned lightly, are likely to serve birds better than neatly manicured beds and large expanses of lawn.

If birds are just one of your gardening interests, con-sider devoting only a portion of your landscape to a bird garden. Wildlife is prolific where different habitats meet; naturalists call this the "edge effect." You can create similar conditions by planting a small woodland on one corner of your property or along a fence line. Place trees at the very back and then shrubs of various types and sizes extending to the lawn. Or instead of lawn, create a strip of meadow where native grasses mingle with wildflowers. The following pages provide more ideas for supplying the three elements birds seek in the landscape: food, shelter, and water.

FOOD

You can attract a lot of birds simply by providing a bird feeder year-round. But feeders are the fast-food stop of the avian world. To provide more types of birds with a more varied diet, make your landscape into a bird feeder. Grow plants that provide a wide-ranging menu of seeds, fruit, and nuts or attract insects, a favorite bird food.

Food from the Garden. Try to match the birds you want to attract with the plants they desire. Hummingbirds are especially fond of plants with red or funnel-shaped flowers: fuchsias, penstemons, trumpet vine, and bee balm. It's easy to experiment with annuals and perennials to see which birds they attract. But trees and shrubs require a large investment in time and money, so it's wise to do some research before planting them for the birds.

Here are some general principles to bear in mind as you plan your garden and choose plants:

- **Seek out native plants** (those indigenous to your area), rather than exotic imports. Local birds will have developed tastes for plants with an equally long history in the area.
- **Create a varied menu** with a mix of seed- and berry-producing plants. (See the table opposite.) Include insect harborers (alder, oak, willow). Some of the insects you lure to feed birds may be garden pests, but some will be natural predators of those or other pests. Birds will enjoy the feast regardless.
- **Stock the larder year-round** with selected plants. The dried seed heads of wildflowers and grasses provide fall and winter forage for the birds and winter beauty for you.

Winter food is as likely to come from weeds such as milkweed as from plants in your garden, below left. Wherever possible, leave "wild" spots for birds and other animals.

Stock birds' larders for the winter months by planting seed-producing grasses and berry producers such as this viburnum, below.

Plants That Attract Birds

The following are only some of the many plants useful to birds. Plants are listed by common name; botanical names are included where only certain species are recommended or where they're needed to avoid confusion.

KEY
The listed plants provide food or shelter, as indicated by the following symbols:

Berries   Nectar

Seeds   Shelter

TREES AND SHRUBS

- Alders
- Arborvitae
- Ashes
- Azaleas and rhododendrons
- Barberrys
- Bayberry
- Birches
- Cotoneasters
- Dogwoods
- Elderberries
- Firs
- Hawthornes
- Hemlocks
- Hollies
- Junipers
- Oaks
- Pines
- Shrub roses
- Serviceberries (*Amelanchier*)
- Spruces
- Viburnums
- Yews

PERENNIALS

- Asters
- Bee Balm
- Black-eyed Susan
- Penstemon
- Purple coneflower
- Scarlet sage

VINES

- Honeysuckle (*Lonicera heckrottii* and *L. semper virens*)
- Trumpet vine
- Virginia creeper

GROUND COVERS AND GRASSES

- Ivy
- Miscanthus
- Northern Sea Oats (*Chasmanthium latifolium*)
- Fountain grass (*Pennisetum* species)
- Pampas grass (*Cortederia selloana*)

ANNUALS

- Cosmos
- Fuchsia
- Salvia
- Sunflower
- Quaking grass (*Briza maxima*)

The berry-like fruit of yews (top) and hollies (above) make good winter bird food.

SHELTER

Different bird species have distinct shelter preferences, but all need a place to rest and sleep, as well as protection from driving wind, rain, snow, and—especially—predators. When under attack from a hawk, any bird will welcome the sanctuary of a nearby thicket.

Birds also need a secure spot to raise their young, and nesting requirements are the most specific. Birds can be fussy about where they will nest. The ovenbird, for instance, constructs a little domed hut on the forest floor, while orioles weave a delicate bag high in the branches of a tree such as an elm or maple.

Many of the same plants that provide food also provide shelter. Yet because birds may not always nest where they feed, a landscape of varied plantings will accommodate a greater range of birds. Choose plants of differing heights and densities. A few large trees can dominate a residential lot but won't attract the diversity of birds that shrubs and smaller trees will. Evergreens are particularly attractive to birds: hollies, junipers, pines, hemlocks, and cedars all provide year-round shelter and food. In warmer climates, evergreen oaks and southern magnolia do the same.

Shelter doesn't need to be a living plant. Dead trees, piles of brush, hollow logs, and roof eaves attract birds. To encourage wildlife, you may need to curb some of your desire for orderliness. "Messy" landscapes are more attractive to birds and other creatures.

Birdhouses. A birdhouse may be the answer when you can't provide the natural cover that a particular bird requires for nesting. Almost anyone can build satisfactory birdhouses (or nesting boxes, as they are more accurately called). All you need is a handsaw, a brace-and-bit or electric drill, a hammer, and a few nails or screws. A small supply of new or scrap ¾-inch lumber works just fine.

Birds don't really care what style the structure assumes, but they're particular about the accommodation's interior dimensions, the size of the entrance and its height above the box floor, and the box's height above the ground. The table below provides critical dimensions for a number of North American birds.

In addition to making the box the right size, make it easy to clean out so you can offer it year after year. A removable floor or a hinged roof or wall works best for cleaning. Because a birdhouse may be used more than once in a season, clear out the old nest after the young birds have fledged (left the nest), and it will be ready for another nesting pair.

Don't make the box airtight; remember how hot and stuffy a tightly enclosed room can be on a warm day. Add slits if necessary for ventilation. To allow rainwater to drain, drill ¼-inch-diameter holes in the floor.

Birds are more likely to nest in a stationary box than in one that swings in the breeze. If you put it on a pole, add a baffle as described for feeders to discourage unwanted guests. When you place a box, try to think like a bird—where will the box be safest from predators?

Shelter for birds can be provided by bushes such as this densely growing barberry that also provides breakfast, lunch or dinner.

Birdhouses, or nesting boxes, must be built to the specifications, including height off the ground, of the particular bird you are trying to attract.

BIRDHOUSE DIMENSIONS

BIRD	INTERIOR (Length x width x height in inches)	ENTRANCE (Diameter x height from floor)	HEIGHT (Aboveground, in feet)
Bluebird	4 x 5 x 8 to 12	1½ x 6 to 10	5 to 10
Chickadee	4 x 4 x 8 to 10	1⅛ x 7	6 to 15
Carolina wren	4 x 4 x 6 to 8	1¼ x 4 to 6	5 to 10
Common flicker	7 x 7 x 16 to 18	2½ x 14 to 16	6 to 20
Downy woodpecker	4 x 4 x 9	1¼ x 7	5 to 15
House wren	4 x 4 x 6 to 8	1¼ x 4 to 6	6 to 10
House finch	6 x 6 x 6	2 x 1	8 to 12
Nuthatch	4 x 4 x 8 to 10	1¼ x 7	12 to 15
Purple martin	6 x 6 x 6	2¼ x 1	10 to 20
Screech owl	8 x 8 x 12 to 15	3 x 9 to 12	10 to 30
Titmouse	4 x 4x 8 to 10	1¼ x 7	5 to 15
Tree swallow	5 x 5 x 6 to 8	1½ x 4 to 6	10 to 15

WATER

The final requirement, water, can be simple or challenging to provide—it's your choice. A traditional pedestal birdbath is relatively inexpensive and can be set up in a few minutes. Like a small bird feeder, it will serve the needs of a transient population of birds. At the other end of the bath spectrum is a backyard pond, fully integrated into a naturally land-scaped wildlife habitat and garden.

Effective birdbaths offer the same features as the baths provided by nature—puddles. The bottom slopes gently, so birds can find a depth at which they feel comfortable—a fraction of an inch for some. A small "island" partially sub-merged in the middle of the water can provide shallow wading if your bath has sides that slope too steeply. Not all puddles are on the ground, and birdbaths can be at any height. Raised above the ground, they make bird-watching more difficult for feline stalkers.

All sorts of shallow receptacles can be used for bird-baths. Once you've satisfied the birds' requirements, feel free to please yourself—a large steel disk from a farmer's disk-harrow is surprisingly elegant. Birds appreciate fresh, clear water as much as we do, so bear in mind that you'll need to replace stale or dirty water regularly and make up for evaporation. Making a drip-feed bath or trickle waterfall

Water for feathered friends should be clean. Scoop out plant debris and change the water daily to keep it inviting.

can answer most of those needs as well as being a delight in itself. Such creations range from a dripping garden hose to a recirculating pump feeding an elaborate landscaped pool and waterfall.

Bird Feeders

Like the seeds they hold, feeders vary according to the type of bird you wish to attract or discourage and the landscape in which you place them.

■ **Platform.** The simplest bird feeder is merely a flat platform, with a low lip, raised above the ground on a pole. It will attract all sorts of birds—as well as squirrels and possibly other animals. To discourage squirrels, make a baffle by inverting an aluminum piepan on the pole beneath the feeder. To keep rain from making a mess of the seeds, roof the feeder.

■ **Hopper.** These feeders offer several improvements over a platform. The plastic-sided hopper holds a quantity of seeds, which are kept dry by a roof and are gravity-fed to the birds as they eat. Make sure the space between the plastic sides and the platform is no more than ½ inch because larger openings may trap the head of a small bird. Unfortunately, hopper feeders mounted on poles or hung from trees can be easy prey for squirrels, so attach some type of baffle if possible.

■ **Tube**. Tube feeders are ideal for hanging next to a window because they're small and don't block the view. They are less vulnerable to squirrels too. You'll find them particularly useful for thistle seeds for finches and other small birds. Look for sturdy construction and good-quality materials. Remove attached trays, which tend to become fouled with hulls and droppings, and fill the bottom of the tube almost to the level of the bottom hole with small gravel. This prevents a layer of rotting seed from building up.

■ **Nectar.** Hummingbirds are among nature's most fascinating creatures—tiny, jewel-colored birds whose wings beat up to 80 times per second as they fly up, down, forward, backward, upside down, or hover in place. Hummingbirds are found in many regions; entice them to visit with an inexpensive feeder containing a sugary liquid that mimics the nectar they seek in plants. Hang the feeder during frost-free months; change the fluid often to keep it clear of fungi and bacteria; and keep your eyes peeled for the tiny visitors. Hummingbird feeders often have red plastic, trumpet-shaped "flowers" that prove irresistible lures.

FEEDER FOOD FOR THE BIRDS

FOOD	BIRDS ATTRACTED	COMMENTS
Sunflower seeds	Chickadees, cardinals, finches, grosbeaks, nuthatches, titmice	Smaller, black oil seeds are cheaper, easier for birds to handle, and more nutritious than striped seeds.
Millet	Ground feeders (doves, juncos, sparrows), cardinals, pine siskins, purple finches, some waterfowl	These tiny round seeds are inexpensive.
Safflower seeds	Cardinals	Squirrels, crows, and grackles don't like these seeds.
Thistle	Finches, juncos, indigo buntings	These tiny black seeds, high in oil and protein, are expensive. They are also called Niger seeds because some kinds come from Nigeria.
Corn, whole or coarsely cracked	Large birds (bluejays, crows), various fowl (ducks, wild turkeys)	Doesn't readily absorb water; you can scatter it on the ground.
Corn, finely cracked	Mourning doves, other medium-size birds	Protect from water.
Suet	Woodpeckers, nuthatches, chickadees	Good winter bird food; hang from a feeder or tree in a vinyl-covered wire basket.

Butterfly Gardens

Butterflies are like jewels on the wing. Flitting among flowers or floating on a breeze, admirals, skippers, fritillaries, swallowtails, monarchs, and other butterflies bring delight to a garden. Of all wildlife, butterflies are among the easiest to accommodate. They need sun to warm their muscles, and they need protection from strong winds. They need plants that provide larval food and nectar for adults. They'll appreciate a shallow puddle where they can get a drink. Like birds, specific butterflies have specific needs and preferences; local experts are likely to be the best sources of information about the butterflies in your area and what plants attract them. The box on page 146 notes other sources of information.

You don't need to plant a separate garden for butterflies. You may already be growing many of their favorite plants, and you can add others to existing borders or beds. (See pages 146–147.) Scatter groups of butterfly plants around the yard instead of putting them all in one garden. Add a rock or two in a sunny spot on which butterflies can bask. If you want to devote a planting to butterflies, start small. The first year, plant a shrub such as butterfly bush, a few perennials—bee balm, coreopsis, and garden phlox—and annuals such as cosmos and zinnia. Enlarge the garden gradually in the second and subsequent years, adding larval plants as well as nectar sources.

Butterflies aren't particular about design. They won't care if the garden is formal or informal, as long as it contains the plants they prefer. Butterflies are attracted by flower color and form. In general, they like flowers in the yellow, red, and blue-to-lavender spectrum. Plant in large groups if possible—butterflies are more likely to land if they

Butterfly gardens can be as simple as a patch of wildflowers in a corner of your yard.

see a wash of color rather than sparse dots here and there. Choose tubular or flat-topped flowers, and single rather than double forms. If you'd like to attract moths, include some night-blooming plants with sweet-scented white- or pale-colored flowers: nicotianas, night-scented stocks, bouncing Bet, and dame's rocket.

You can also attract butterflies to your garden by including plants on which they lay their eggs; these plants then provide food for the developing larvae. All butterflies and moths are particular about these plants, most often frequenting just a few species for egg-laying purposes. Many use woody plants as host plants, but few gardeners are likely to plant a tree or shrub for the purpose of feeding caterpillars. Dill, parsley, and Queen Anne's lace all host the black swallowtail, and all kinds of milkweeds host monarchs.

When you ponder pest control for your garden, remember that the caterpillars munching on your plants may one day be lovely butterflies. Butterfly larvae don't cause a lot of leaf damage in gardens, but you need to be mindful of them when making decisions about controlling other insect pests. The cost of a butterfly-rich garden includes a few more chewed up plants than you might otherwise like. A pesticide-free environment is safest for butterflies. Try preventive methods first when trying to control a pest; if you do need to use a botanical or chemical control, use the least toxic and apply it selectively.

smart tip

DESIGNING FOR WILDLIFE

The National Wildlife Federation offers information on creating wildlife-friendly gardens. You will learn how to provide food, supply water, create cover, and give wildlife a place to raise their young. You can also get an application for NWF's certification program, which provides formal recognition to those who create wildlife-friendly habitats. Call the National Wildlife Federation at (800) 822-9919, or write to NWF, Certified Wildlife Habitat, P.O. Box 1583, Merrifield, VA 22116-1583, or visit the Web site at www.nwf.org.

Butterfly gardens often provide sun, shade, water, and plants such as scabiosa, allium, phlox, aster, and daisy.

LEARNING ABOUT BUTTERFLIES

To learn which butterflies frequent your area—either passing through or staying for the season—be observant. Take a field trip around your neighborhood, into nearby fields and parks, along open woods. Note the butterflies you see and the plants they are frequenting. If you don't know the names of either, write down descriptions or photograph them so you can look up the names later. Local nature centers are excellent sources of information about the butterflies in your area. Some useful books

- *Butterflies of North America* by Jim P. Brock and Kenn Kaufman (Houghton Mifflin Harcourt)
- *Attracting Native Pollinators: Protecting North America's Bees and Butterflies* (Xerces Society/ Storey Publishing)
- *Attracting Butterflies and Hummingbirds to Your Garden* by Sally Roth (Rodale Books)
- *Butterflies, How to Identify and Attract Them to Your Garden* by Marcus Schneck (Rodale Books)

Two useful organizations concerned with conserving butterflies are

- The Xerces Society, 628 NE Broadway, Ste. 200, Portland, OR 97232; xerces.org
- North American Butterfly Assn., 4 Delaware Rd., Morristown, NJ 07960; naba.org

PLANTS FOR BUTTERFLIES

These plants produce nectar that attracts butterflies. The plants are listed by common name. Botanical names are included only when a specific designation is important.

Allium	Lavender
Aster	Milkweed
Bee balm	Pentas (*Pentas lanceolata*)
Black-eyed Susan	Purple coneflower
Butterfly bush	Phlox
Butterfly weed	Red valerian (*Centranthus ruber*)
Coreopsis	Scabiosa
Cosmos	Stoke's aster
Daisy	Sunflower
Joe-Pye weed	Verbena
Lantana	Zinnia

Butterfly bush, Monarch butterfly

Purple coneflower, Long dash skippers

Chives, Tiger swallowtail

New England aster, Monarch butterfly

Swamp milkweed, Great spangled fritillary

Mayapple, Mourning cloak

Butterfly weed, Black swallowtail

Water Gardens

A garden pond is a pleasing addition to almost any home landscape. Water has a soothing quality; a few minutes spent contemplating a garden pond can wash away the cares of the day. In hot weather, the sight of a small pond can be refreshing, particularly in regions where water is scarce. In addition to the charms of water, garden ponds provide an opportunity to grow some intriguing and beautiful plants. Stocked with a few fish and visited by local frogs and birds, a pond can be the hub of a thriving ecosystem and a source of continual fascination for both children and adults.

Constructed water gardens can provide a cool restful spot in any landscape, formal or informal.

PLANNING A WATER FEATURE

Even a small backyard pond involves considerable effort and expense. And once installed a pond is difficult, if not impossible, to move. Take time to think about how a pond will fit into your landscape and into your family's activities. Talk with established water gardeners and learn from their experiences. While you're pondering, consider the following practical details:

- Water plants are sun lovers, so site your pond where it can receive at least six to eight hours of sun daily.
- Avoid siting the pond on your property's lowest spot, where it will catch the runoff and debris of every rainstorm. You need some land that is lower than the pond to receive both overflow and drain water from the pond when you clean it.
- Avoid areas filled with tree roots, rocks, or other impediments to digging.
- Remember that water finds its own level; a relatively flat spot will save you a lot of grading.
- Before digging, check with local building authorities to learn whether a permit is required or if restrictions, such as safety fencing, will apply.

how to: Install a Pond

Tools and Materials: shovel, carpenter's level, stakes and string or garden hose, powdered limestone, long board,

1 Lay out the perimeter of the pond. Plot a formal, geometric shape with stakes and string. (Drive a stake and stretch a string from it for a radius to make a circle.) A length of garden hose is useful for making curves for free-form shapes. Establish the shape with the hose; then mark it on the ground with powdered limestone.

2 Dig the hole with sides sloped at about a 75-degree angle. You may want to make part of the perimeter a much shallower, gradual slope; this mimics many natural ponds and may attract birds. Leave a shelf near the edge for shallow-water bog plants and another two feet deep for water lilies. Remove debris that might puncture the liner.

3 To level the pond perimeter, lay a board across the hole at several spots, and rest a carpenter's spirit level on it. Fill any low spots you find with earth from the hole, and tamp it down. Dig a ledge around the hole's perimeter to accommodate the thickness of the capstones you are using plus the builder's sand or mortar in which they will rest.

Pond size and shape depend largely on personal preference, but plants and fish do impose certain requirements. Water plants grow at specific depths, ranging from a few inches to several feet below the surface. Many pond designs incorporate a ledge for shallow-water plants and a bottom about 2 feet deep to accommodate water lilies and lotuses. For fish, plan an area more than 2 feet deep. In warm climates, the extra depth provides cool water in summer; in cold climates it provides a place under the ice for plants and fish to overwinter.

INSTALLING A POND WITH A FLEXIBLE LINER

Modern materials have made pond construction possible for anyone with a shovel and a generous supply of elbow grease. Two kinds of pond liners are common. Preformed liners of rigid fiberglass are convenient, but they are expensive and available only in a limited number of shapes and sizes. Sheets of thin, flexible plastic (polyvinyl chloride, called PVC) or EPDM (Ethylene Propylene Diene Terpolymer) rubber (another synthetic material) offer far more design possibilities at less cost. For all but the smallest ponds, these flexible pond liners are easier for homeowners to install. Nonetheless, allow a couple of weekends for the job.

Your first task is determining how much liner you'll need. Calculate by adding twice the pond's maximum depth plus 2 feet (for overlap) to the pond's maximum length; do the same for the width. To make a pond 2 feet deep, 15 feet long, and 7 feet wide, the liner length needs to be 4 feet + 2 feet + 15 feet = 21 feet total. The width would be 4 feet + 2 feet + 7 feet = 13 feet.

Buy a liner specially made for ponds, not ordinary plastic sheeting. Thicker liner material is more expensive but more durable and longer lasting—20-mil PVC (0.020 inch thick) should last about 10 years before ultraviolet radiation degrades it. PVC that is 32 mil thick will last 15 to 20 years, and EPDM rubber for 40 years or longer if it's bonded to an underlayment.

Natural ponds made into water gardens become the hub of a thriving ecosystem.

DIFFICULTY LEVEL: CHALLENGING

stones and pebbles, builder's sand, mortar (optional), pond liner, underlayment, capstones

4 Make an overflow outlet to accommodate runoff after a rain. This outlet can be as simple as a channel cut at water level to lower ground nearby or a buried drainpipe or drain tile that empties into a rock-filled dry well. If you cut a channel, add stones and pebbles later to hold the liner in place and obscure it from sight.

5 Before laying the liner, cushion the surfaces of the hole with a ½- to 1-inch layer of builder's sand on the bottom. Use carpet underlayment or fiberglass batting on the sloping walls. When you install the liner, let it sag to touch the bottom and walls, but keep it taut enough to prevent bunching. Weight the edges with stones.

6 Fill the pond, smoothing the liner around the perimeter and trimming it to cover the surrounding soil by about 1 foot. The simplest pond edge is made by laying flat-bottomed capstones on top of the liner, setting them in sand to level the surfaces and prevent rocking. Extend the capstones about 2 inches over the water.

STOCKING THE POND

The plants and fish in your new pond will require clean water. After you finish all stages of construction, drain the pond. Siphon and bail out the water, and clear out all construction debris; then fill it with clean water. Let the water sit for a week or so before you add plants or fish, so any chlorine in the water can dissipate. Check with local pet stores to determine whether the local water contains any chemicals that require the addition of commercial conditioners to make the water safe for fish.

Make a Self-Sustaining Ecosystem. A well-balanced mixture of plants and aquatic creatures will keep themselves healthy and the water clear. When you select water plants, remember that some, such as irises and pickerel weed, grow vertically above the water surface. Other plants, such as water lilies and lotuses, float on the water surface and can take up considerable water-surface space.

Ponds require a certain mix of plant and animal life to be self-sustaining. When you first stock your pond, balance it by growing two bunches of submerged plants and one water lily for each square yard of pond surface area. If the pond has two or more square yards of surface area, grow enough floating plants (water lilies and lotuses) to cover 50 to 70 percent of the surface during the summer months. (The submerged plants release oxygen into the water, and the floating plants shade it, restricting the growth of algae.) Add 8 to 10 small snails or 6 to 8 large snails per square yard of pond surface and enough fish so that their combined lengths equal 2 inches for every square foot of pond surface if the pond is 18 to 24 inches deep. (The snails and fish eat algae and release nutrients that act as fertilizers for the plants.)

PLANTING WATER PLANTS

Water plants are no more difficult to plant than garden plants. They are usually grown in containers; pots make the plants easier to maintain and allow easy removal for repotting or overwintering inside. Buy plastic pans or open-lattice baskets designed for pond plants, regular plant containers, or even plastic dishpans in which you've bored drainage holes. Line open-lattice baskets with burlap to keep soil from leaking out of the holes. Most water lilies need at least 4 to 10 gallons of soil, while most other water plants need 1 or 2 gallons.

For all pond plants, use fertile, heavy garden soil. Don't use potting soil or soilless mixes because these media are lightweight and will float out of the containers. Remove undecomposed organic matter, and don't add organic amendments, such as peat moss and compost, because they break down and cloud the water.

Plant water lilies as shown below for lotuses. Hardy lilies grow well when their soil surface is 6 to 16 inches under the water but no more than 2 feet deep. Tropical lilies prefer a more shallow depth—6 to 12 inches under the water surface. Don't put tropical water lilies out until the water has stabilized at about 70°F. To lessen the shock of transplanting, you can lower tropical lilies gradually into the pond, so the developing foliage stays on the surface.

Planting Shallow-Water Plants and Bog Plants. Use heavy soil, as described above, and transplant as usual, much as you'd pot up a begonia for the patio. To keep the soil in the pot, spread a ½-inch layer of washed gravel over the soil surface.

When you buy the plant, check with the supplier to learn how deep to set it. Most shallow-water plants do well on a ledge with the soil surface under several inches of water. Others may be planted with the soil surface at or above the water level. Free-floating plants don't need soil to anchor them. Just set them gently into place. To confine them to a certain spot, anchor them in soil.

Plant lotus rhizomes so that the top of the crown and new leaf shoots are exposed, and spread gravel on the pot. As the plant grows, gradually lower the pot to the correct depth.

GROWING TROPICAL AND HARDY WATER LILIES

There are hardy water lilies for almost any size pond, from miniature plants for a half-barrel to wide-spreading plants that require a good-size pond. All bloom from summer to frost, producing striking, sometimes fragrant flowers. Hardy water lilies can survive winters outdoors in areas as cold as Zone 4 or even Zone 3, as long as the roots don't freeze. They won't need protection unless the pond freezes deep enough to reach the roots. In shallow ponds or extremely cold climates, lift the rhizomes, and store them indoors in damp vermiculite or sand. Hardy water lilies are day-blooming.

Tropical water lilies are hardy outdoors in winter in Zones 10 and 11. In colder zones, you can treat them as annuals, replacing them every spring after the water is 70°F. Or take the tubers out of the pond, and bring them indoors before night temperatures fall below 50°F in fall. Store them in damp vermiculite or sand in a cool location. Tropical water lilies are either day- or night-blooming.

Tropical water lily 'Albert Greenberg'

Hardy water lily 'Margaret Griffith'

CARE AND MAINTENANCE

Like any container-grown plant, water plants need regular feeding. Special tablets formulated for water plants are easy to use—just push them into the soil; follow label directions for how frequently to use them. Hardy water lilies need to be divided every two or three years.

Water plants attract few pests. For these, you will need to decide how much damage you can tolerate before controls are warranted. If your pond contains fish or other wildlife, you can't use most pesticides. Control aphids on water lilies and other plants by knocking them into the water with a well-directed spray from the garden hose. Get rid of caterpillars with the biological control *Bacillus thuringiensis* (BT), as well as by encouraging birds and beneficial insects. Good hygiene helps prevent pest and disease problems; it also keeps the water clear and inviting. Remove faded, diseased, and damaged plant parts as soon as you see them, and keep the water clear of leaves and other debris.

Within the first several weeks, your pond is likely to bloom with algae, even if you have followed the stocking guidelines for self-sustaining ponds. (See page 150.) As the plants mature and shade more of the water, the bloom should subside. If not, try adding additional oxygenating plants that compete with algae for nutrients or more snails to eat the algae. (Garden centers and catalogs that specialize in water plants will sell at least a couple of types of oxygenating plants.) As a last resort, you can try chemical controls designed for controlling algae in ponds—be sure to find one that won't harm other plants or fish.

Winter Care. Plants hardy in your region can be overwintered in the pond as long as the water doesn't freeze to the bottom. The layer of ice on the surface serves as insulation. Cut back foliage after a killing frost, and place plant containers on the pond bottom. Fish can also overwinter under the ice, but you'll need to maintain an unfrozen area with an electric pond deicer to allow harmful gases to escape.

SOME RECOMMENDED WATER PLANTS

PLANT NAMES	COMMENTS
DEEP-WATER PLANTS	
Hardy water lilies (*Nymphaea* species)	Numerous cultivars with striking, slightly fragrant star-shaped flowers in a range of colors. Leaves float on water surface, flowers just above. Hardy to Zones 3 or 4.
Tropical water lilies (*Nymphaea* species)	Numerous cultivars producing larger flowers in greater quantities than hardy water lilies; flowers are intensely fragrant. Look for night-blooming as well as day-blooming cultivars. Hardy in Zones 10 and 11; grow as annuals in the north or overwinter indoors.
MID-DEPTH PLANTS	
Lotus (Nelumbo species)	Large, beautiful flowers and handsome leaves up to 2 ft. across rise above the surface of the water to heights of 5 ft. Equally attractive seedpods. Heat lovers, they bloom in late summer. Need large pots and lots of feeding. Plant 6 to 24 in. deep. Most are hardy to Zone 5 if summers are hot.
SHALLOW-WATER PLANTS	
Arrowhead (*Sagittaria* species)	Named for the distinctive leaf shape; leaves rise several feet above water. Smallish flowers borne on spikes in mid- to late summer. *S. sinensis* contributes oxygen to the water; sword-shaped leaves grow to 3 ft. tall. Zone 4.
Cattail (*Typha* species)	A favorite of children, featuring long grassy leaves and familiar cigar-shaped catkins. For water gardens, look for *T. laxmanii,* which is smaller and spreads less vigorously than common cattail. Zone 3.
Dwarf papyrus (*Cyperus* isocladus)	Large pom-poms of spiky, light green foliage are borne at the ends of thin, reedlike stems 2 to 3 ft. tall. This tropical plant is grown as an annual or overwintered indoors. Zone 8.
Iris (*Iris* species)	Some of the most beautiful flowering plants, yellow flag, blue flag, and Louisiana iris will grow with "wet feet." *I. laevigata* 'Variegata' is grown for its striped leaves. Zones vary with species; most are hardy to Zone 4.

East Indian lotus

Taro (*Araceae*), foreground, and dwarf papyrus

PLANT NAMES	COMMENTS
SHALLOW-WATER PLANTS (Continued)	
Pickerel rush (*Pontederia* cordata)	Lance-shaped leaves are carried on 2-ft. stalks. In late summer, long-blooming spikes of starlike blue flowers appear. Zone 3.
Sweet flag (*Acorus* species)	Grown for grassy, iris-like foliage. There are striped (variegated) types as well as smaller cultivars. Zone 4.
Water snowflake (*Nymphoides* species)	Leaves look like small water lily leaves. Fragrant, star-shaped white flowers appear in summer. These spread aggressively. Zone 7.
WET-SOIL PLANTS	
Cardinal flower (*Lobelia cardinalis*)	Spikes of lovely red flowers rise to 3 to 4 ft. above the soil surface in late summer. Zone 4.
Japanese primrose (*Primula japonica*)	Tall stalks bear red, pink, or white flowers in a whorled candelabra. Zone 5.
Marsh marigold (*Caltha palustris*)	Cheerful buttercup flowers and bright green foliage in spring or early summer. Plant dies back and goes dormant about a month after flowering. Zone 4.
SUBMERGED AND FREE-FLOATING PLANTS	
Anacharis (*Elodea canadensis*)	Excellent, hardy oxygenating plant that grows submerged. In deep water that doesn't freeze, it is hardy to Zone 3.
Water lettuce (*Pistia stratiotes*)	The little lettuces look like a floating salad display. Outlawed in many Southern states because it is highly invasive; check before you purchase. Zone 8.
Water milfoil (*Myriophyllum aquaticum*)	An oxygenator with feathery leaves that are bright yellow-green, tipped red in autumn, and rise several inches out of the water. Zone 6.

Marsh marigold

Water lettuce

CHAPTER 11

Vegetables

One of the great pleasures of gardening is eating tasty vegetables you've grown yourself. This is true whether you harvest tomatoes, potatoes, and melons by the bushel from a quarter-acre plot or pluck the occasional lettuce or pepper from a patio planter. A vegetable garden is the first garden for many people, and an excellent gardening introduction for children. The plants are not difficult to grow and the rewards are quick in coming—a recipe for enjoyment in any age group.

Planning a Vegetable Garden

Few people think of laying out a plot of vegetables as garden design. While the criteria can be very different from those for designing a perennial border, the process is similar: you need to figure out what plants go where, for what purpose, and to what effect. Culinary choices are usually more important than aesthetic ones. Rather than just placing plants to please the eye, you position them to maximize yield, make the best use of available space, avoid pest and disease problems, and provide easy access for maintenance and harvesting. But there is no reason why a vegetable garden can't be a treat for the eye as well as the taste buds. Choosing vegetable plants for their color, texture, or form, as well as their taste, and combining them imaginatively—sometimes along with ornamental plants—can produce strikingly handsome "edible landscapes," as they've come to be called.

If this is your first vegetable garden, start small. When you look out the window in early spring, it's tempting to imagine a bountiful garden that supplies many of your family's food needs. But remember that vegetable gardens are a lot of work—invigorating and rewarding, yes, but work nonetheless. A modest start will keep you from becoming overwhelmed. And you'll be pleasantly surprised

Plan your vegetable garden, above, to be a treat for the eye while it also provides an optimal growing environment.

Vegetable gardens are an introduction to the joys of gardening for many people, opposite.

PLANNING GUIDELINES

- Choose a good garden site.
- Prepare and improve the soil.
- Select pest- and disease-resistant plants suitable for your region and local conditions.
- Plant, space, support, and water the plants correctly.
- Control weeds, pests, and diseases.

at how much foodstuff you can grow in a 10 x 10-foot plot.

Some gardeners plan and record the layout of their vegetable garden on paper; others make a plan in their head or evolve one as they plant. A paper plan provides a handy record where you can jot down notes about what worked and what didn't as well as ideas for next year. Keep your plans in a notebook—it's fun to go over plans and notes from previous years.

Choosing a Site

Putting a vegetable garden in the wrong place can reduce crop yields and cause you headaches, no matter how well you choose and care for your plants. Good soil is an advantage, but most soils can be improved. Location is more important. The garden needs to fit in with other activities and plantings on your property, as discussed in Chapter 1, pages 8–9. But in addition, look for a spot that receives sun for at least six hours a day and is well away from trees, whose roots will compete with vegetables for water and nutrients. A flat or slightly sloping site is best. Avoid steep slopes and low areas where water puddles after a rain. If your property is windy, look for a sheltered spot. In many areas, vegetable gardens require regular watering to supplement rainfall, so convenient access to an outdoor water faucet will cut your work load. Finally, don't hide your garden away. A garden you walk by every day will be better cared for, more attractive, and more productive than one at the far end of the yard where no one ever goes.

If your site isn't ideal, don't despair. Most problems can be solved. You can remove or prune trees to increase sunlight. Where soil is really bad or poorly drained, you can build raised beds and fill them with improved soil or purchased topsoil. Terraces can make steep slopes usable. Dense hedges or vine-covered fences block strong winds. And lastly, if your property poses just too many problems or you want to grow only a few vegetables, you can make a containerized vegetable garden on a deck or patio.

Raised beds transform sites with poor soils but good exposure into ideal gardening areas.

Good Soil

Like their ornamental counterparts, healthy, high-yielding vegetables thrive in healthy soil—fertile and well drained but moisture retentive. The methods of soil evaluation and improvement discussed in Chapter 2, pages 28–31, apply equally to vegetable gardens. The main difference between beds for vegetables and those for perennials and shrubs is that you can extensively rework and improve the soil in a vegetable garden every year. You can conduct regular soil tests to check on pH and levels of various nutrients, and add amendments to correct problems when you prepare the bed in autumn or spring.

Gardeners in cold-winter areas often prepare vegetable beds in two stages. After cleaning up debris from the fall harvest, they turn the soil with a spade or rotary tiller to incorporate manure, straw, or chopped-up leaves that will begin decomposing during the winter. They may plant a winter cover crop of rye or a similar "green manure" plant. (See the box below.) In spring, they redig the bed as soon as

smart tip

GREEN MANURE

If you want to save money or don't have easy access to other sources of organic matter, you can improve soil with a "green manure." For the price of a few seeds, you can grow large quantities of organic matter right where you need it, no hauling needed. Common green manures (also called cover crops) are quick-growing grains, such as winter rye or buckwheat, and nitrogen-fixing legumes, such as clover or soybeans. Planted in the fall or spring or between vegetable crops, these green manure crops are mowed short and then dug or tilled into the beds a few weeks before you want to plant vegetables. (A rotary tiller makes this job much easier.) While growing, green manures protect the soil surface from erosion by wind or water, and their roots help loosen compacted soil. Turned into the soil, they provide lots of organic matter as they decompose, improving soil tilth and fertility.

Green manures are excellent for improving poor soils as well as for adding organic matter. They occupy the soil for at least a month, depending on the crop and its purpose, so it takes some planning to use them well. To learn how to use these crops in your region, ask for information from the local Cooperative Extension Service.

the soil can be worked. At this time, they turn in any cover crops that have been growing and incorporate compost and any fertilizers they might be using. While lime works best if added in the fall, fertilizers are best added in spring; otherwise, many of their immediately available nutrients will leach away with winter snows and spring rains.

In warm-winter regions, gardeners often grow vegetables throughout the year. Organic matter decomposes faster and must be replenished more often where winters are warm. Without a cold fallow period, warm-winter gardeners amend and work the soil between the harvest of one crop and the planting of the next.

There are many schools of thought on soil preparation for vegetable gardens. Some people add only organic amendments and organic fertilizers; others use synthetic fertilizers. And still others build the soil with compost and organic amendments and then keep tilling to a minimum. The methods of soil preparation and maintenance outlined in Chapters 2 and 3, pages 22–31 and 36–37 will get you started and can serve for years.

Good soil for vegetable gardens is guaranteed with a steady supply of organic mulch. Organic mulches improve the soil structure and provide plant nutrients as they decompose.

WHAT TO GROW?

Vegetable gardeners often cherish tradition. It's a pleasure to grow the same beans your grandmother planted—particularly if you grow them from seeds saved year after year. But it's also fun to try something new. The number of different vegetables is much broader than the usual supermarket fare, and the variety within each type is remarkable. Don't be afraid to explore this cornucopia. Plant a salad garden with a dozen different leaf lettuces, or try some of those intriguing purple potatoes. How about the world's hottest chili pepper? Or the coolest watermelon? An increasing number of nurseries and garden centers are offering a greater range of vegetables and varieties on their seed racks. If you wish to search even farther afield, there are numerous specialty mail-order suppliers.

When making choices, remember that plants adapted to conditions in your region will give the greatest yields with the fewest problems. A local Cooperative Extension Service will be able to recommend crops and cultivars that are proven performers in your area. Each region also has nurseries that specialize in

Heirloom vegetables, such as these 'Moon and Stars' watermelons, often have better flavor than modern hybrids but may be less disease-resistant.

plants adapted to local conditions. Plant breeders have developed disease- and pest-resistant cultivars of many common vegetables. Their hard work can save you from battles in the garden.

Laying Out the Beds

Most of us imagine a vegetable garden as a rectangle with rows of plants. This layout is easy to tend, water, and harvest. But vegetable gardens can be different shapes and configurations to suit the layout of the property or the habits or whims of the gardener. When planning your bed, keep the following considerations in mind.

Ensure Access. Be sure to provide adequate access for planting, maintenance, and harvest. Establish permanent walkways wide enough to accommodate a wheelbarrow or basket. Lay out beds and paths so that you can reach most plants (sprawlers like squash and melons excepted) without walking on the beds.

Consider Height and Spread. Plant tall crops (corn, tomatoes, and trellised cucumbers or pole beans) on the north side of the garden, so they won't shade the other vegetables. Be sure to give sprawling plants such as squashes, cucumbers, and melons enough room, or they'll engulf the rest of your garden. If space is at a premium, consider growing these plants on trellises. (You'll need to support heavier fruit. Some people wrap them in old panty hose tied to the trellis.)

Try Intercropping. To make best use of limited space, consider intercropping. Sow fast-growing plants, such as radishes, among slower-growing crops, such as tomatoes or zucchini. The fast growers will be harvested before the slowpokes have taken over the space. You can combine aboveground crops with root vegetables, too. Plant lettuce, for instance, among the carrots or beets. Midsummer lettuce and other salad crops can also profit from tall plants. Plant them to the east of a row of corn or pole beans so that they'll be shaded from afternoon heat.

Use Succession Planting. If your climate permits, plan to use space in a bed for crops planted in succession. Gardeners in warm-winter regions, for example, often grow vegetables throughout the year. In spring they plant warm-season crops such as corn, tomatoes, peppers, squash, cucumbers, okra, and eggplants. These plants thrive in hot weather and are harvested throughout the summer and fall. In fall and very early spring, they plant cool-season crops such as lettuce, spinach, salad greens, cabbage, broccoli, cauliflower, peas, and onions. These crops grow best in cooler temperatures and can even survive some frost. They are harvested through the winter and into summer, before temperatures rise too high.

Northern gardeners can plant some cool-weather crops in early spring for harvest in late spring, and plant others in midsummer to late summer for harvest in late fall—if the winter cold and summer heat don't interfere. Where the growing season is short, you either grow everything at the same time or rely on season-extending practices and equipment. (See page 160.)

Provide Proper Spacing. Proper spacing is particularly important for vegetable crops. These plants tend to be more enticing to pests and diseases than many ornamentals; when crowded, they become particularly vulnerable. Yields are also reduced as a consequence of increased competition for water, nutrients, and sunlight. Follow the recommendations on seed packets for spacing. In free-form gardens or those in which you can reach everything from a path, you may wish to plant in blocks. If so, ignore the wider row-spacing recommendations, but maintain the recommended spacings between plants within the block.

Intercropping flowering ornamentals among the vegetables gives beneficial insects nectar, pollen, and protected niches where they can lay eggs, pupate, and find midday shade.

Planting and Care

The techniques for planting vegetable seedlings and seeds, whether inside in containers or direct-seeded in the garden, are the same as those described in Chapter 4 for ornamentals. Remember that frost or cool soil temperatures kills or retards the growth of many plants and seeds. Seed packets and plant tags provide planting times and all the other basic information you need about how to sow seeds or space seedlings.

Vegetable and ornamental plantings have many of the same requirements for ongoing care—support, feeding, weeding, and watering—as discussed in Chapter 3, pages 32–38. Some vegetables need to be staked, caged, or trellised to take up less space or to keep the fruit clean and healthy.

NUTRIENTS

Vegetables are hungry plants. Even with rich, fertile soil and a mulch of good-quality compost, you may need to provide additional nutrients to boost size or yield. Use the same fertilizers as for ornamentals, as described in Chapter 2, pages 24–25. Follow package recommendations for timing and amounts. As a general rule, fruiting crops such as tomatoes and peppers perform best if given supplemental fertilization when their first flowers are opening. Leafy crops such as spinach and lettuce thrive if their soil is fertilized a week or two before they are planted. Root crops, on the other hand, respond best to soils that were heavily fertilized with slow-release organic materials the year before they are planted. It's wise to plant them where you grew (and fertilized) squash or corn, both heavy feeders, the year before.

WATER

Vegetables do best with a steady supply of moisture. An average of 1 inch of water a week is ideal for most, though many vegetables can survive for two or three weeks with no rain or watering at all. In most areas of the country, vegetables do best with more water than nature usually delivers. You can water young seedlings and individual plants by hand with a watering can or hose, but these methods are impractical for all but the smallest plots. Overhead sprinklers can be left running until enough water has been delivered. But they waste water in hot or windy weather, and they wet leaves

VEGETABLE SUPPORTS

Stake or cage tomatoes to keep them from sprawling all over the garden and to protect the fruit from damage. You can tie the stems to a sturdy wooden, bamboo, or metal stake. Or surround the plants with a homemade cage or one bought at a nursery or garden center. Install stakes and cages when you first set the plants in the garden.

Support pole beans and cucumbers with tepees or mesh trellises. To make a tepee, form a tripod or circle with three or more 6- to 7-ft.-tall poles (bamboo works well). Push the bottom ends about 1 foot into the soil, gather the top ends together, and tie with twine. Staple mesh trellises to sturdy posts set 1–2 ft. into the soil.

Support low-growing plants such as dwarf peas with twine or mesh trellises. You can also poke some twiggy brush into the row when you sow the seeds. The plants will grow through the brush. Supports keep stems and pods off the ground, allow easier harvesting, and promote healthier, more disease-free growth.

as well as roots, providing a breeding ground for fungal diseases in dense foliage. The most practical and healthful way to water vegetables is with a soaker hose or drip-irrigation system. (See Chapter 3, pages 34–35.) Both methods deliver water to the root zone, and some drip systems can be set up to supply individual plants as well as rows. Set up a timer with a soaker hose or drip system; you can save time while providing plants with a reliable water supply.

Water your vegetable garden with a drip irrigation system to provide reliably good growing conditions while conserving water.

EXTENDING THE SEASON

Gardeners in areas where spring and fall frosts circumscribe the growing season can employ a number of materials and techniques to extend the season. While these practices add some cost and labor, many gardeners find that the pleasure of eating home-grown vegetables through more of the year is ample reward.

In the spring, protect crops from late frosts by covering them with polyester row covers, plastic tunnels, fiberglass cones, or homemade devices such as plastic gallon jugs with the bottoms cut out. An innovative product also protects against frosts by enclosing plants in a circle of insulating water-filled tubes. As soon as the weather warms sufficiently or the flowers begin to open, remove the season extension devices so that insects can pollinate the blooms.

Northerners whose growing season is too short and whose soil is too cool for heat-loving plants such as watermelons, eggplants,

and peppers, can grow these crops by mulching with black or infra-red transmitting (IRT) plastic film or black mulching paper. Lay the mulch one to two weeks before planting, and insert the transplants through Xs cut in the mulch. Remove plastic mulch at the end of the growing season, or it will degrade into small shards that you'll be picking out of the soil for years to come.

In midsummer, plastic or fabric shade cloth creates a cooler environment for cool-season crops such as lettuce or broccoli. You can buy plastic shade netting from a garden supplier or make your own from hoops and burlap that has not been treated with fungicides.

In mild-winter areas, such as coastal portions of the Northwest, all but the most tender crops can grow through the winter when protected by row covers or plastic tunnels. In more northern areas, winter gardeners often use insulated cold frames or two plastic structures, one inside the other, to carry cold-hardy leafy crops such as kale, spinach, and Brussels sprouts through the winter.

Season-extending technologies can create a warmer or cooler environment. The plastic tunnel in the foreground raises temperatures for the cucumbers, while the shadecloth in the rear keeps the greens cool.

Cold frames extend the growing season long into the winter for cold-hardy crops such as lettuce, spinach, and some of the oriental greens.

Weeds

Weeds are generally a greater problem with new rather than established beds. After a few years of intense gardening, you'll have removed most of the perennial weeds and developed an eye for weed seedlings, which are easy to pull when young. With a sharp shuffle hoe you can work out weeds without even bending down. In a large vegetable garden you can till between rows to control weeds. If you use a herbicide, make sure it is approved for use with food plants, and follow instructions on the label to the letter.

You can reduce water consumption and weed problems simply by mulching your vegetable garden. After harvest, digging- or tilling-in an organic mulch helps replenish the soil. Straw (not hay, which harbors weed seeds), shredded leaves, dry grass clippings, compost, and even shredded newspapers make good mulches. Where you're transplanting seedlings, you can spread the mulch and then plant through it, keeping the mulch away from the plant's stems. You can mulch between rows and around hills when you sow seeds or after the plants are a few inches tall. Mulching with plastic sheeting is effective for heat-loving commercial vegetable crops, but unless you're in the North, these mulches are usually far more trouble than they're worth for home gardens. See "Extending the Season" (opposite) for more information.

Black plastic mulch is useful in northern areas where soils are too cool for fast healthy growth of warm-weather tomatoes and squash. Remember to remove plastic mulches at season's end.

Straw mulch reflects light back onto the plants, helping to keep the soil cool while increasing their light exposure.

Pests and Diseases

Techniques used to control insects and diseases in vegetable gardens are the same as those for ornamental plants. (See Chapter 3, pages 39–41 and 44–47.) However, you must be certain that any pesticides you use are approved for food crops. Also, you have an advantage over ornamental gardens: because production rather than beauty is your priority, you can use row covers to protect plants from invading insects. Prevention, rather than control, is always wisest in the vegetable garden. Pests or diseases can sometimes get out of hand, though, particularly during the first years when you're building soil health and creating a balanced ecosystem. If you find that you need to control a pest or disease, choose the least-toxic methods or substances first; try handpicking bugs into a jar of soapy water or hosing off plants. Save pesticides, even those that are botanical or mineral, as a last resort.

Praying mantids are known for their pest-hunting prowess but they're just as likely to eat a ladybug as an aphid.

Gallery of Vegetables

This gallery contains the most common and easy-to-grow vegetables. Start with these crops, and add the more difficult ones, such as globe artichokes and Belgian endive, after you've learned to grow these basic types.

Descriptions include comments on common pests and diseases, but not all the pests and diseases that may afflict the plant. Cultural or least-toxic controls are also given. If your plants suffer from a problem you can't identify or if you would like to learn about additional controls effective in your area, take samples to a local nursery or Cooperative Extension Service.

BEAN (*Phaseolus vulgaris* var. *humilis*)
String, or green, beans are easy to grow and harvest. Gardeners often grow both bush and pole types as well as yellow, purple, and green cultivars. Beyond this, you can choose the flat-podded romanos, thin little filet verts, or yard-long Chinese beans.

Plant beans after the frost-free date; they won't germinate in cold soil. They require **full sun** and well-drained soil of moderate fertility and a pH of 6.3 to 6.8. To increase yields, apply "garden pea and bean innoculant" to the soil when you plant. Mexican bean beetles are the most common pests. Remove the vines at the end of the season, and practice good garden sanitation to decrease the beetles' overwintering sites. Handpick or use a botanical insecticide derived from the neem tree to control heavy infestations.

BEET (*Beta vulgaris* species *vulgaris*) and
SWISS CHARD (*Beta vulgaris* var. *flavescens*)
Beets are a double-duty crop, providing edible greens as well as roots. Swiss chard is grown only for its leaves. Both crops grow best in moderatelyfertile soils with steady moisture supplies and a pH of 6.0 to 7.0. The **sunny days and cool nights** of spring and fall stimulate the best growth, but both crops tolerate summer conditions.

In spring, direct-seed these crops a week or two after the soil can be worked. Space seeds about 3 inches apart in the row. Because each seed is actually a fruit that contains several seeds, this spacing will yield more than enough plants. Thin out the extras once they're big enough to eat as greensor baby beets.

Time the planting of fall beet and chard crops so that they will mature near the first expected frost. (Seed packets usually indicate days to maturity.) Harvest beets before severe frost. You can leave the Swiss chard in the garden, harvesting the outside leaves of each plant as long as possible. Use row covers or plastic tunnels to protect plants from the snow (and deer), and you can extend the season many months past frost.

BROCCOLI, BRUSSELS SPROUTS, CABBAGE, AND CAULIFLOWER
(*Brassica oleracea*)
Diverse as they appear to be, broccoli, cauliflower, cabbage, and Brussels sprouts all belong to the same species. Gardeners often refer to these crops as "brassicas" and save "crucifer," the family name (which designates a much larger group of plants), for the smaller family members,

Beans

Beets

which include arugula, kale (page 165), kohlrabi, mustards, radishes, rutabagas, and turnips.

Brassicas all require the same growing conditions—**full sun,** high soil fertility, steady moisture, a pH of 6.0 to 6.8 and cool temperatures. Different cultivars perform better in different regions and at different times of year. Local suppliers usually provide seeds selected for your region or particular seasons. Specialty mail-order suppliers can also advise you.

Most people grow or buy seedlings to transplant into the garden. All crucifers, including the brassicas, tolerate cool temperatures and can be planted two to three weeks before the last expected frost. To extend the summer harvest, direct-seed some heat-resistant cultivars, such as 'Saga' broccoli, when you transplant the spring seedlings. These plants will mature a month to six weeks later than the transplants. For fall crops, check the "days to maturity" listing on seed packets and direct-seed or transplant so that plants will mature 1 to 2 weeks after the first expected frost.

Common pests include cabbage root fly maggots, flea beetles, imported cabbage moth caterpillars, and cabbage loopers. Cover spring and early summer crops with row covers to prevent cabbage root flies from laying eggs near the plants. These covers should also protect against flea beetles. Pick off all the caterpillars you see. If they become truly damaging, apply an insecticide containing *Bacillus thuringiensis.* This bacterium, commonly called "BT," kills young caterpillars.

Club root is the most damaging disease. A soil-borne fungus that survives for years even without a host, it produces swollen, "club-shaped" roots in infected plants. Avoid it by planting in soil with a pH of 6.5 to 7.0 and using only healthy transplants. Other diseases include powdery mildew and black rot, both of which can be avoided by good garden sanitation and adequate spacing so that plants are not crowded.

CARROT (*Daucus carota* species *sativus*)
Homegrown carrots taste so much better than store-bought that even children ask for them. Carrots require **full sun,** deep, light soils with high fertility, a pH of 5.5 to 6.8 and steady moisture levels. To avoid forked roots, remove rocks from the soil where they will grow. Carrots will grow well in most climates if provided with adequate moisture.

Plant carrot seeds when the spring soil is beginning to warm. Seeds can take up to three weeks to germinate. Mix the seeds with dry sand or vermiculite to make proper spacing easier. After the first or second true leaves appear, thin plants to an inch or two apart. Harvesting baby carrots gives the remaining plants more room to grow. In good soil, you can grow carrots in a broadcast fashion; thin to 2 inches between plants.

Problems are rare for carrots growing in good soil, although many pests and a few diseases attack them. Carrot rust-fly maggots eat long channels on the root surfaces. A 2-foot-high "fence" of row cover material can exclude the low-flying mother flies. Beneficial nematodes are another control. Split roots are a sign of inconsistent soil moisture levels. Green shoulders occur when the top of the carrot pushes out of the soil.

Carrot

Broccoli

Cabbage

Brussels sprouts

Cauliflower

SWEET CORN (*Zea mays*)

Garden-fresh sweet corn is a treat, with a taste even better than "fresh" corn from a roadside stand. Corn is easy to grow but a heavy feeder. Even in fertile soil, you'll need to provide additional nutrients, especially nitrogen.

In general, sweet corn requires a long growing season with **full sun,** plenty of warm or hot weather, a pH of 5.5 to 6.8, and consistently moist soil. There are good cultivars for shorter growing seasons and cooler climates, so seek out cultivars adapted to your region. To extend your harvest, plant several cultivars with staggered maturity dates.

After all danger of frost is past, plant corn in blocks of at least four rows each so that the wind-blown pollen will reach the silks. Once the plants are 4 to 6 inches tall, thin them to the spacing recommended on the packet. Hill up soil around the stalks periodically to stabilize plants. Harvest ears when the kernals are plump and the liquid in them is milky-colored.

A number of pests and diseases attack corn, particularly in less-than-ideal soils. Corn earworms and European corn borers are both caterpillar pests. To discourage earworms, wrap rubber bands tightly around the tip of each ear, or apply about 10 drops of mineral oil just inside the husk tips. Many beneficial insects attack these pests, so avoid using any pesticides if you can. Try *Bacillus heliothis* against earworms and *Bacillus thuringiensis* (BT) for corn borers; both will spare beneficial insect predators. The best defense against corn diseases is highly fertile soil. For many people, raccoons are the bane of the corn patch. Fence the garden as shown in Chapter 3, page 42. If that fails and you're truly desparate to eat a few ears of your own crop, wrap nearly mature ears with small paper sacks and chicken wire.

CUCUMBER (*Cucumis sativus*)

Grown for use fresh in salads and sandwiches or for pickling in brine, cucumbers are traditional garden staples. All cucumbers were once vining crops, growing 10 to 15 feet in length. But today, bush types, ideal for small gardens or containers, are also available.

Cucumbers require at least **six hours of bright sun** a day and grow best in rich, well-drained soils with a pH of 6.5 to 7.5 and steady moisture levels. They like hot, humid weather and can be grown almost anywhere, but have a short growing season and can be damaged by temperatures below 50°F. Direct-seed in rows or hills after all danger of frost has passed. If you buy seedlings, get those in peat pots—cucumbers don't tolerate root disturbance during transplanting. Allow ample room for the plants to spread. Or grow them on a fence or trellis.

Pests and diseases love cucumbers. You'll see squash bugs, aphids, and cucumber beetles on your plants. Handpick the squash bugs, and let ladybugs and other native beneficial insects prey on the aphids. To avoid cucumber beetles, use floating row covers until the flowers open and need to be pollinated by flying insects. If these measures fail, ask at your nursery for a pyrethrin-based insecticide. Cucumbers are susceptible to scab, mosiac virus, and several mildews. Fortunately, disease-resistant cultivars are available. Another lethal disease, bacterial wilt, is transmitted by feeding cucumber beetles. Gardeners who have lost plants to this disease plant a second crop of cucumbers each year, generally at the end of June or in July, depending on location. This crop prolongs the harvest until frost. In most years, a double layer of plastic or floating row covers will protect plants through the first fall frosts.

Sweet Corn   Cucumber

EGGPLANT (*Solanum melongena*)

With their shiny, taut-skinned fruits in shades of deep purple, rose, white, orange, or bicolors, eggplants are worth growing just for their appearance. They're indispensable if you like Mediterranean-style cooking. This close relative of tomatoes, potatoes, and petunias requires a long growing season, high temperatures, **full sun,** steady moisture, and a pH of 5.5 to 6.8.

Starting from seeds can be tricky, so most novices and many veteran growers buy seedlings. (To start your own, sow seed indoors 8–10 weeks before the last frost, and wait to harden off the plants until a week or so later.) Set plants in the garden when daytime temperatures have reached 70°F. Northern gardeners can plant fast-maturing varieties or extend the season by warming the soil with a plastic mulch and protecting seedlings during the first part of the season. (See "Extending the Season," page 160.) Uncover plants when they bloom, but replace the covers if nights cool below 60°F.

Eggplant tastes best when it's young, so harvest it while the skin is still glossy. White fruits and the slender Japanese types tend to be sweeter than the traditional "eggplant-shaped" fruits. See "Tomato," page 171, for common pests and diseases.

KALE (*Brassica oleracea,* Acephala group)

Eaten young and tender as salad greens or cooked when mature, kale is among the most nutritious of vegetables. Some colorful cultivars are grown as ornamentals or used as attractive garnishes. You can thank Ben Franklin for introducing this Scottish native to America. In keeping with its origins, kale is remarkably hardy. It grows year-round in areas where winter temperatures remain at 40°F or above and survives temperatures of –10°F. Even in northern areas, gardeners who use season-extending methods can expect to harvest mature plants long into the winter.

Kale has the same growing requirements as its close relatives, broccoli and the other brassicas. (See pages 162–163.) Direct-seed as soon as the soil can be worked in the spring and, for a fall crop, again in midsummer. Kale tastes best once it's been touched with frost, so most people grow their main crop in the fall. The cultivars 'Red Russian' and 'Wild Garden' are particularly tender. Kale is usually free of pest and disease problems; those from which it may suffer are the same as for broccoli and other brassicas.

LEEK (*Allium porrum*)

The sophisticate of the onion family, leeks are surprisingly easy to grow. They require **full sun,** high fertility, a pH of 6.0 to 7.0, long growing season, and cool temperatures, but will tolerate heat if kept well-watered. To grow from seed, sow indoors 10 to 12 weeks before the last frost date, and transplant to the garden when seedlings are 4 to 8 inches high. If severe late frosts are predicted, protect seedlings with a covering. In warmer areas (Zone 6 and higher) or when planting short-season cultivars, you can plant seed directly in the garden in early spring.

To produce long, tender white stems, blanch them by planting the seedlings in a deep furrow and backfilling to cover only the roots and stem bottom. As the plants grow, continue to heap soil around the stems. You can also grow leeks without blanching. The white area will be a little shorter, but the leeks are still tasty.

Leeks stand fall frosts extremely well, surviving over the winter in many parts of the country. In the North, prolong your harvests by piling mulch over the plants once temperatures are routinely below freezing. The mulch keeps the soil warm enough so that you can continue to dig them into the winter months.

Leeks are generally trouble-free but can develop some of the same problems as onions. (See page 167.)

Kale

Leek

Eggplant

LETTUCE (*Lactuca sativa*)

Homegrown lettuce is one of the delights of the home vegetable garden. You can grow far more types than are available in grocery stores and eat them garden-fresh. A wide range of leaf types—crinkled and smooth, tender and crisp, loose and tightly bunched—in a selection of reds, bronzes, or greens will make your salads as pleasing to the eye as to the palate. Specialty seed companies offer the widest range of lettuce types.

Lettuce requires rich, well-drained soil, con-sistantly high moisture levels, and a pH of 5.8 to 7.0. Lettuce prefers cool weather but can toler-ate temperatures into the 80s. It thrives in **full sun (cool climates) to partial shade (warm climates).** In hot weather many varieties *"bolt,"* rapidly flowering and setting seed, and the leaves wilt or become tough and bitter. Heat-tolerant cultivars are available.

Baby leaves can be harvested in as little as 28 to 35 days from seeding. Long-season types take 75 days to mature, but the majority of let-tuces need only 45 to 55 days. This short season makes succession planting practical. Start the first crops inside about 8 weeks before the frost-free date, and transplant them 2 weeks before that date. Start successive crops every week to 10 days after that. (You can also buy seedlings or direct-seed into the garden.)In mild-summer cli-mates, succession planting will guarantee salads through the summer and into fall. In mild-winter climates, fall-planted crops can provide harvests through the winter.

In good soil, lettuces suffer very few prob-lems. If possible, spread a layer of compost 1 to 2 inches deep before you plant. Bottom leaves often rot in soils that are not well-enough drained and in plantings that are too crowded. (If rotting begins, remove and destroy the crop to avoid a spread of problems.) Allow a square foot for every plant of head lettuce. For leafy types, plant seed-lings or thin direct-sown plants to about 3 inches apart; thin further by harvesting small plants. Extend your harvest of leafy lettuces by picking outer leaves from mature plants.

Lettuce

Muskmelon

Watermelon

MELONS: MUSKMELON (*Cucumis melo*, Reticulatus group), CANTALOUPE (*C. melo*, Cantalupensis group), HONEYDEW (*C. melo*, Inodorus group), AND WATER-MELON (*Citrullus lanatus*)

Homegrown melons fresh from the garden are a splendid summer treat, much tastier than store-bought melons that are picked long before they're ripe. Melons require **full sun,** a long growing season, high temperatures, constant moisture, and well-drained, fertile soils high in organic mat-ter with a pH between 6.5 and 7.0. They need nighttime temperatures of 50°F or above and day-time temperatures of 80°F or more. If your climate doesn't provide these conditions, try one of the faster maturing hybrids, and extend the season with plastic mulch and tunnels or row covers as described on page 160.

Most cultivars are vining and take a great deal of space, but some of the newer hybrids are bushy or relatively small. You can also train melon vines on trellises or fences, but you have to support the heavy fruit. Depending on your location and the plant's days to maturity, you can start seeds indoors 4 weeks before the last frost. Transplant seedlings (purchased or home-grown), or sow seeds directly after the last frost and when day and night temperatures are warm.

Harvesting vine-ripened melons justifies the effort and space these plants require. So learning when to harvest is important. Most cantaloupes "slip" from the vine when they're ripe, mean-ing they will come off the vine if you apply slight pressure with your thumb where the fruit and vine meet. To harvest other melons (and some canta-loupes), you have to learn to gauge ripeness. Fra-grance is the best indicator for cantaloupes. For watermelons and other thick-skinned types, you can use three measures. First, check to see that the small tendril just above the fruit has shriveled and browned. Then look to see that the yellow spot on the bottom of the fruit is large and really yellow. Third, knock on the fruit and listen for a deep, resonant tone. With practice, these indica-tors will become easy to read.

Melons suffer from the same pests and diseases as cucumbers and squashes. (See pages 164, 170.)

ONION (*Allium cepa*), **GARLIC** (*A. sativum*), **AND SHALLOT** (*A. cepa*, Aggregatum group)

Onion and garlic are indispensable ingredients in cuisines from the rustic to the most refined. Young onions, called scallions or green onions, are harvested when their bulbs are small and the aromatic, grassy foliage is tender. Mature onions are harvested for the large bulb. You can harvest any onion for use as scallions, but certain cultivars are valued for that purpose, as others are valued for their mature bulbs. Shallots form clumps of up to a dozen bulbs. Garlic bulbs form meaty wedge-shaped sections instead of concentric layers.

Onion-family plants require well-drained, fertile soil and a pH of 6.0 to 6.5. Day length, temperatures, and moisture levels all affect onions; choose cultivars adapted to your conditions. (Purchase seeds, sets, and plants locally.) In most areas, onions require **full sun,** although they tolerate partial shade in warm-weather regions.

Onions are planted as seeds, seedlings, and sets (small bulbs), depending on type and gardener's preference. Shallots are usually planted as sets. To grow onions from seeds, sow inside 8 to 10 weeks before the frost-free date. Transplant purchased or home-grown seedlings into the garden 2 weeks before the last frost date. If your growing season is long or you've chosen fast-maturing types, you can direct-seed in the garden 2 weeks before the last frost date.

Many gardeners prefer onion sets to seeds or seedlings. They're easier to handle and mature more quickly than seed-grown onions. Plant both types to harvest fresh onions over a longer period. Selection of cultivars is more limited using sets. Plant sets as soon as the ground can be worked in the spring.

Scallions can be harvested as soon as they are large enough to eat. For fresh eating, you can harvest mature onions this way too. However, if you want to store an onion crop, bend the leaves to the ground a few weeks before you plan to pull the bulbs. The tops will brown and dry, and the necks will shrink. After you pull the bulbs, let their skins dry in a warm, bright spot for approximately a week or so. Once the skins rustle, store the bulbs in net bags in a cool but not freezing area.

Shallot sets are planted in early spring or, in mild-winter areas, in late fall. In recent years, shallot seeds have become available. Direct-seed them in the garden as soon as the soil can be worked in the spring. Harvest and cure shallots as you would onions.

Garlic bulbs are best planted in the fall, just about tulip-planting time. Mulch after the ground has frozen. In spring, pull the mulch back once the tops have begun to grow, but be ready to cover the plants up if severe frost threatens. Harvest fall-planted garlic in mid-July, without knocking over the tops. Cure and store as you would onions.

Onion maggots and thrips are common onion-family problems. Once maggots infest a crop, it is lost. Destroy infected plants, and treat the soil with beneficial nematodes (available at many garden centers). Onion thrips eat the interior parts of the leaves, giving them a silvery appearance. Insecticidal soap kills them. A number of fungal diseases attack onions. The best defense is good prevention. Plant resistant varieties, grow only in well-drained soil, and space plants properly. If fungal problems are serious, treat with copper- or sulfur-based fungicidal sprays.

Onions

Garlic

Peas

Pepper

PEA (*Pisum sativum*)

Fresh peas are a new taste sensation for most people. Eat tender snow peas, crunchy snap peas, or robust, freshly shelled English peas straight from the garden. Peas also freeze well and can be dried for use through the year. English, or shell, peas were once the most commonly grown. Today, gardeners are just as likely to grow snow peas and sugar (or snap) peas, both edible-podded.

Peas prefer cool temperatures, **full sun,** consistently moist, well-drained soil of moderate fertility, and a pH of 5.5 to 6.8. Plant them as soon as you can work the soil in the spring. (Late planting in hot-summer regions is risky, as peas don't mature after temperatures consistently rise above 70°F.) Some pea seeds are treated with fungicide to prevent their rotting in cool, damp soil. At planting, you can also add a soil innoculant (available at nurseries) which helps these legumes supply their own nitrogen. Peas will survive moderate frosts and can live through light snows with only a row cover for protection. Harvest peas at least every other day. Fresh peas are tender. If you let many pods mature, the vines will stop making flowers. In warm-winter regions, gardeners often plant peas in the late summer for a fall crop. This is ideal timing if the weather is not so humid that the plants get fungal diseases.

You can choose between bush and tall cultivars. It's tempting to think that the bush plants will not need support. However, yields are always higher and the peas healthier if they don't trail on the ground. Set up appropriately sized supports for all peas.

Fungal diseases are a major pea problem. The easiest way to prevent them is to move peas to a different part of the garden each year. Serious outbreaks can be treated with copper- or sulfur-based fungicides. Aphids carry pea mosaic, a fatal disease. You can help ladybugs and other indigenous beneficials keep aphids in check by washing the pests off leaves with a spray of water. To help avoid mildew during cool, damp weather, keep water off leaves by using drip irrigation or soaker hoses.

PEPPER (*Capsicum annuum* var. *annuum*)

Homegrown peppers are surprisingly flavorful and beautiful. You can choose sweet peppers in an array of vibrant greens, reds, or yellows, or grow hot peppers that range from mild to three-alarm. With a homegrown crop, you can enliven salads, add flavor to sauces, and make a variety of dishes from every corner of the world.

Peppers grow best when nighttime temperatures reach 60° to 65°F and days are hot, 85° to 90°F. They prefer **full sun** and moderately fertile soils with excellent drainage and a pH of 5.5 to 6.9. You can buy seeds and plants locally, but the greatest variety of peppers is offered as seeds by mail-order specialists. Start plants inside about 8 weeks before the frost-free date, and set them out about a week after the last frost. Where growing seasons are short, choose early varieties and extend your season. They thrive with the same sorts of season-extension practices as eggplants.

The characteristic grocery store "green" pepper is actually immature. As they ripen (which usually takes 10 to 15 days after reaching full size), some peppers will turn yellow or another exotic color, but most will turn red. Many people think the sweeter, more nutritious, and more colorful ripe peppers are worth the wait. Ripening peppers can be more vulnerable to pests and diseases. Avoid problems by cutting peppers off the vine when they are about half-colored and letting them finish ripening indoors.

Pests and diseases are similar to those for tomatoes. (See page 171.)

POTATO (*Solanum tuberosum*)

Growing enough potatoes to contribute much to a family's yearly supply takes a lot of garden space. But there are two good reasons to devote precious garden space to the lowly potato. The first is strictly culinary. Young potatoes harvested and eaten fresh from the garden have a delightful flavor and texture not found in a store-bought spud. The second is for fun and variety. There are potatoes of all colors except black and green, in sizes ranging from long skinny fingerlings to big fat bakers, and with textures running from waxy to dry. You won't find these at the store—or at the local nursery. Check specialty catalogs (advertised in the back of gardening magazines) to find unusual varieties.

Potatoes tolerate cool temperatures (but not frost) and can be planted about two weeks before the last frost date in the spring. They prefer **full sun** and fertile, well-drained acid soil with a pH between 5.5 and 6.5. They can be grown from sections cut from a large seed potato or from small seed potatoes planted whole. (Most grocery store potatoes have been treated with substances that inhibit sprouting—buy seed potatoes from a nursery or mail-order supplier.) A few days before you plant, cut large seed potatoes into pieces that weigh at least 3 ounces, with a minimum of one eye on each piece. Lay the seed pieces in a single layer on newspaper, and let the cuts callus over and dry. Plant the callused sections or whole small seed potatoes 1 to 2 feet apart (the supplier usually provides spacing recommendations). Cover them with 1 to 3 inches of soil.

Once sprouts are 5 to 6 inches tall, hill soil over the plants so that only the top two to four leaves show. Repeat this hilling procedure every 10 days to 2 weeks until the hills are about a foot high or the plants are beginning to bloom.

Maturity times vary with the cultivar. For the longest harvests, plant early, midseason, and late varieties. (Check with a supplier or local Cooperative Extension Service to determine the cultivars and planting schedules best for your region.) When the plants bloom you can begin to harvest tender young potatoes, called "new potatoes." To harvest full-grown potatoes, wait until the vines die back. Most potato vines die back naturally, but if they don't, cut them at ground level in early fall. You can dig the tubers immediately when vines die back or are cut. But if you want to store the potatoes, wait two weeks; this delay allows the skins to thicken enough to withstand long storage. After digging, cure potatoes by laying them out in a single layer, generally on top of a pad of newspaper, in a totally dark place. Do not wash them. Let the skins dry completely before carefully packing them in burlap bags or cardboard boxes. Store in a dark spot where temperatures remain just above freezing during the winter.

Exposing the skins of growing or harvested potatoes to light stimulates the tubers to produce certain compounds, including solamine, that can make you sick if you eat them in large quantities. Green-colored skin is the tip-off to this problem. To avoid having potatoes turn green, keep them well hilled while they are growing and, after harvest, put them in the dark immediately.

Potatoes are prey to many pests and diseases. Colorado potato beetles are the most common pest. Avoid them by mulching plants with dry straw, squash any orange eggs you might see on leaf undersides, and handpick the adults. Insecticidal soap and a strain of *Bacillus thuringiensis* (BT) offer additional protection. Fungal diseases are also common. To minimize problems, plant potatoes only in well-drained soil, and don't grow them in the same spot for at least four years. Treat the foliage with copper- or sulfur-based fungicides if necessary. Scab, a warty-looking disease of the skin, can usually be prevented by keeping the soil acidic (pH 6.0 or less). See "Tomato," page 171, for additional pests and diseases.

Potatoes

SPINACH (*Spinacia oleracea*)

Tasty crisp spinach leaves are a salad lover's delight. Spinach prefers **full or partial sun,** rich soil with high nitrogen content, a pH of 6.0 to 7.0, and high moisture levels. It is the first crop that many gardeners plant each year. As soon as the soil can be worked, long before the last frost date, spread an inch or two of fully finished compost over a bed and sow spinach. Plant again every week to 10 days. Spinach is a cool-weather crop. Where summers are mild, gardeners can harvest well into the summer fromsowings that are made until daytime temperatures consistently reach 70°F. In midsummer to late summer, they can begin planting fall crops.

(Continued on next page)

Spinach

Zucchini squash

Acorn winter squash

Butternut winter squash

(*Continued from previous page*)

Spinach quickly goes to seed once temperatures get hot, so where summers sizzle, gardeners grow true spinach as an early spring and fall crop, hoping to harvest when temperatures are cool. Or they plant New Zealand spinach, which is not true spinach but is heat-tolerant. If your summers are hot and winters are mild, plant spinach in September and October for late-fall and early-winter harvests.

To speed germination and growth, cover all the early plantings with floating row covers. Remove the covers once nighttime temperatures are 45°F or above and days exceed 60°F. Cover fall crops when nighttime temperatures dip below 40°F.

Spinach can be harvested several ways. Thinnings are the first harvest; eat the tender young plants you pull to establish 8-inch spacing between the remaining plants. As plants mature, pick off their outside leaves. If the weather is cool enough, you can continue in this way for two to three harvests. When a central leaf stalk starts to form, it's time to pick the whole plant.

If you buy disease-resistant cultivars you'll have very little trouble with spinach.

SQUASH (*Cucurbita pepo, C. maxima, C. argyrosperma, C. moschata*)

Squash are among the most commonly grown garden vegetables. In part, this is because there are so many different kinds. Summer squash—yellow, green, and white in various shapes and sizes—usually form sprawling bushes and are harvested before the fruit reach maturity. Winter squash—such as acorn, butternut, buttercup, and pumpkin—are harvested when their rinds are tough, which allows them to be stored.

Of the summer squash, zucchini, or green squash, is the most widely grown. With **full sun,** deep, fertile soil, a pH of 5.5 to 6.8, and consistently high moisture levels, this plant justifies its reputation as a huge producer. Unless you really like zucchini bread, zucchini pickles, zucchini pancakes, zucchini casseroles and zucchini

everything-else, plant only one or two hills of two plants each at a time. Cultivate zucchini and other summer squash as you do cucumbers in all respects. (See page 164.)

Most summer squashes can be picked 50 to 60 days after planting. But because they're harvested when immature, you can pick them when they suit your taste or purposes. For eating fresh, harvest zucchini when it is no more than 8 inches long and yellow squash when it is a maximum of 5 to 6 inches. Patty pan and other globe types are best when they are 4 to 5 inches in diameter. Take the time to look under the leaves, from several vantage points, every day when harvesting. If you'll be away for a few days, pick all the baby squash you see.

Winter squashes are easy to grow in high light, heat, fertility, and moisture conditions. If space is tight, bush types are available, but if you can afford the room include some vining types such as 'Delicata'. Treat these crops as you do melons. (See page 166.)

Winter squashes have a much longer season than summer squashes. The clues to determining when to harvest vary with the cultivar; tough skin, color changes, and a yellow spot where the squash touches the soil are all good indicators. With the exception of butternut, these squashes can take a light frost. You can store winter squash for many months if you cure them first. After you pick, set them on elevated screens or a table in bright sunlight. Turn them daily for about a week. If light frost threatens, cover them with a tarp, but if the frost is likely to be severe, bring them inside for the night. Store them in a dark spot that maintains temperatures of 50° to 60°F.

Pests and diseases are similar for all members of this family. In addition to the pests and diseases discussed on page 164, watch for powdery mildew, particularly at the end of the season. At the very first sign of this disease, spray plants every few days with 1 tablespoon of baking soda and 1 tablespoon of dishwashing detergent or insecticidal soap mixed into 1 gallon of water. You can also use sulfur-based fungicides.

TOMATO (*Lycopersicon lycopersicum*)

Tomatoes are, hands down, the most popular vegetable in home gardens. (Technically, tomatoes are a fruit.) Taste, productivity, and convenience are all responsible. No store-bought tomato can rival the flavor of a homegrown one; a single plant can produce from 10 to 20 pounds of excellent fruit; and they are easy to grow. Mail-order specialists offer lots of interesting cultivars that you're unlikely to find at local suppliers, including heirloom types. These varieties may be more disease-prone than modern hybrids, so include some disease-resistant cultivars in your planting.

Tomatoes require **full sun,** and moderately fertile, well-drained, consistently moist soil with a pH of 6.0 to 6.5. Buy plants, or start them 6 to 8 weeks early inside. If you have artificial lights, set the timer for a 14- to 16-hour day. Seedlings grow best at daytime temperatures of 60° to 65°F and nighttime temperatures of 50° to 55°F. If you'll be growing them on a windowsill, start them 8 weeks ahead of time; with lights, 6 weeks will give the same results.

Transplant tomatoes once all danger of frost is past. In cool-summer areas use plastic mulches and row covers. In warm-summer areas, mulch with straw and use row covers only during the beginning and ends of the season.

Tomatoes can be *indeterminate,* meaning that they continue to grow from the top as long as they are alive, or *determinate.* Determinate plants grow to a certain height and stop. Many early-bearing tomatoes are determinate. Stake indeterminate types, pruning them to only one or two main stems. Indeterminate types also grow well in cages; do not prune off their branches.

Tomatoes have a vine-ripened flavor when they're picked after their color is about half as deep as it will eventually become. When you pick at this stage, place the fruit in a warm, dark place until it is fully colored.

Tomatoes can host many different pests and diseases. Common diseases include early blight, late blight, septoria leaf spot, and bacterial spot, all of which cause spotted leaves and can eventually kill the plant if left unchecked; bacterial wilt, fusarium wilt, and verticillium wilt, diseases which plug the interior vessels, blocking water and nutrient transport; anthracnose and botrytis rot, which cause spots and rotting of fruit; and various virus diseases that cause everything from distorted growth to mottled leaves and stunted growth. Several measures help to avoid these diseases. Buy resistant cultivars; fusarium- and verticillium-wilt resistant varieties are widely available. On seed packets, look for F and V, respectively. Do not plant tomatoes in the same spot in successive years (or if space permits, more than once every 4 years). Throw out all diseased plant tissue rather than composting it. If diseases prove problematic, ask the local nursery or Cooperative Extension Service for least-toxic measures.

In addition to aphids, which often spread tomato diseases, common pests include flea beetles, which eat tiny round holes in leaves; Colorado potato beetles, which skeletonize leaves; spider mites, which suck cell sap; tobacco (tomato) hornworms, which devour leaves and fruit; and nematodes, tiny worms that destroy the plants' roots. Row covers protect plants against many of these pests, and beneficial insects in your garden usually keep aphids under control. If spider mites become a problem, wash them off the leaves, and use a misting nozzle on the hose to add humidity to the area each morning. Pick off hornworms, with a pair of kitchen tongs if necessary, and drop them into a can of water with a film of soap on top. Buy nematode-resistant varieties (labeled N on seed packets) to control that pest. To control serious infestations of any pest, seek advice from nursery staff or the Cooperative Extension Service.

Tomatoes

Tomato varieties

Glossary

Amendments. Organic or inorganic materials that improve soil structure, drainage, and nutrient-holding capacity. Some add nutrients.

Annual. A plant that completes its entire life cycle in a year.

Axil. The upper angle between a stem and its branches or leaf petioles.

Biennial. A plant that completes its life cycle in two years. Most biennials form a rosette of leaves the first season and a flower stalk the second.

Bulb planter. A metal hand tool designed for digging holes of the correct width and depth for planting bulbs.

Central leader. The dominant stem or branch of a tree.

Collar. The enlarged portion of a stem formed at the point of origin of branches growing from it.

Crown. The part of the plant where roots and stem meet.

Cultivar. Short for cultivated variety. Rather than occurring naturally in the wild, cultivars are developed. Cultivar names are enclosed in single quotes.

Deadheading. Removing flowers after they have faded.

Exposure. The intensity, duration, and variation in sun, wind, and temperature that characterize any particular site.

Foliar feed. To spray a plant's leaves with a fertilizer containing immediately available nutrients.

Full shade. A site that receives no direct sunlight.

Full sun. A site that receives six or more hours of direct sunlight a day.

Fungicide. A substance that kills fungi.

Genus (plural: genera). A closely related group of species that share similar characteristics and probably evolved from the same ancestors. Genus names in text are italicized and capitalized.

Hardy annual. An annual that can tolerate cool temperatures. Some hardy annuals tolerate freezing temperatures for short periods of time.

Herbicide. A chemical that kills plants.

Humus. A material derived from the almost completely decomposed remains of organic matter. Highly complex in makeup, humus buffers soil acidity and alkalinity, holds water and nutrients, improves soil aggregation and structure, and contains many compounds that enhance plant growth.

Hybrid. A plant resulting from cross-breeding parent plants that belong to different varieties or cultivars, species, or sometimes even genera. Hybrids are sometimes indicated by a times sign (x) between the genus and species name.

Indigenous. Native to a particular area or region.

Invasive. A plant that spreads easily and thus invades adjacent areas.

Microclimate. Site-specific conditions of exposure, wind, and drainage.

Node. The point along a stem from which a leaf or roots emerge.

Organic gardening. A gardening system that imitates natural systems. Standards for organic growers, including a list of approved and disapproved materials, are available from organic growers' associations.

Perennial. A plant that normally lives for three or more years.

Pesticide. A substance that kills insect pests. The term is also used to describe other agricultural toxins, including fungicides and herbicides.

Petiole. The stem of a leaf.

Plant habit. The form that a plant naturally takes as it grows, such as spreading, columnar, or rounded.

Propagate. To create more plants. Plants also reproduce, or propagate, themselves.

Rhizome. A creeping, often enlarged, stem that lies at or just under the soil surface. Both shoots and roots can form at nodes along the rhizome.

Seed leaf. The first leaf or set of leaves produced by the embryo of a plant during its germination period. Also called a cotyledon.

Species. A group of plants that shares many characteristics and can interbreed freely. The species name follows the genus name, is italicized, and is not capitalized.

Stem cutting. A portion of the stem that is removed and used to propagate a new plant. Stem cuttings can be stimulated to root in water or a moistened medium.

Sucker. A stem arising from the rootstock of a woody plant.

Tender perennial. A plant that is perennial in mild, frost-free climates but dies when it is exposed to freezing winter temperatures.

True leaf. The second and subsequent leaves or sets of leaves that a plant produces. The first leaf or set of leaves are seed leaves, or cotyledons. True leaves have the distinctive shape of the leaves of the mature plant.

Watersprout. An upright stem growing from a branch of a tree. In fruit trees, these stems do not bear fruit.

Variegated. Foliage that is marked, striped, or blotched with a color other than the basic green of the leaf.

Index

Note: Page numbers in **bold italic** refer to pages on which the subject is illustrated

Have a home gardening, decorating, or improvement project?
Look for these and other fine Creative Homeowner books
wherever books are sold

GARDEN SECRETS FOR ATTRACTING BIRDS
Provides information to turn your yard into a mecca for birds.

Over 250 photographs and illustrations.
160 pp.
8½" x 10⅝"
$14.95 (US)
$17.95 (CAN)
BOOK #: CH274561

SUCCESSFUL CONTAINER GARDENING
Information to grow your own flower, fruit, and vegetable "gardens."

Over 240 photographs.
160 pp.
8½" x 10⅞"
$14.95 (US)
$17.95 (CAN)
BOOK #: CH274857

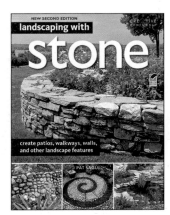

LANDSCAPING WITH STONE
Ideas for incorporating stone into the landscape.

Over 335 photographs.
224 pp.
8½" x 10⅞"
$19.95 (US)
$21.95 (CAN)
BOOK #: CH274179

BACKYARD HOMESTEADING
How to turn your yard into a small farm.

Over 235 photographs.
256 pp.
8½" x 10⅞"
$16.95 (US)
$18.95 (CAN)
BOOK #: CH274800

DECORATING: THE SMART APPROACH TO DESIGN
A go-to how-to guide on decorating, explaining fundamental design principles, for real people.

Over 375 photographs.
288 pp.
8½" x 10⅞"
$21.95 (US)
$24.95 (CAN)
BOOK #: CH279680

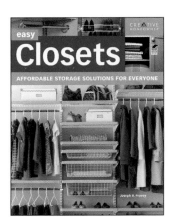

EASY CLOSETS
Introduces homeowners to the variety of closet types and closet systems available.

Over 275 photographs.
160 pp.
8½" x 10⅞"
$14.95 (US)
$16.95 (CAN)
BOOK #: CH277135

For more information and to order direct, go to **www.creativehomeowner.com**